Cut
Here

COME VISIT!

King Henry's

Olde Faire

A fun time for peasants and nobles

...shire's
...N Faire!

Exit 4 off Rt. 93 in Derry.

Faire

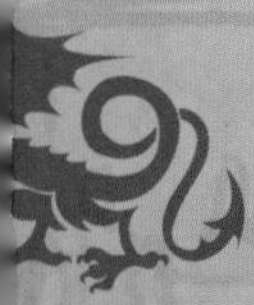

RAGON!

stic and dastardly dragons to King Henry's
elf! Send your drawing in an envelope to:

ersham
ntertainment
et, Suite 1010,
CA 90028.

his squires deem the most worthy
d in the songs of the bards!

Cut
Here

A New Hampshire tradition:

King Henry's

Great for young princes, princesses and squires!

Meet the Knights of the Round and test your mettle!

GOODS
SWOR

Fill your bellies with the food of yore!

Admission & Hours

Adult: $28.00 Child: $16.00
Senior: $18.00

Open every weekend July 1st thru October 31st. Gates open at 10:00AM and close at 7:30PM.

Parking is FREE in the lot east of the fairgrounds.

Olde

DRAW a D

INSTRUCTIONS: Send in your most maje
most trusted knight—Sir Habersham hims

Sir Hab

c/o Archaia E
1680 Vine Stre
Los Angeles,

Those dragons Sir Habersham and
will be shared with the worl

King Henry's Olde Faire

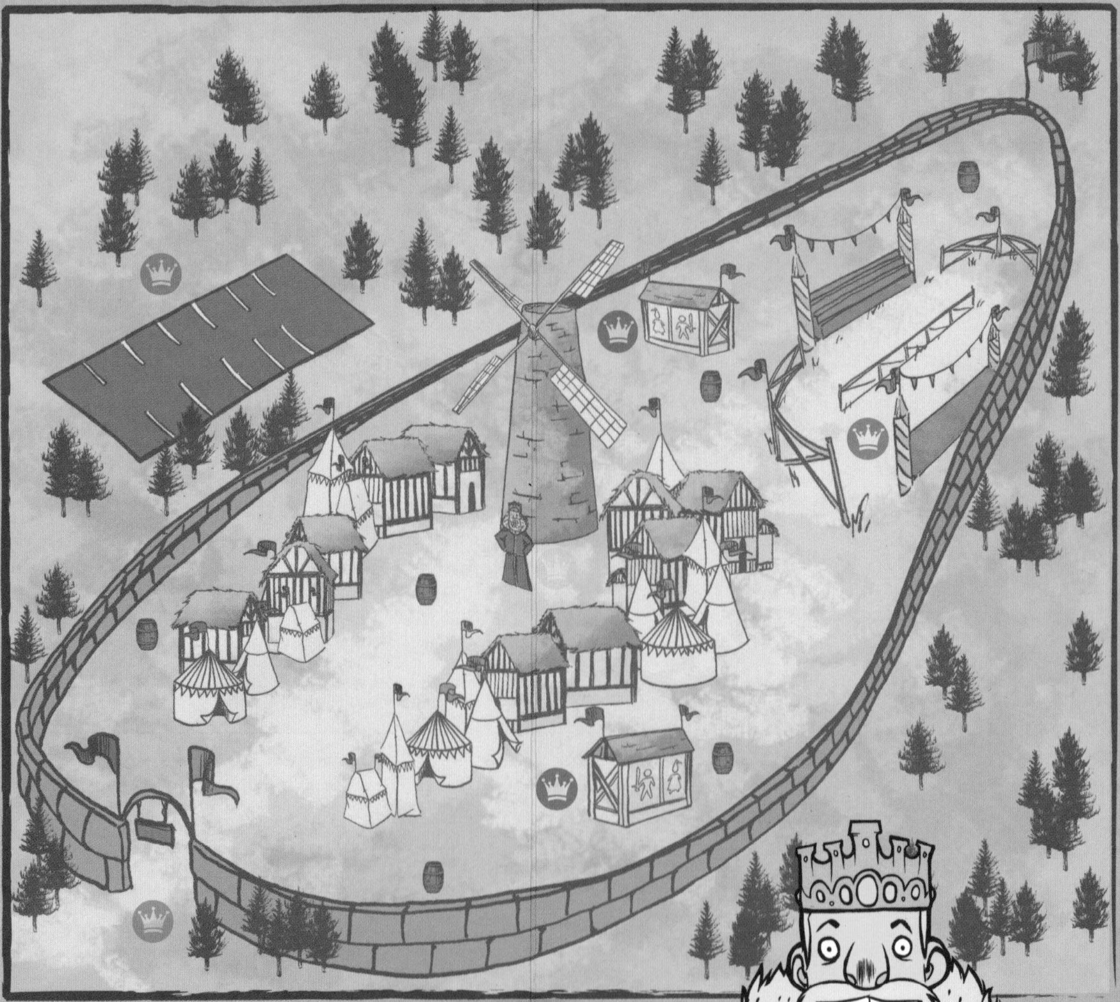

Map Legend

- Ye Olde Lot of Parking
- Jousting Field
- King Henry/ Windmill
- King's Passing
- Little Knights and Princesses Restrooms

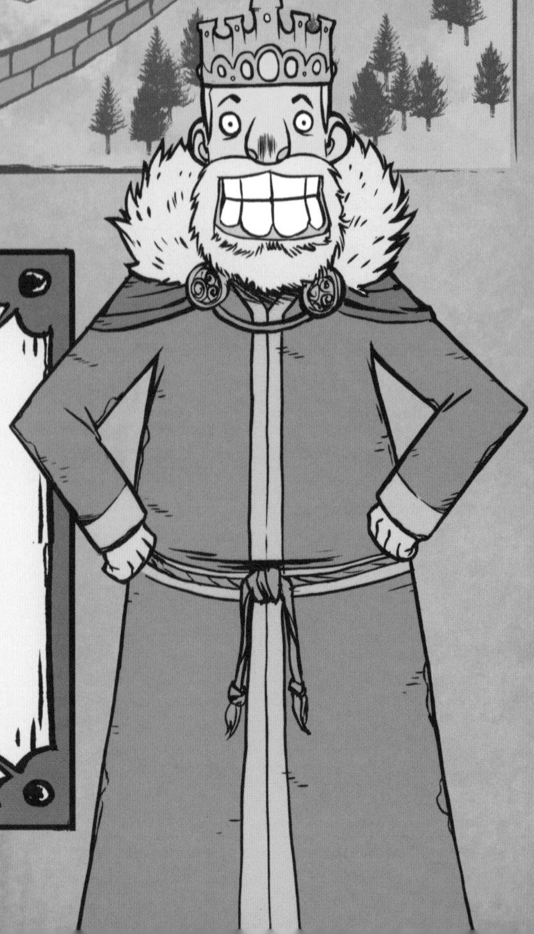

THE REASON FOR DRAGONS™

Created by
CHRIS NORTHROP

Art by
JEFF STOKELY

THE REASON FOR DRAGONS

Written by **CHRIS NORTHROP**
Art by **JEFF STOKELY**
Color by **CHRIS NORTHROP** and
ANDREW ELDER

Lettering by Chris Northrop | Story Assistance by Jeff Stokely
Design by Fawn Lau | Edited by Rebecca Taylor

Based on Concepts by Chris Northrop and Sean Murphy 2007

Archaia Entertainment LLC
Jack Cummins, *President & COO* | Mark Smylie, *CCO*
Mike Kennedy, *Publisher* | Stephen Christy, *Editor-in-Chief*
Mel Caylo, *Marketing Manager* | Scott Newman, *Production Manager*

Published by **Archaia**

Archaia Entertainment LLC
1680 Vine Street, Suite 1010
Los Angeles, CA 90028
www.archaia.com

THE REASON FOR DRAGONS.
Original Graphic Novel Hardcover.
May 2013. FIRST PRINTING.

10 9 8 7 6 5 4 3 2 1

ISBN: 1-936393-74-3
ISBN-13: 978-1-936393-74-9

Printed in **China**.

Table of Contents

TAKE
ONE

SOCK!

Introduction by

Sean Murphy

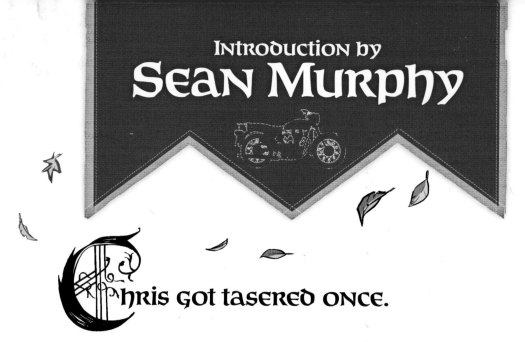

Chris got tasered once.

He was walking alone at night near Pink's Hot Dog stand in Hollywood. Two men jumped him, tasered him, stole his laptop, and drove off. Police arrived along with two choppers armed with spotlights, but they never found the men, nor did they find the laptop with all the work we'd saved onto the hard drive: all the files for an animated Flash cartoon called *Fanboyz.*

We never finished the cartoon, but Chris did eventually get around to doing something with the story. It's now called *The Reason for Dragons*, and you're holding the first edition.

That night, Chris showed up at my place after he'd filed a report with the police. He was finishing up a phone call with his mother back in Queens, assuring her that he was safe and that his recent move to LA was a good thing. Soon he'd find a job in animation, so she didn't need to worry. But overprotective moms are hard to get off your back.

Finally, he was off the phone. He started flipping through my recent Teen Titans pages while telling me about everything that happened. We both started laughing hysterically when he described what it was like being tasered. But once the adrenaline wore off, it finally happened: he had a breakdown.

We'd met six months earlier at a local Starbucks. He was sitting alone while drawing a picture of Spider-Man, so I sat down and started chatting about comics and the Teen Titans book I would soon be drawing.

We quickly bonded over our mutual dislike of Hollywood: the orange tans, the unpronounceable coffee-hybrids you found at Starbucks. Most people who arrive in LA are hipsters and ex-prom queens who only want to get famous. But most of them are too lazy to take a single acting class. Some of the more creative ones try writing a crummy screenplay. Most amount to nothing, and they leave the city in the same state that they came: boring.

Chris and I were different. We wanted to work. I wanted a job in concept art/storyboarding, and he wanted to be an animator—we had no choice but to be in **LA**. At least with each other, we could keep our sanity. Yes, we were judgmental and elitist, but we didn't care. Hating Hollywood was fun. It gave us the illusion of control.

Control is a hard thing to come by when you're pursuing a creative career. As a comics freelancer, it's rare to choose your projects and have a voice. It's easy to become a cog if you're not careful. When it comes to animation, it's even harder. 99% of animators probably never get to do their own thing, whereas it's a bit easier in comics.

Between projects, **Chris** and I came up with our cartoon—a short about a small-town nerd who's coming of age. I'd draw the backgrounds by hand, while Chris would animate the characters.

We'd spent long hours working on it—he'd come over in the morning and we'd work long into the night while listening to Law and Order reruns (it reminded us of the East Coast). Chris would pitch it here and there when he got small animation gigs, but no one ever bit. After the files were stolen, we tried to put some of it back together, but it never became anything. A little while later, I moved to Manhattan to be with an ex-girlfriend (my current wife). Chris has been there ever since, plugging away at different creative outlets to get by: animating, teaching, coloring comics, etc. Eventually he wanted to do something new with Wendell's story—turn it into a graphic novel.

I'm really proud that Chris followed through with this. While we always treated each other as equals, I was a few years older than Chris when we met, so there might have been an older brother role I inherited at times. Seeing him complete this project is like seeing him grow older and finally find the elusive element of "control" that most animators never see.

I'd never seen Jeff Stokely's art before this, but I was in love right away. What a perfect artist to carry the torch. If I was to draw this book, it would never look as good as how Jeff is drawing it, I promise you. His stuff is way more appropriate for the story. I see big things in his future, and would love to write something for him one day.

The Reason for Dragons is a heart-warming masterpiece. Its wandering evolution truly did help develop the story into something unique.

And I can honestly say that I'm glad Chris got tasered.

-Sean Murphy 2013

Lilly

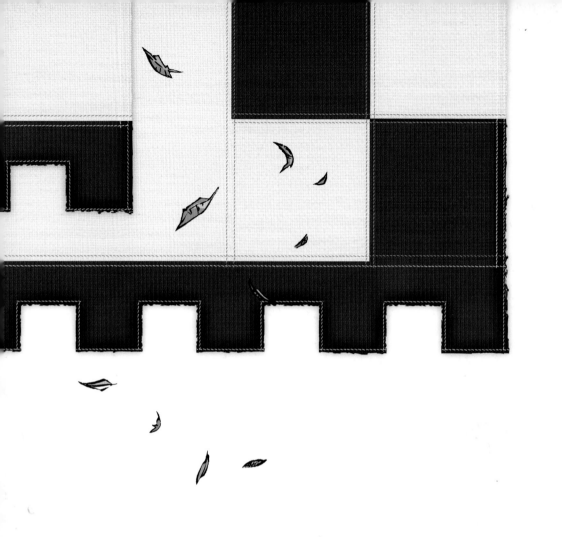

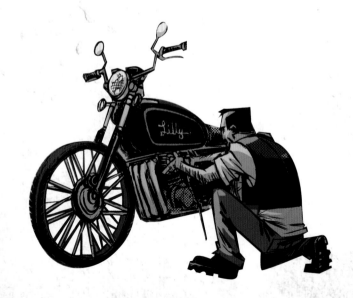

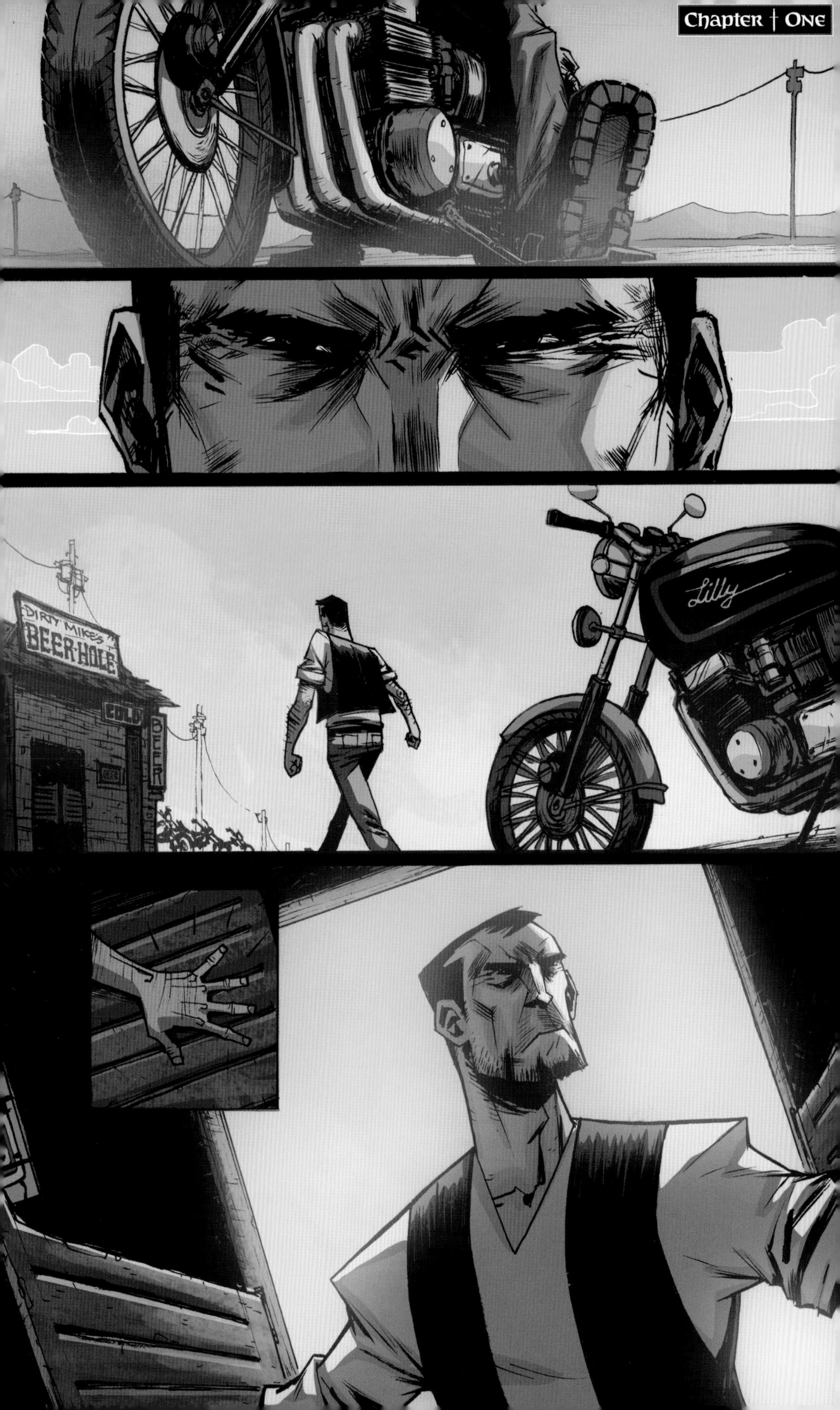
DIRTY MIKE'S
BEER-HOLE
COLD
BEER
Lilly

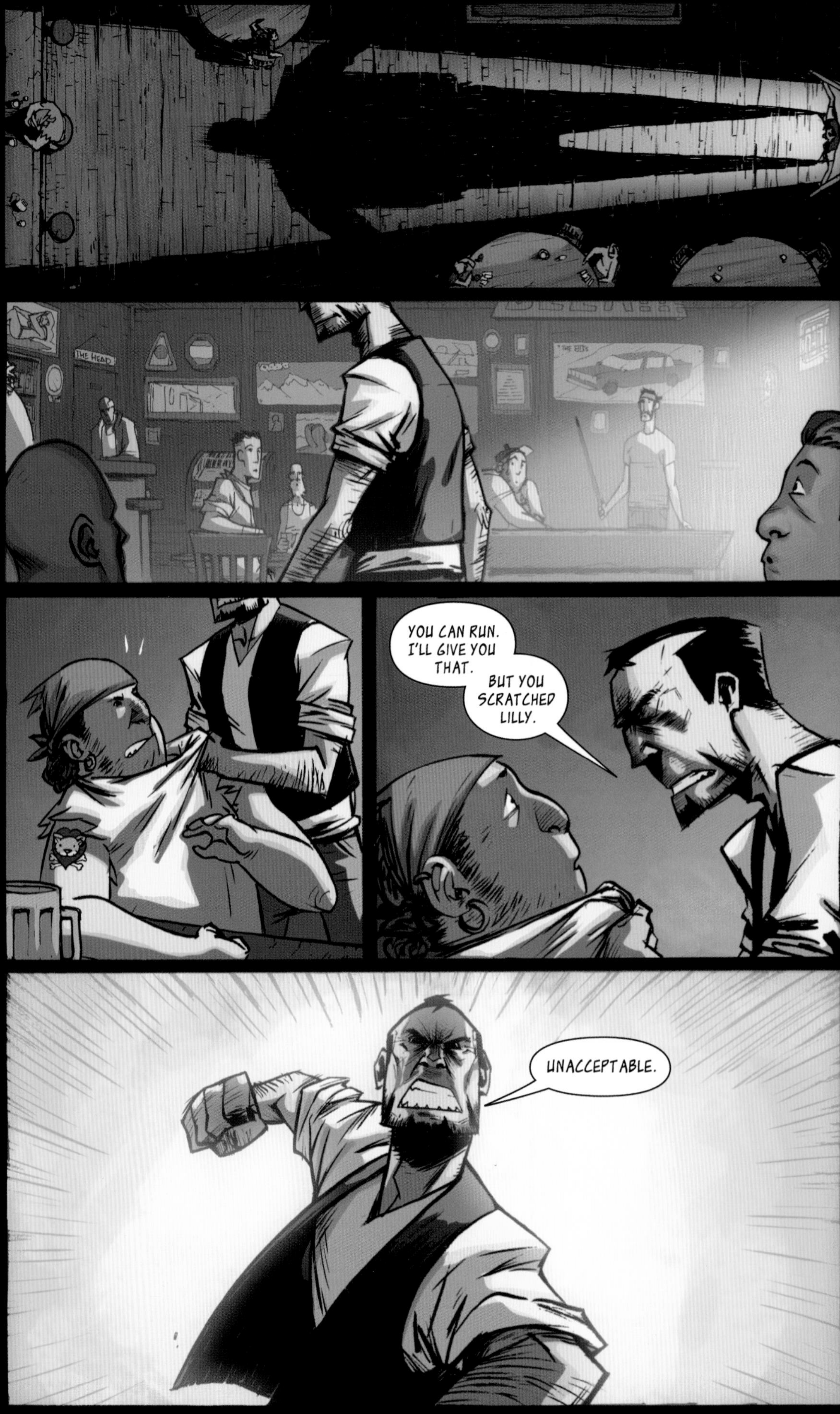
THE HEAD
YOU CAN RUN. I'LL GIVE YOU THAT.
BUT YOU SCRATCHED LILLY.
UNACCEPTABLE.

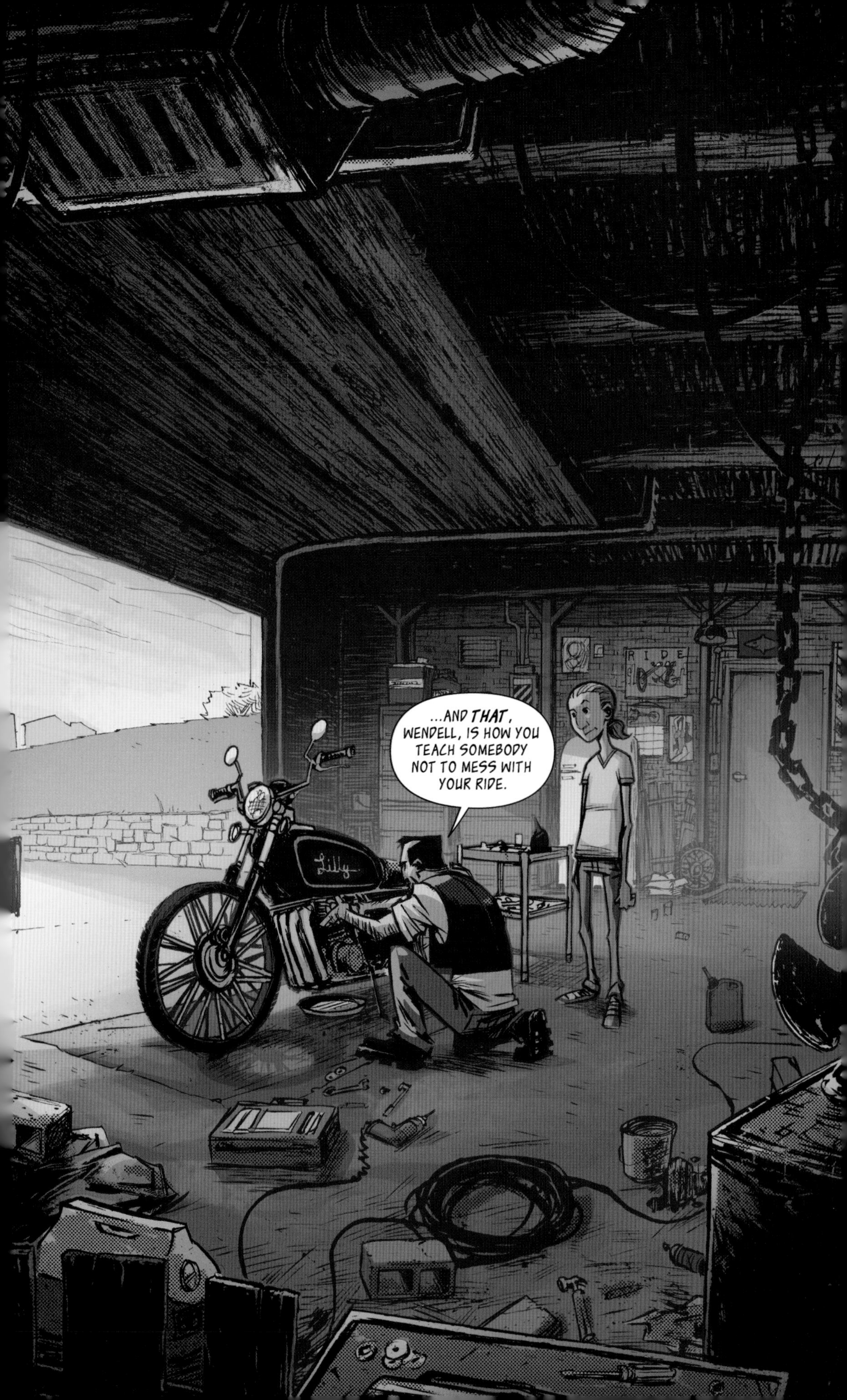
...AND THAT, WENDELL, IS HOW YOU TEACH SOMEBODY NOT TO MESS WITH YOUR RIDE.
RIDE
Lilly

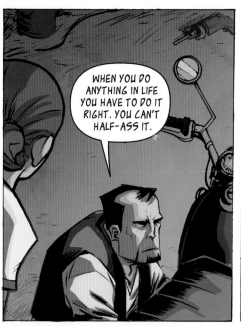

Chapter One

WHEN YOU DO ANYTHING IN LIFE YOU HAVE TO DO IT RIGHT. YOU CAN'T HALF-ASS IT.

THIS IS WHERE THE OIL IS AT. IT KEEPS EVERYTHING RUNNING SMOOTH.

NOW GIVE IT A GO. IT'S EASY. I PUT THE PAN DOWN THERE ALREADY. JUST OPEN THE BOTTOM AND LET IT DRAIN OUT.

I DON'T KNOW, TED. I DON'T EVEN WANT TO *TOUCH* YOUR BIKE AFTER THAT STORY YOU JUST TOLD ME.

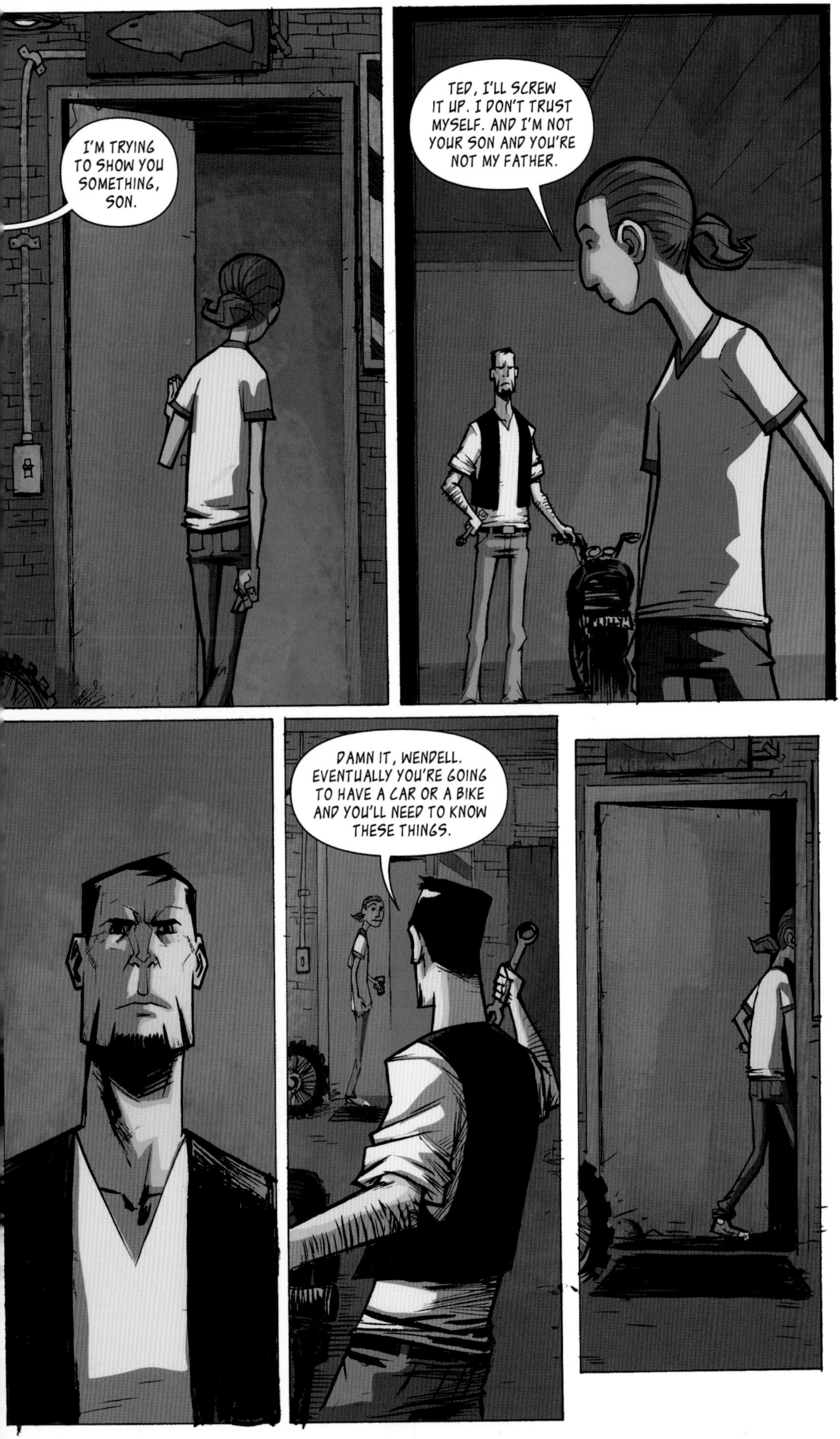
I'M TRYING TO SHOW YOU SOMETHING, SON.
TED, I'LL SCREW IT UP. I DON'T TRUST MYSELF. AND I'M NOT YOUR SON AND YOU'RE NOT MY FATHER.
DAMN IT, WENDELL. EVENTUALLY YOU'RE GOING TO HAVE A CAR OR A BIKE AND YOU'LL NEED TO KNOW THESE THINGS.

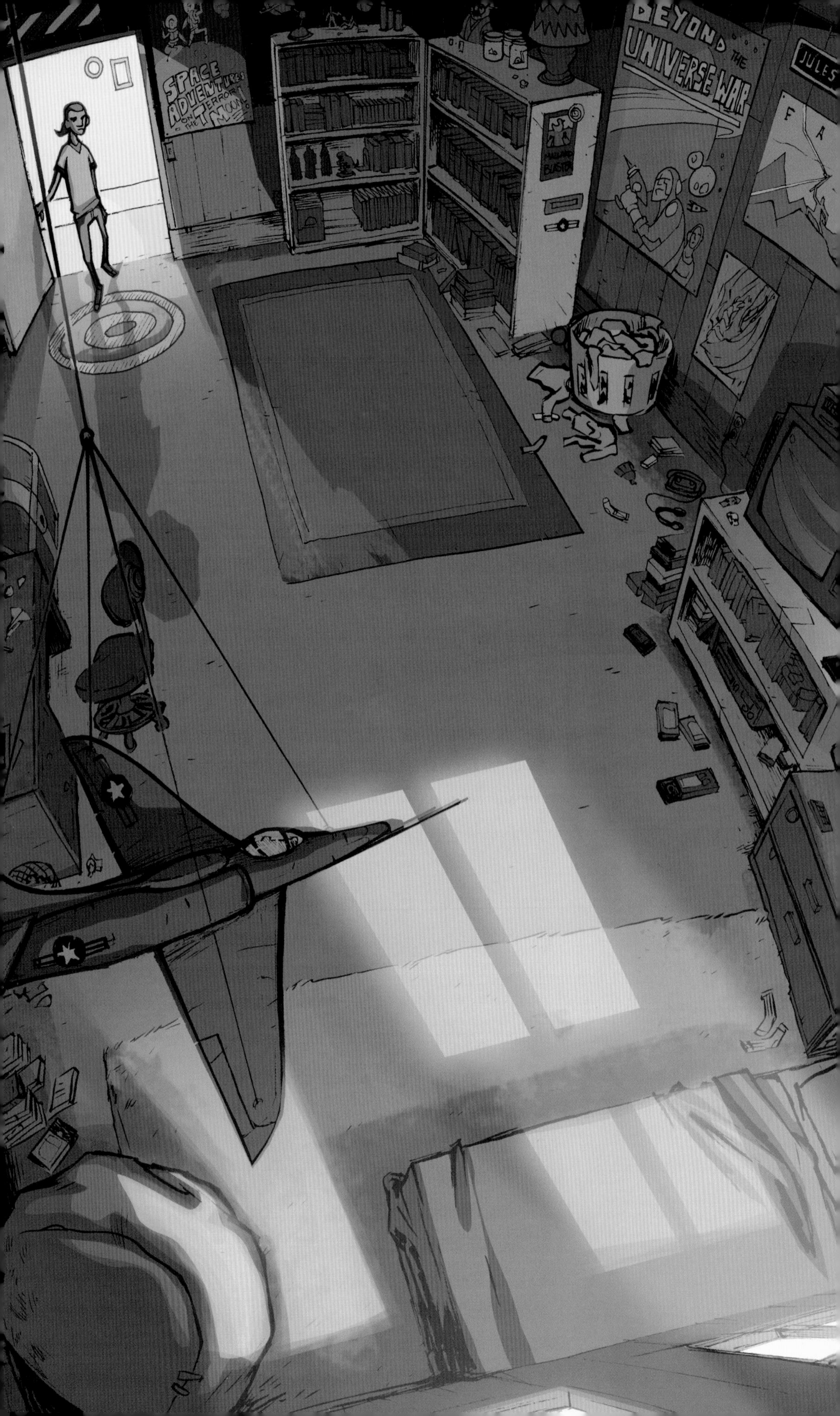
SPACE ADVENTURES ON THE TERROR MOON!
BEYOND THE UNIVERSE WAR
JULES

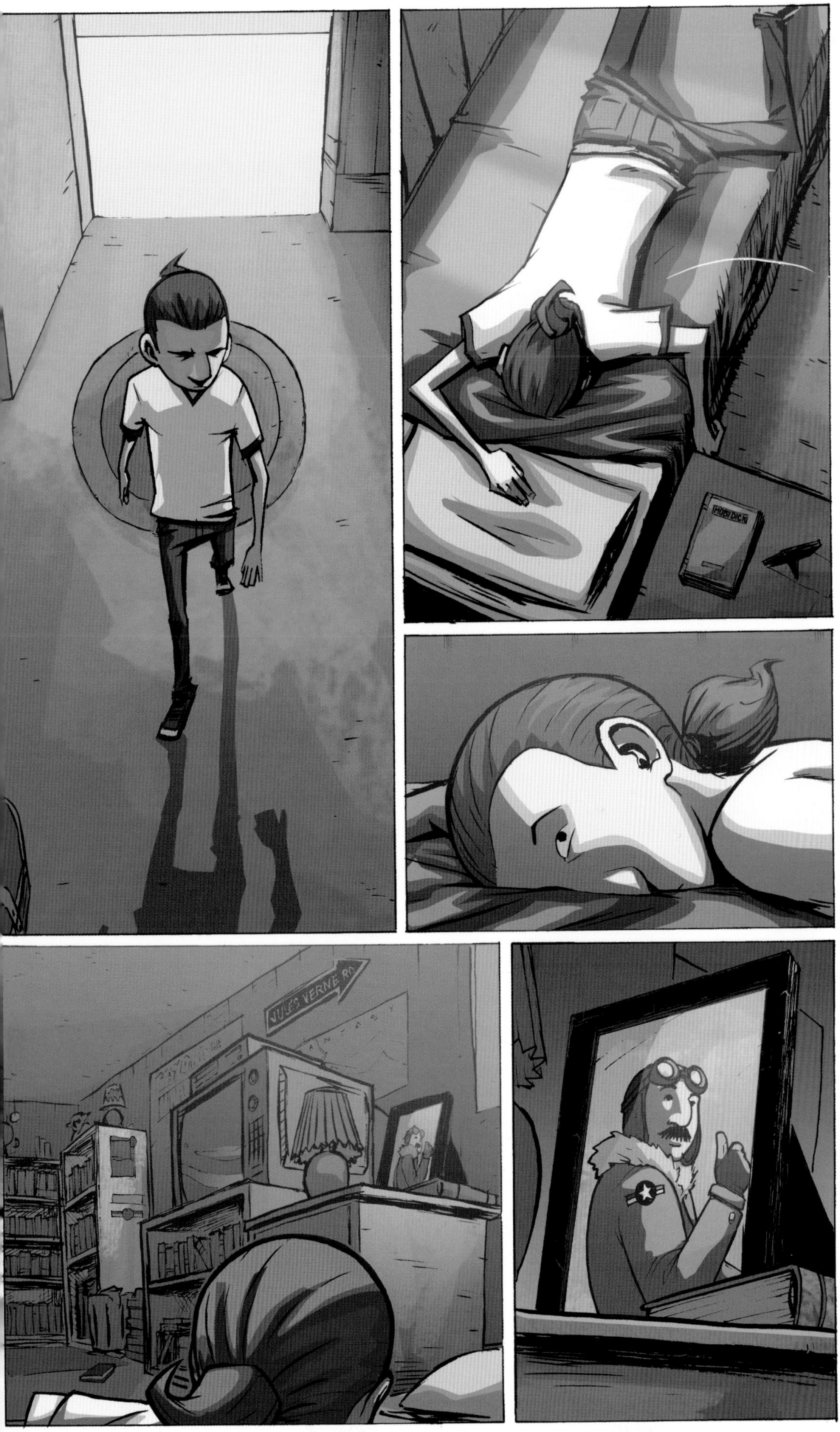
MOBY DICK
JULES VERNE RD

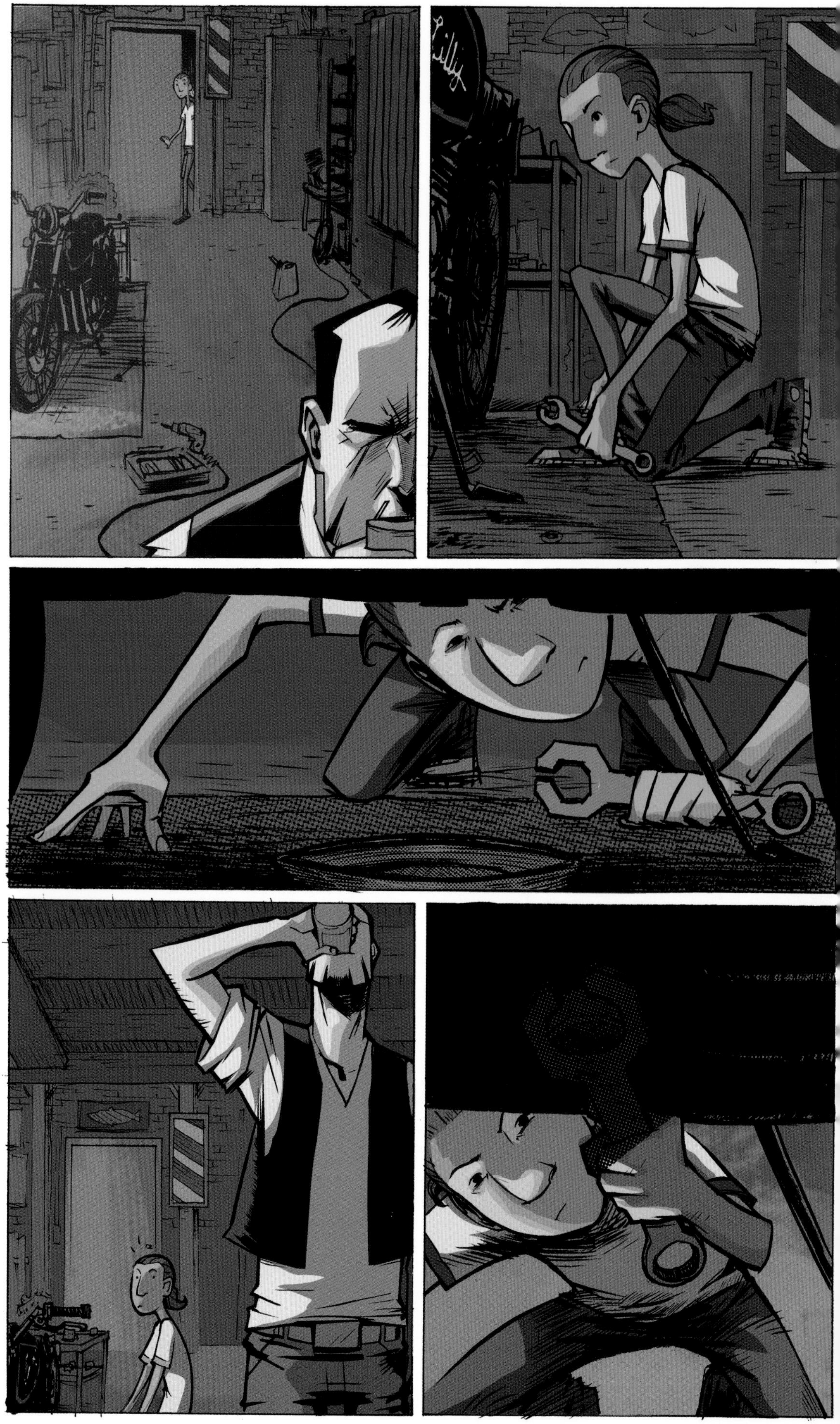
Lilly

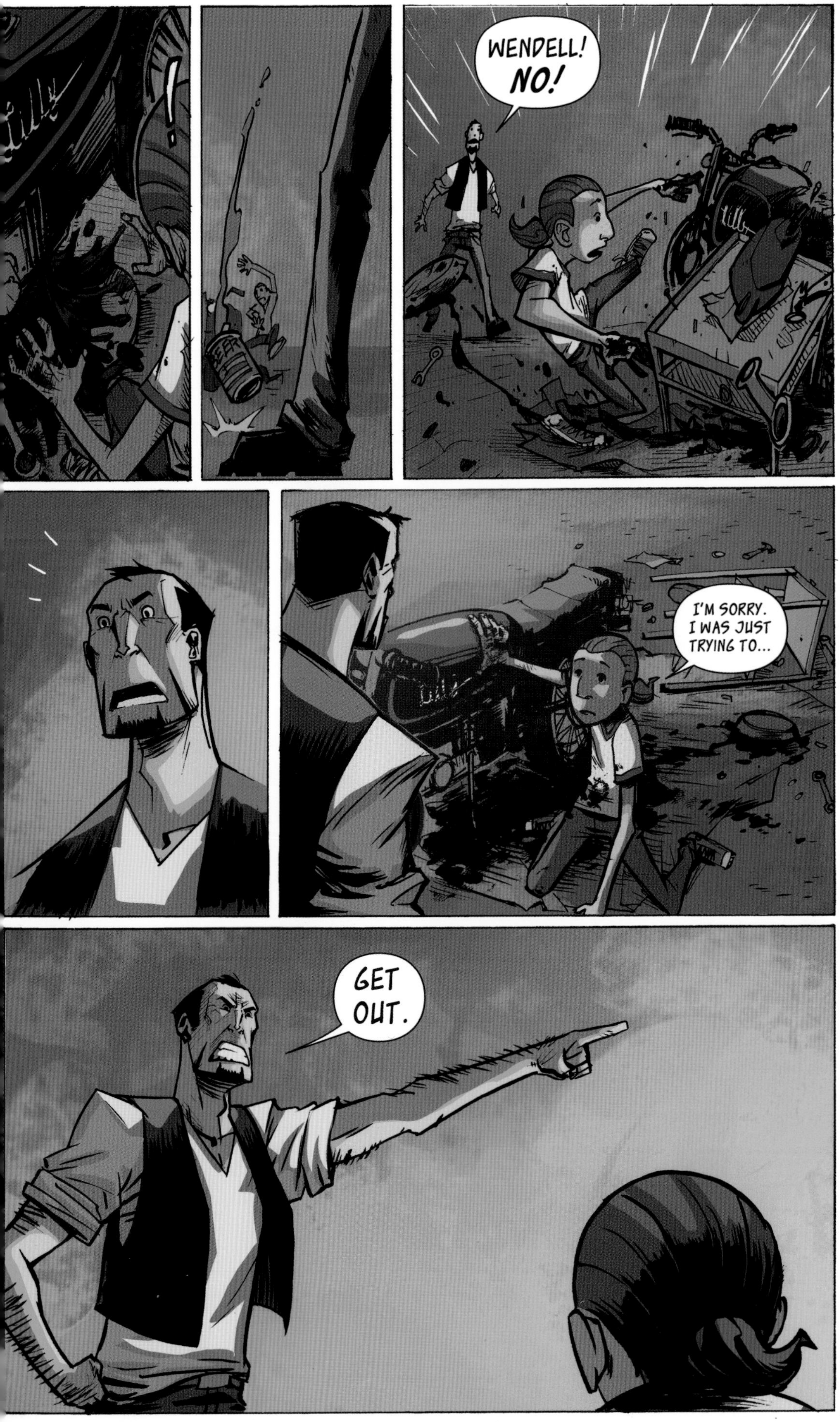
WENDELL! NO!
I'M SORRY. I WAS JUST TRYING TO...
GET OUT.

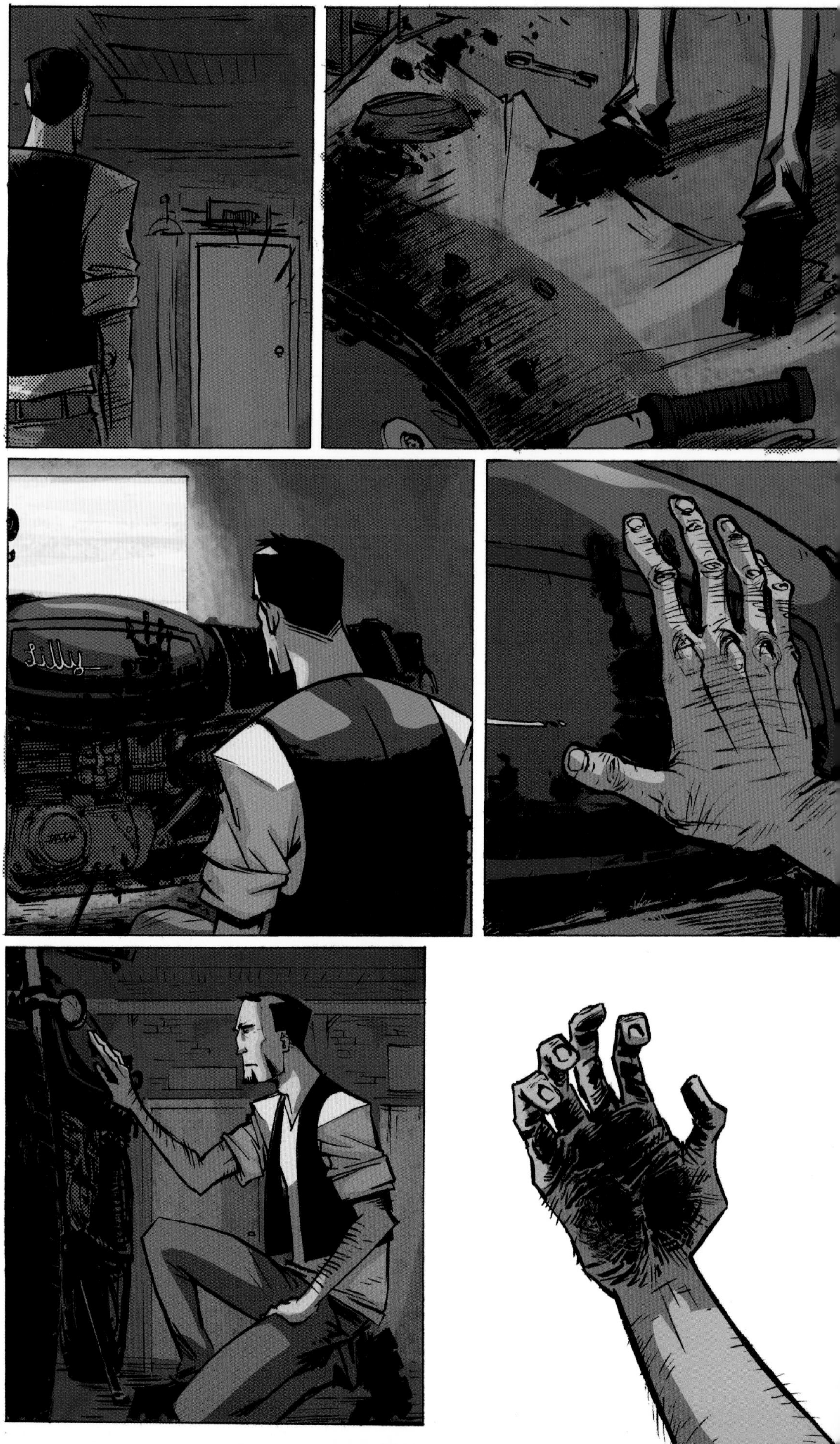
Lilly

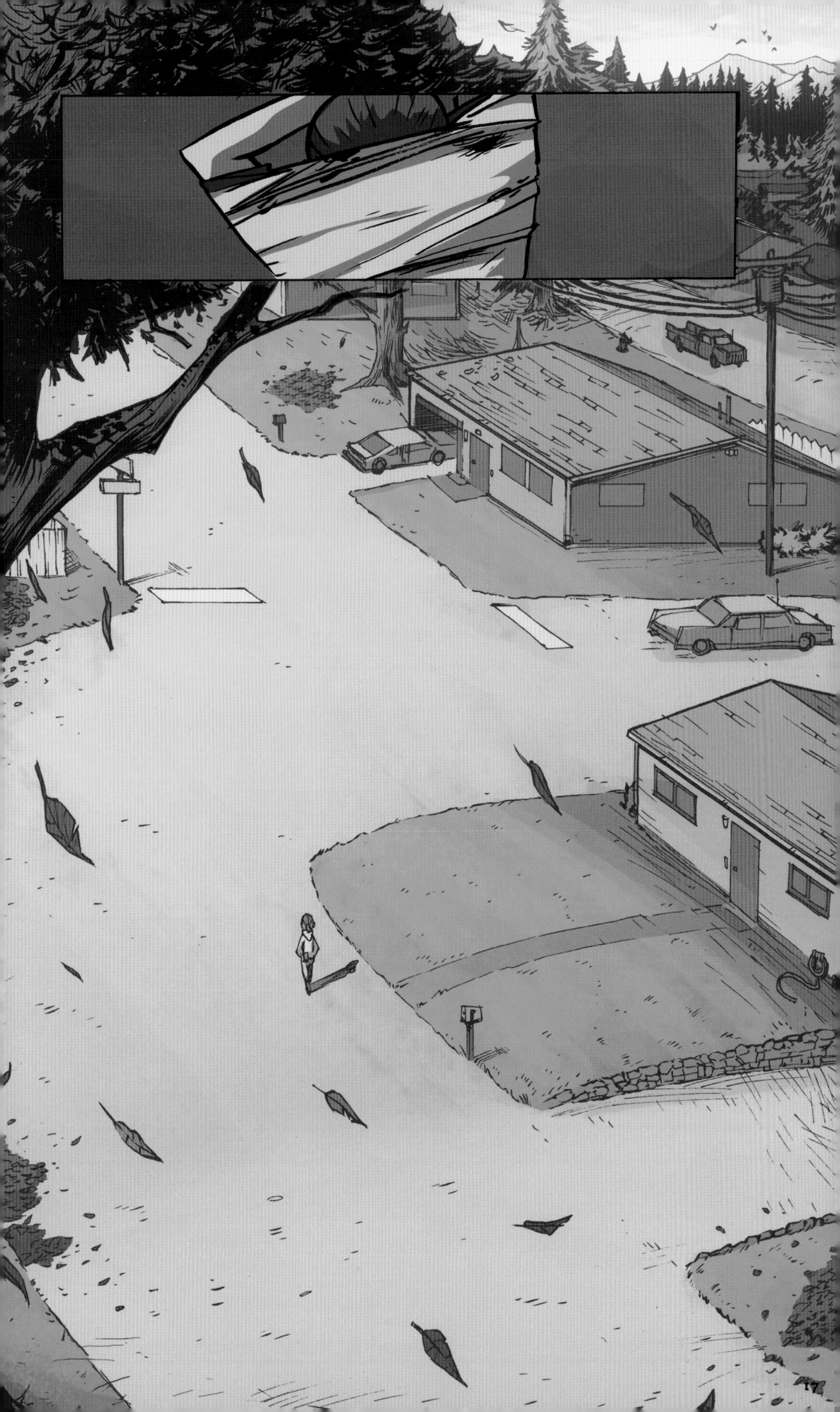

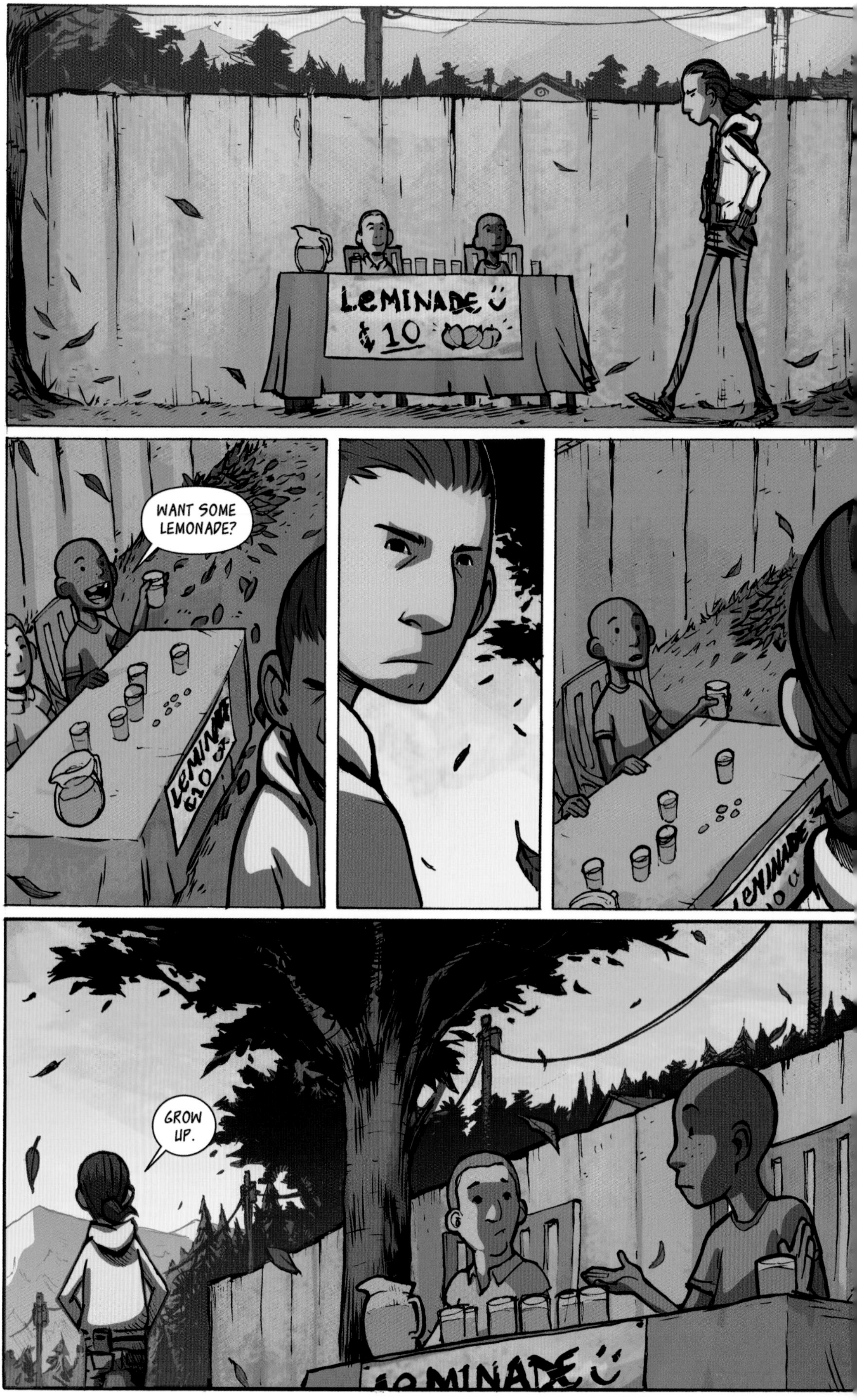
LEMINADE ☺
¢10
WANT SOME LEMONADE?
LEMINADE ¢10
LEMINADE
GROW UP.
LEMINADE ☺

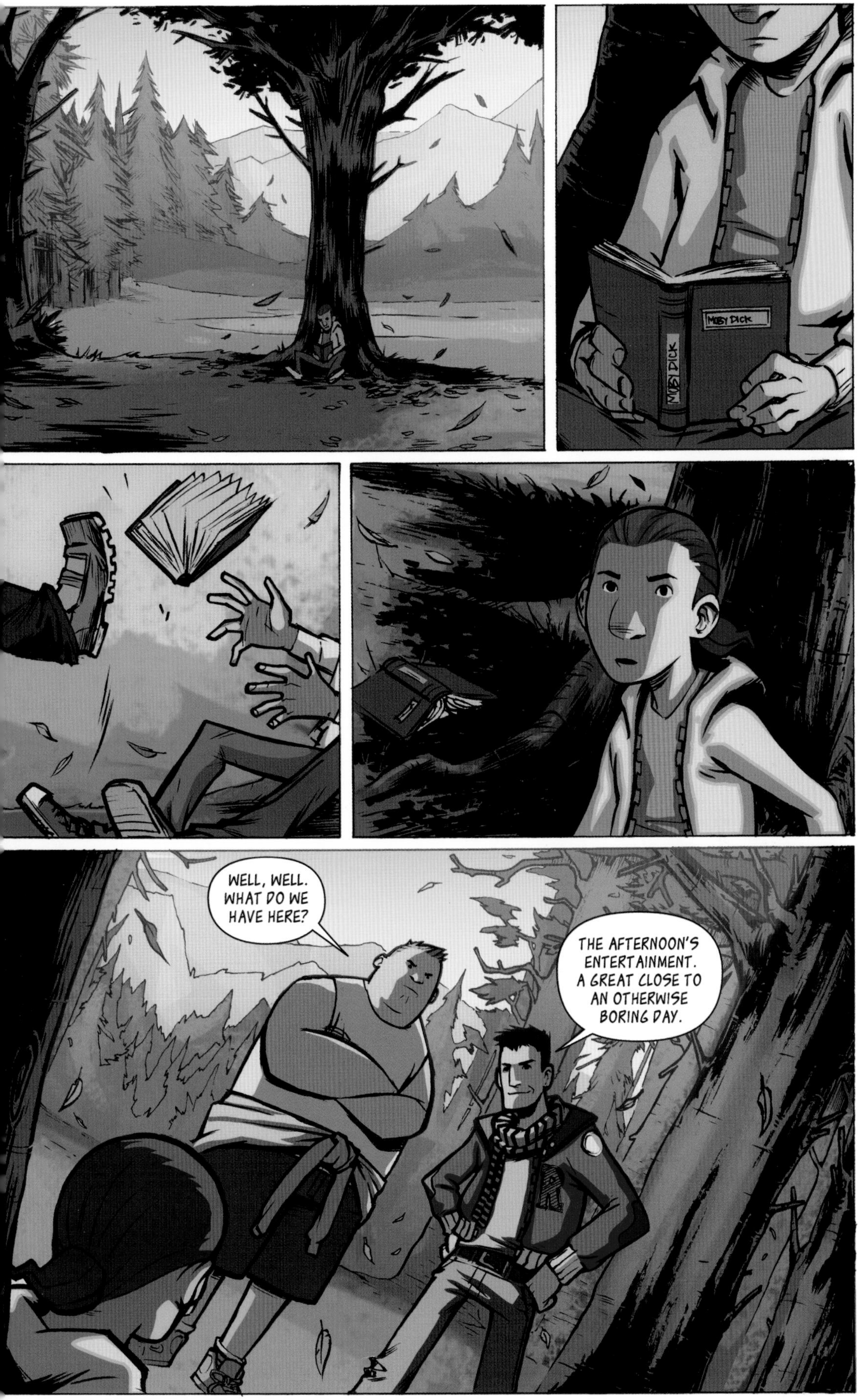
MOBY DICK
MOBY DICK
WELL, WELL. WHAT DO WE HAVE HERE?
THE AFTERNOON'S ENTERTAINMENT. A GREAT CLOSE TO AN OTHERWISE BORING DAY.

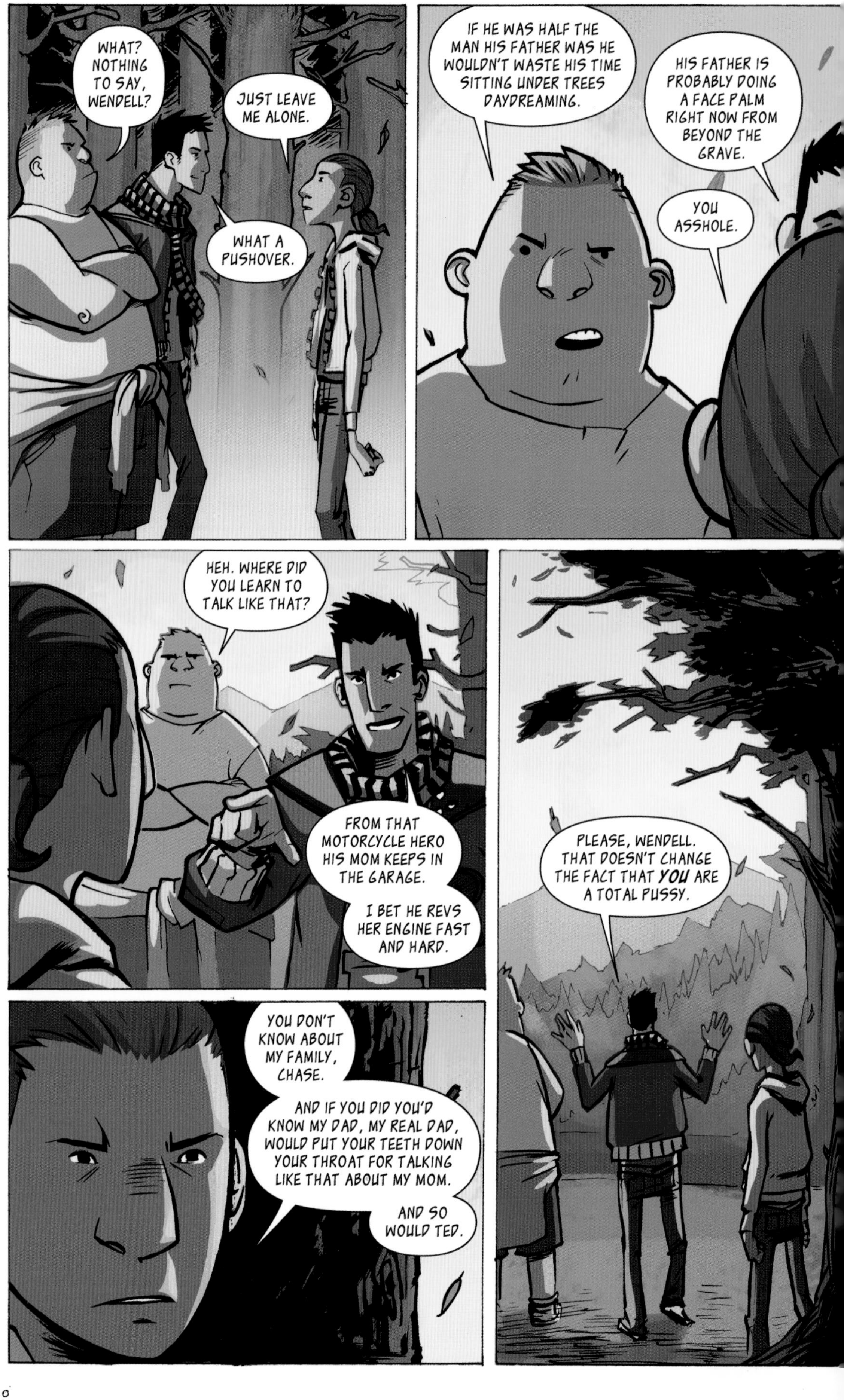
WHAT? NOTHING TO SAY, WENDELL?
JUST LEAVE ME ALONE.
WHAT A PUSHOVER.
IF HE WAS HALF THE MAN HIS FATHER WAS HE WOULDN'T WASTE HIS TIME SITTING UNDER TREES DAYDREAMING.
HIS FATHER IS PROBABLY DOING A FACE PALM RIGHT NOW FROM BEYOND THE GRAVE.
YOU ASSHOLE.
HEH. WHERE DID YOU LEARN TO TALK LIKE THAT?
FROM THAT MOTORCYCLE HERO HIS MOM KEEPS IN THE GARAGE.
I BET HE REVS HER ENGINE FAST AND HARD.
PLEASE, WENDELL. THAT DOESN'T CHANGE THE FACT THAT *YOU* ARE A TOTAL PUSSY.
YOU DON'T KNOW ABOUT MY FAMILY, CHASE.
AND IF YOU DID YOU'D KNOW MY DAD, MY REAL DAD, WOULD PUT YOUR TEETH DOWN YOUR THROAT FOR TALKING LIKE THAT ABOUT MY MOM.
AND SO WOULD TED.

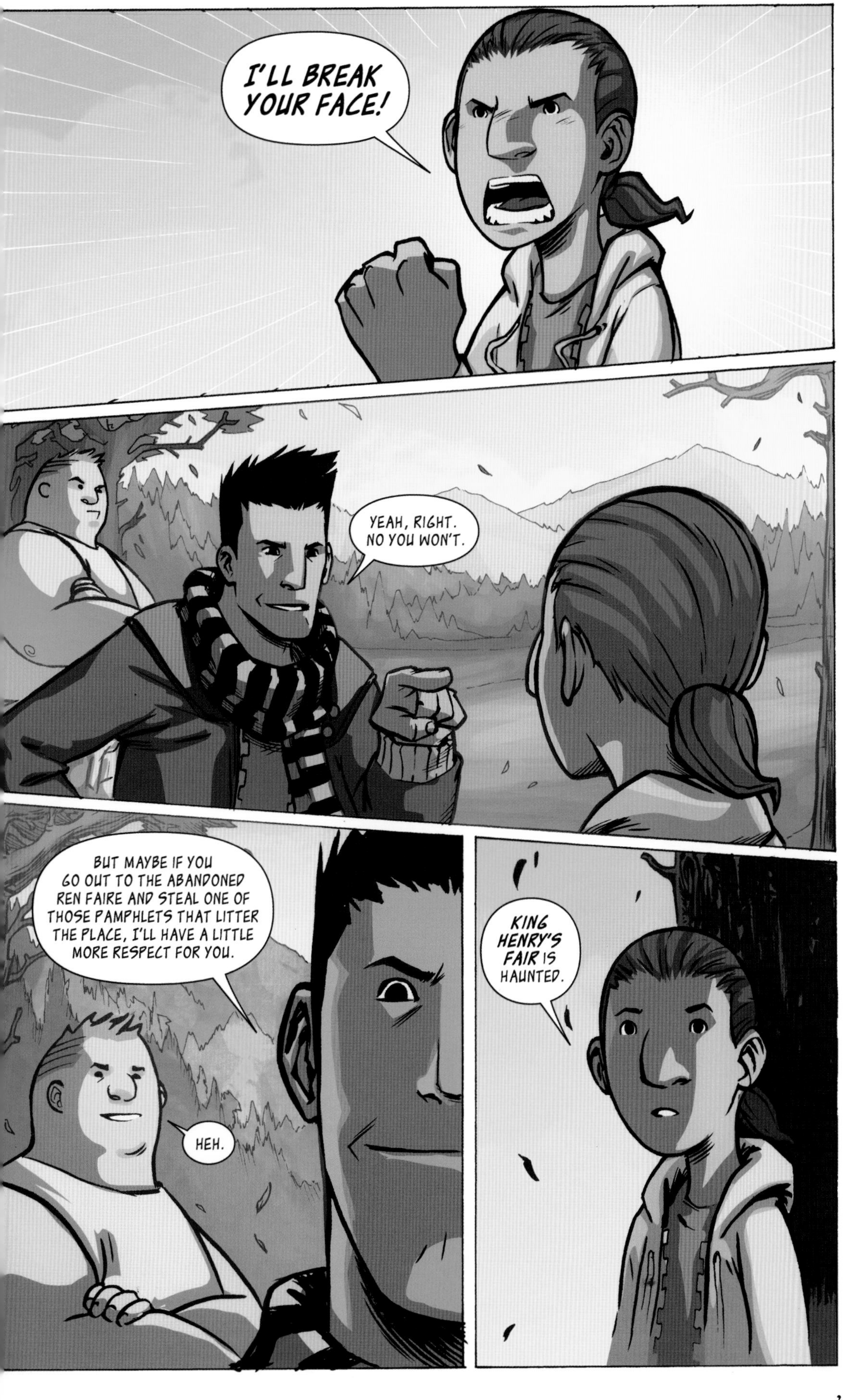
I'LL BREAK YOUR FACE!
YEAH, RIGHT. NO YOU WON'T.
BUT MAYBE IF YOU GO OUT TO THE ABANDONED REN FAIRE AND STEAL ONE OF THOSE PAMPHLETS THAT LITTER THE PLACE, I'LL HAVE A LITTLE MORE RESPECT FOR YOU.
HEH.
KING HENRY'S FAIR IS HAUNTED.

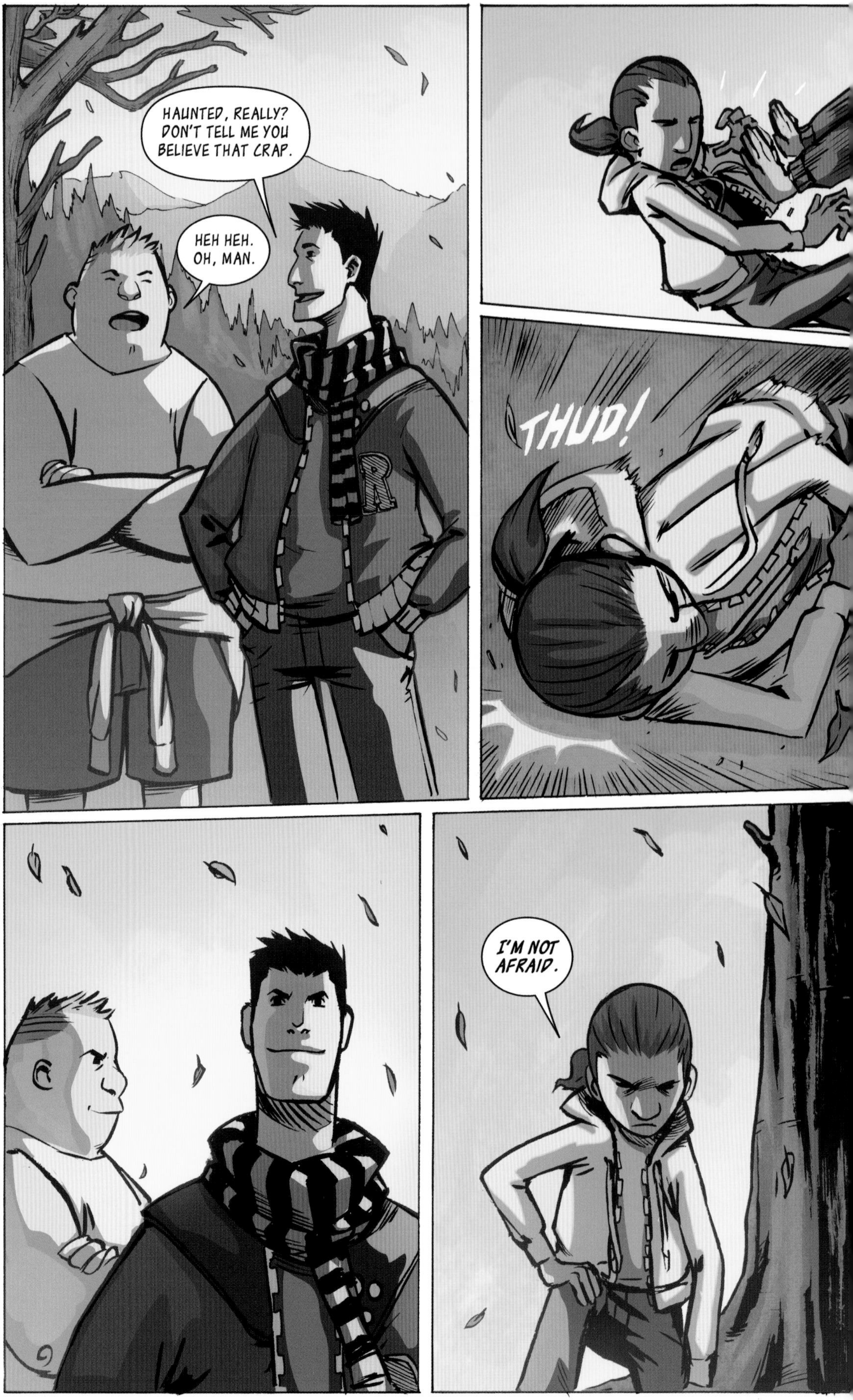
HAUNTED, REALLY? DON'T TELL ME YOU BELIEVE THAT CRAP.
HEH HEH. OH, MAN.
THUD!
I'M NOT AFRAID.

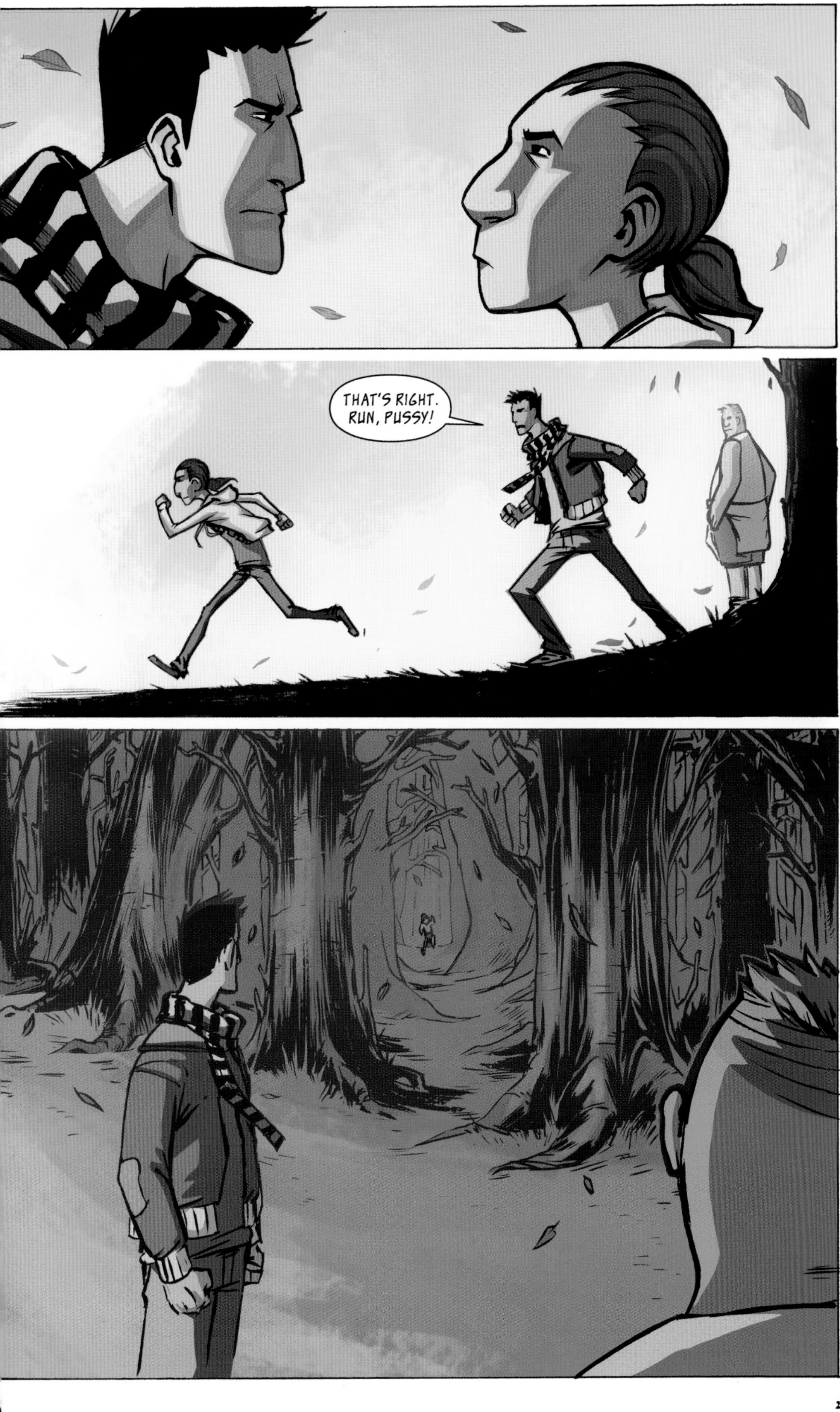
THAT'S RIGHT.
RUN, PUSSY!

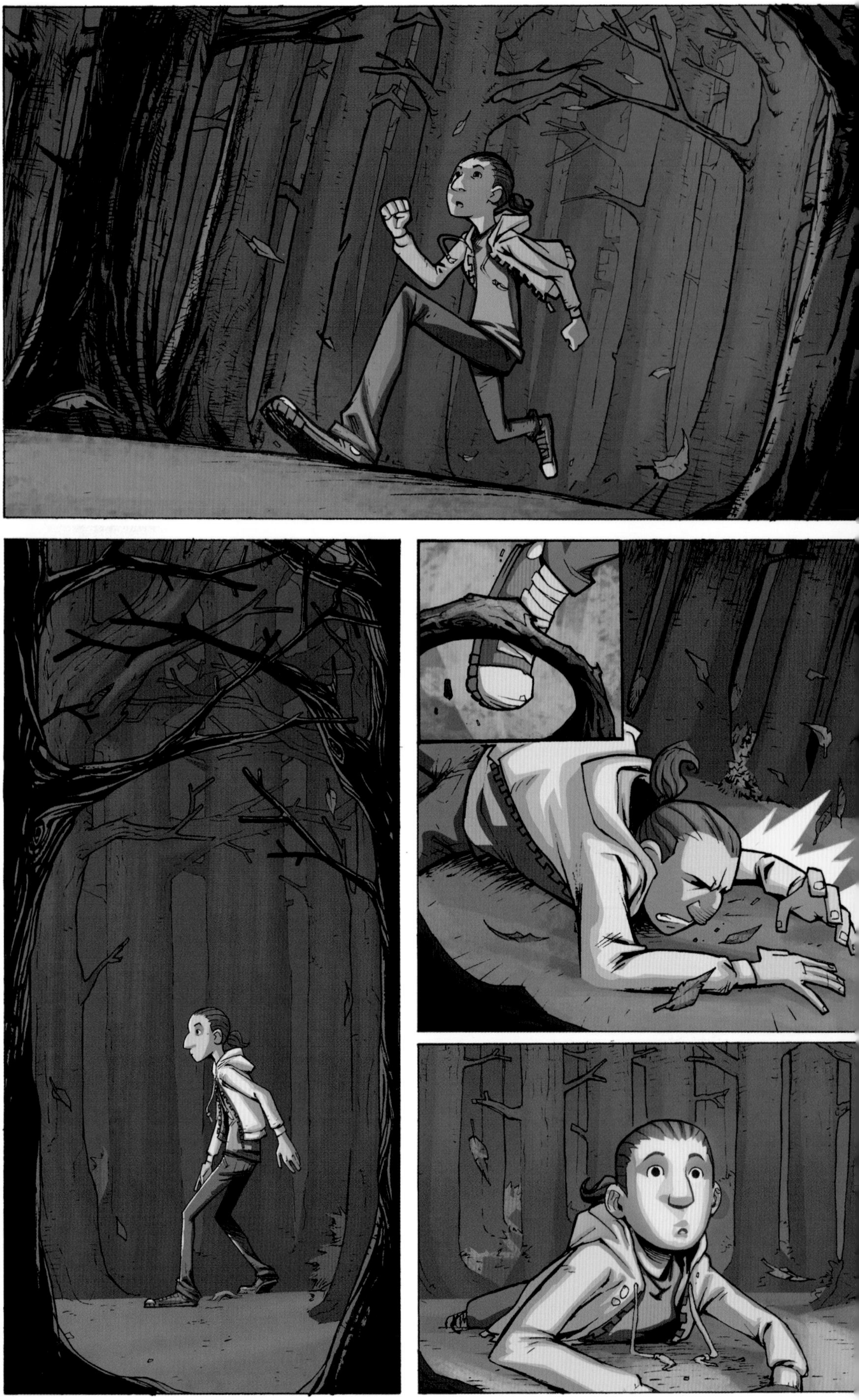

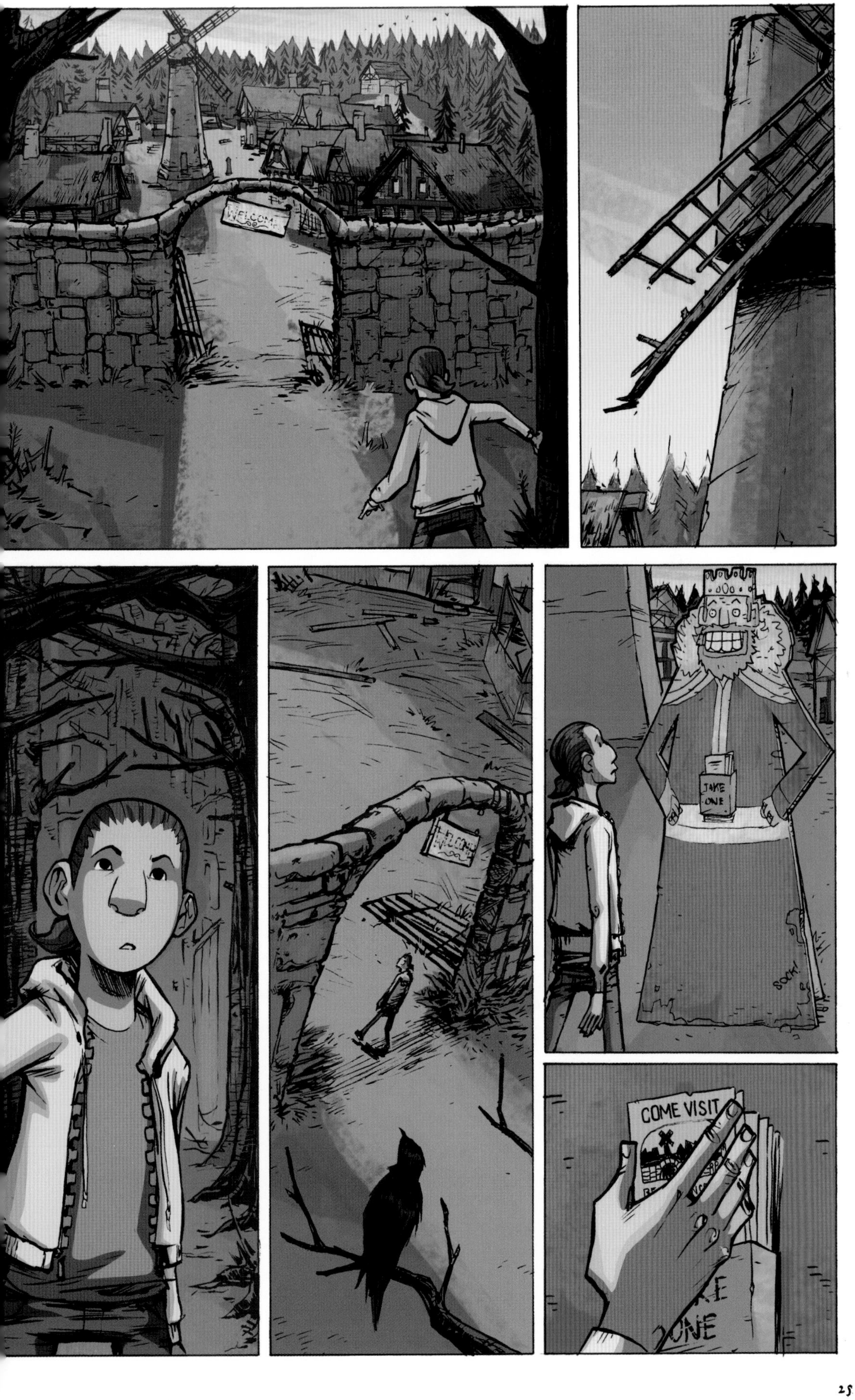
TAKE ONE
SOCK!
COME VISIT

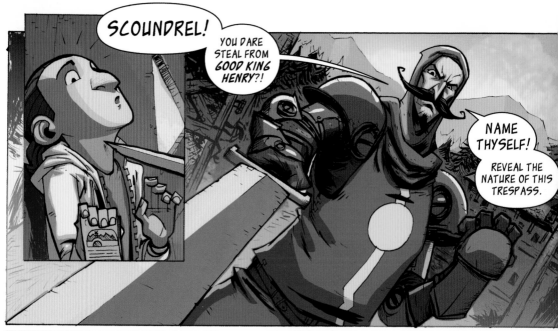

SCOUNDREL!

YOU DARE STEAL FROM *GOOD KING HENRY*?!

NAME THYSELF!

REVEAL THE NATURE OF THIS TRESPASS.

WENDELL.

HA HA HA HA HA!

OK, I GET IT. YOU'RE OUT HERE WITH SOME FRIENDS PLAYING DRESS UP.

"DRESS UP?"

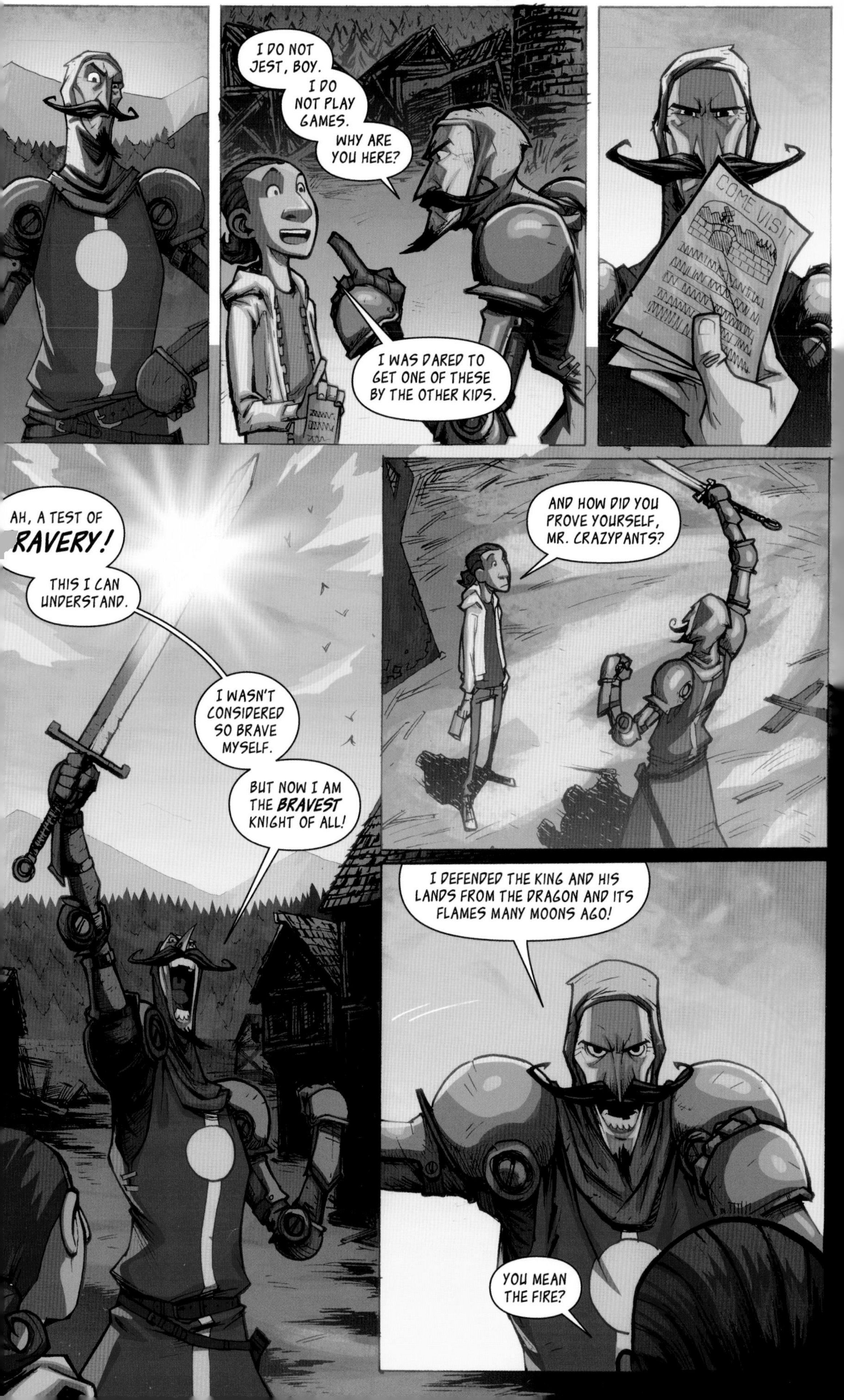
I DO NOT JEST, BOY.
I DO NOT PLAY GAMES.
WHY ARE YOU HERE?
I WAS DARED TO GET ONE OF THESE BY THE OTHER KIDS.
COME VISIT
AH, A TEST OF BRAVERY!
THIS I CAN UNDERSTAND.
I WASN'T CONSIDERED SO BRAVE MYSELF.
BUT NOW I AM THE BRAVEST KNIGHT OF ALL!
AND HOW DID YOU PROVE YOURSELF, MR. CRAZYPANTS?
I DEFENDED THE KING AND HIS LANDS FROM THE DRAGON AND ITS FLAMES MANY MOONS AGO!
YOU MEAN THE FIRE?

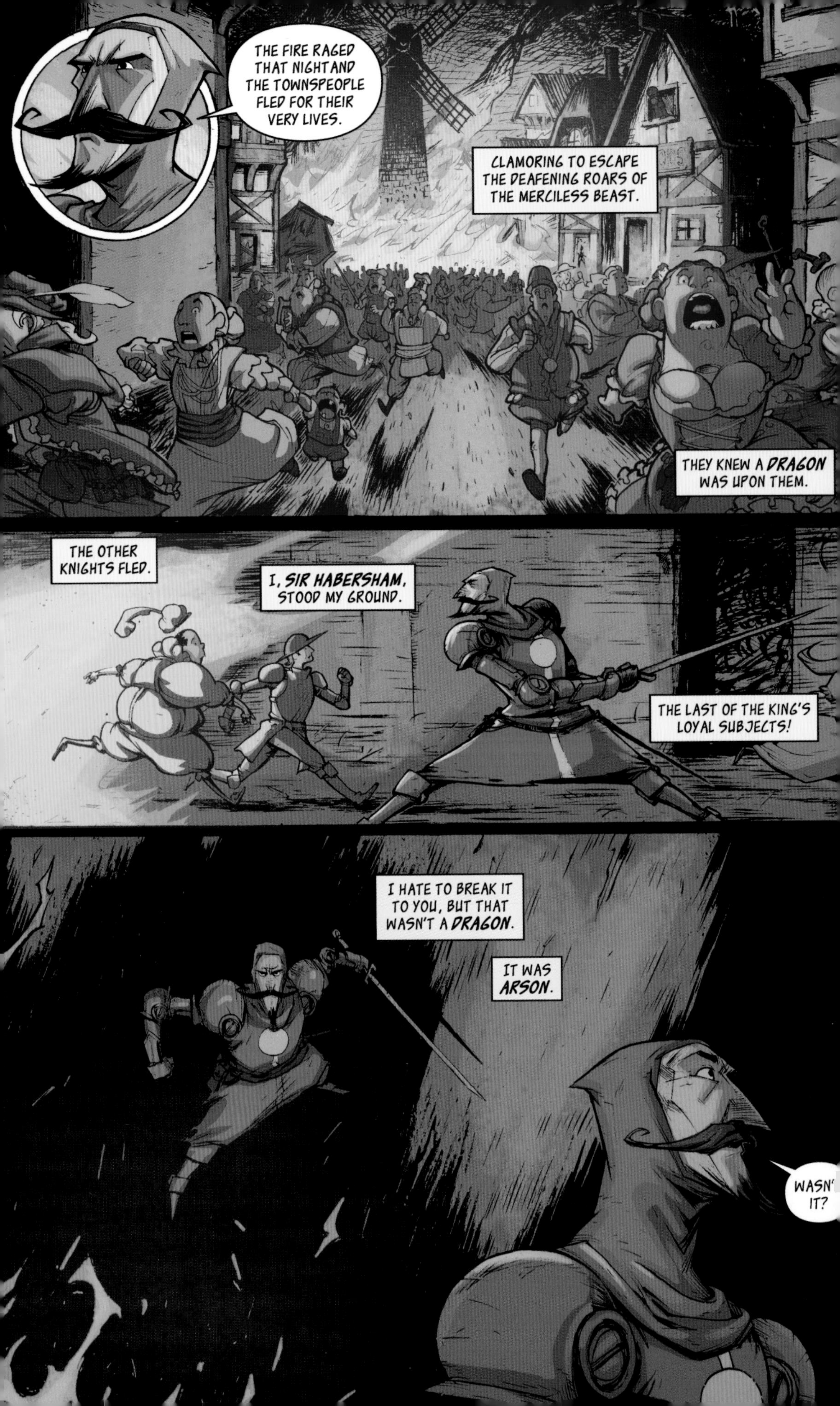
THE FIRE RAGED THAT NIGHT AND THE TOWNSPEOPLE FLED FOR THEIR VERY LIVES.
CLAMORING TO ESCAPE THE DEAFENING ROARS OF THE MERCILESS BEAST.
THEY KNEW A DRAGON WAS UPON THEM.
THE OTHER KNIGHTS FLED.
I, SIR HABERSHAM, STOOD MY GROUND.
THE LAST OF THE KING'S LOYAL SUBJECTS!
I HATE TO BREAK IT TO YOU, BUT THAT WASN'T A DRAGON.
IT WAS ARSON.
WASN' IT?

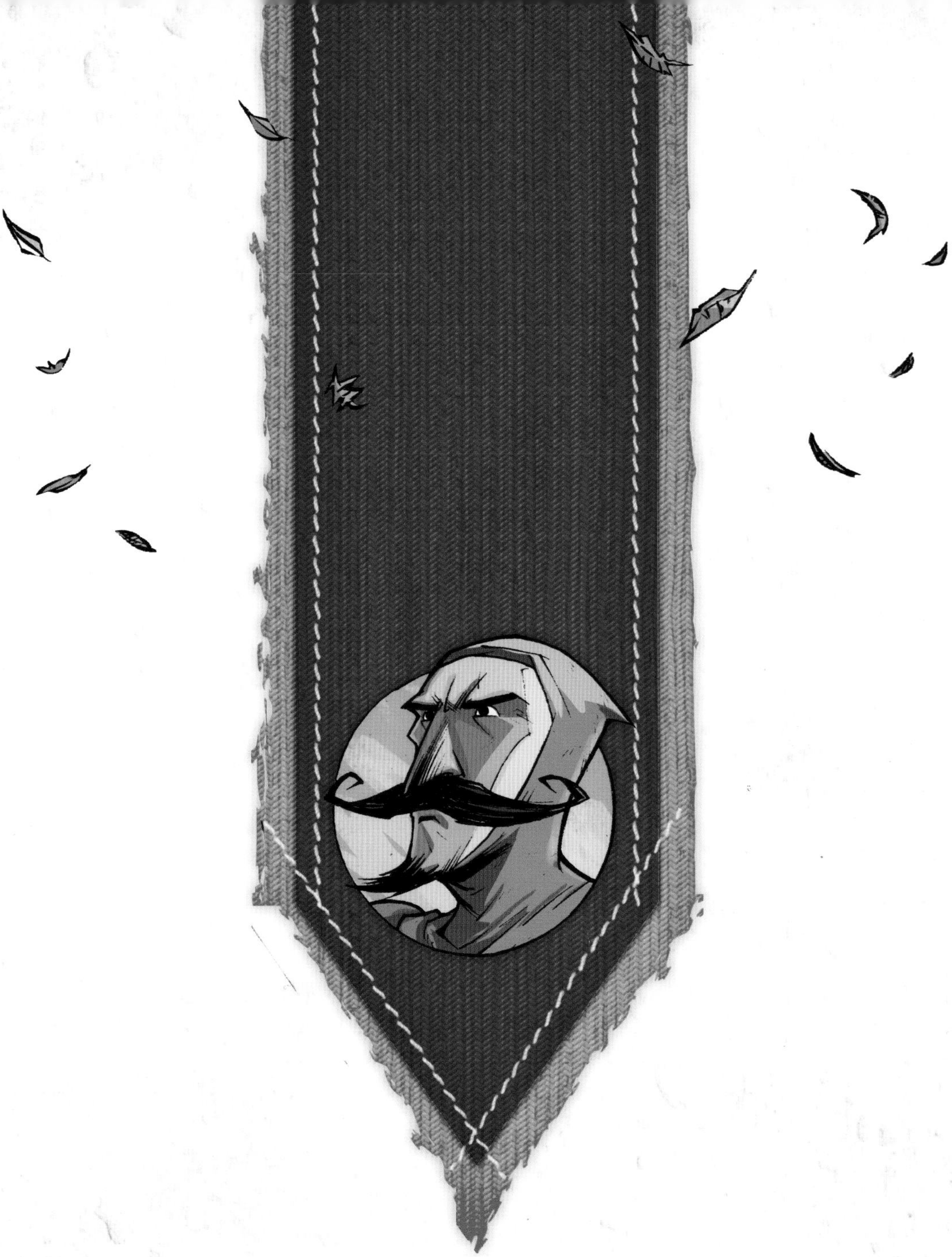

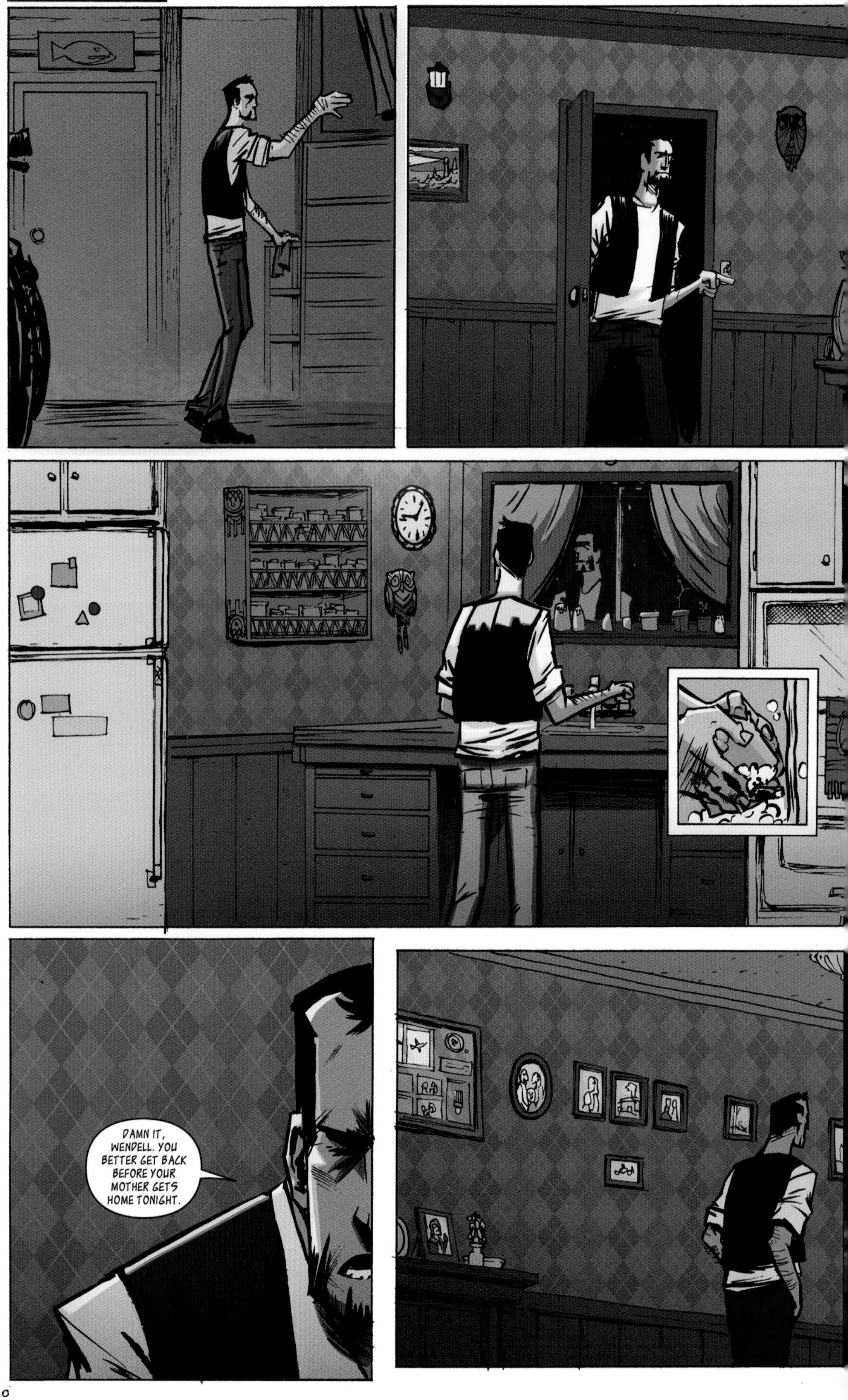
DAMN IT, WENDELL. YOU BETTER GET BACK BEFORE YOUR MOTHER GETS HOME TONIGHT.

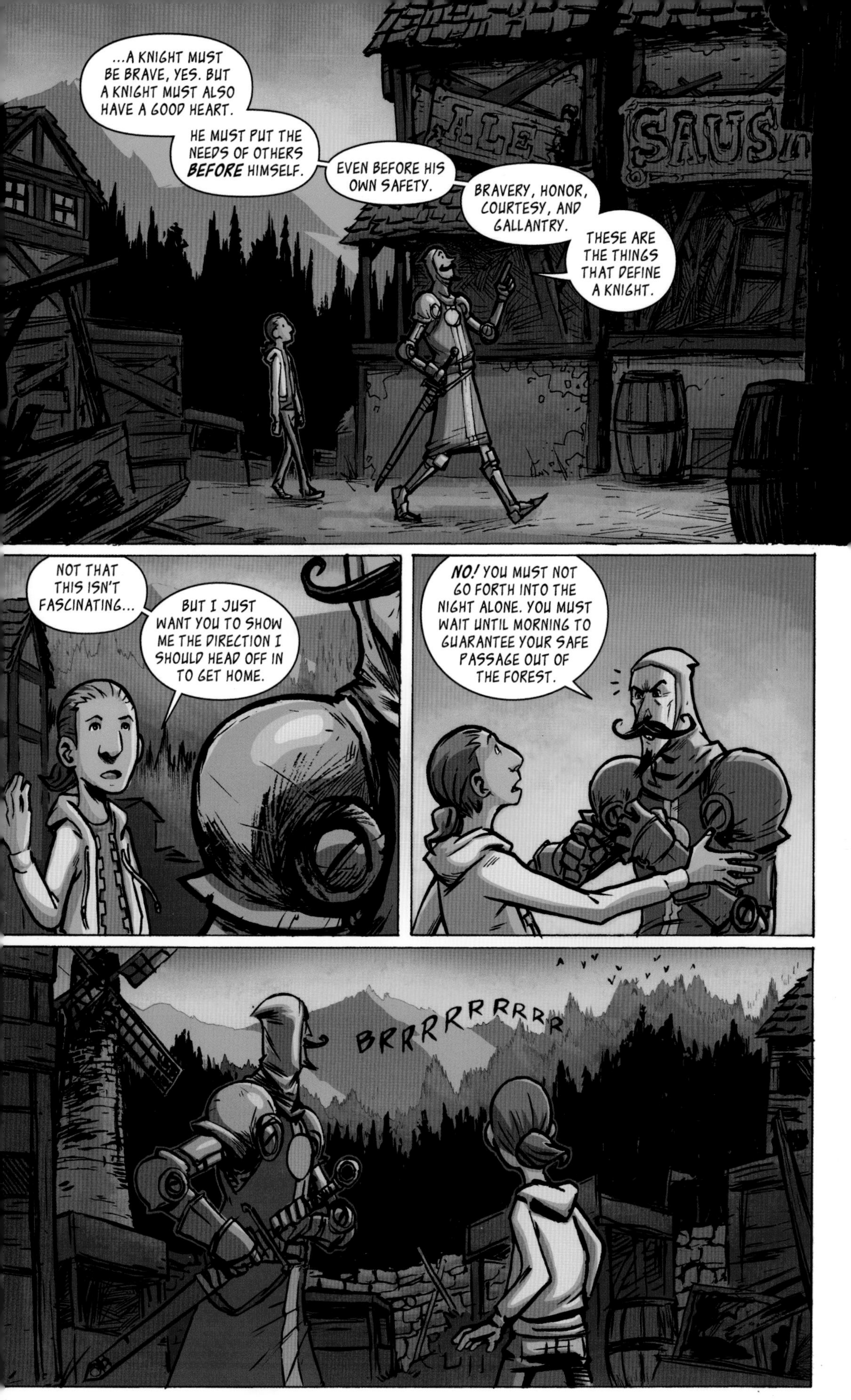

...A KNIGHT MUST BE BRAVE, YES. BUT A KNIGHT MUST ALSO HAVE A GOOD HEART.
HE MUST PUT THE NEEDS OF OTHERS **BEFORE** HIMSELF.
EVEN BEFORE HIS OWN SAFETY.
BRAVERY, HONOR, COURTESY, AND GALLANTRY.
THESE ARE THE THINGS THAT DEFINE A KNIGHT.
ALE
SAUS
NOT THAT THIS ISN'T FASCINATING...
BUT I JUST WANT YOU TO SHOW ME THE DIRECTION I SHOULD HEAD OFF IN TO GET HOME.
NO! YOU MUST NOT GO FORTH INTO THE NIGHT ALONE. YOU MUST WAIT UNTIL MORNING TO GUARANTEE YOUR SAFE PASSAGE OUT OF THE FOREST.
BRRRRRRRRRR

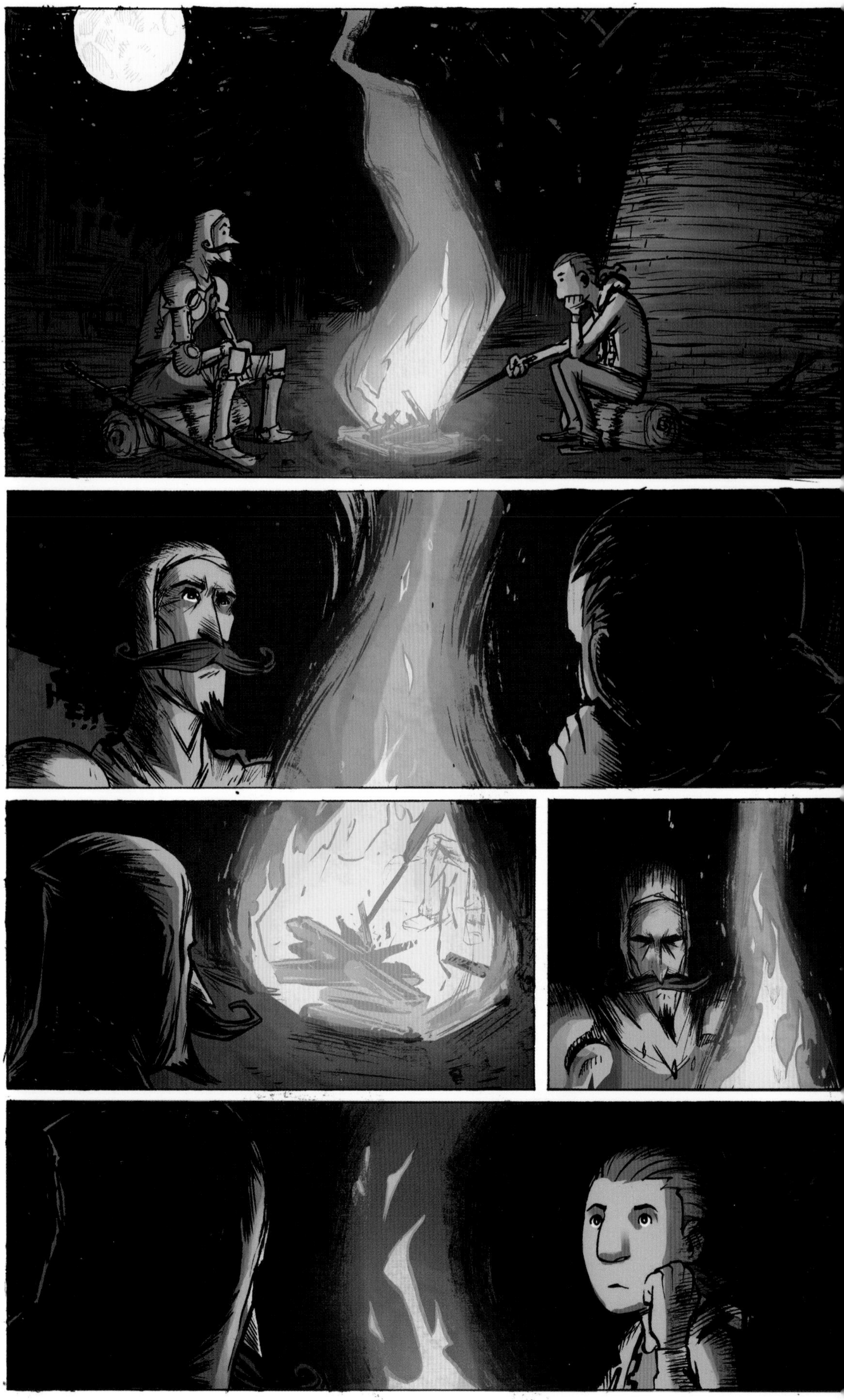

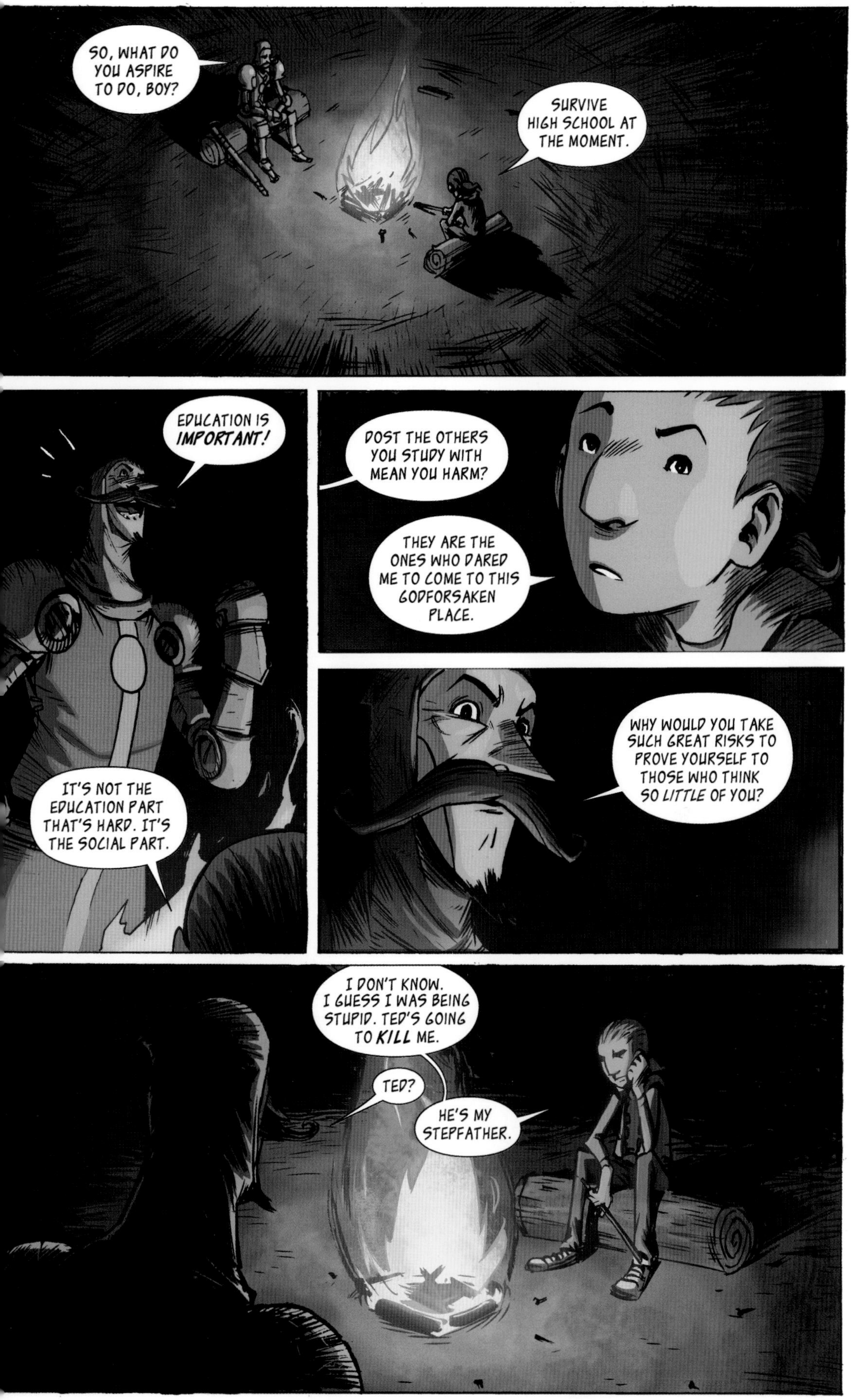
SO, WHAT DO YOU ASPIRE TO DO, BOY?
SURVIVE HIGH SCHOOL AT THE MOMENT.
EDUCATION IS *IMPORTANT!*
IT'S NOT THE EDUCATION PART THAT'S HARD. IT'S THE SOCIAL PART.
DOST THE OTHERS YOU STUDY WITH MEAN YOU HARM?
THEY ARE THE ONES WHO DARED ME TO COME TO THIS GODFORSAKEN PLACE.
WHY WOULD YOU TAKE SUCH GREAT RISKS TO PROVE YOURSELF TO THOSE WHO THINK SO *LITTLE* OF YOU?
I DON'T KNOW. I GUESS I WAS BEING STUPID. TED'S GOING TO *KILL* ME.
TED?
HE'S MY STEPFATHER.

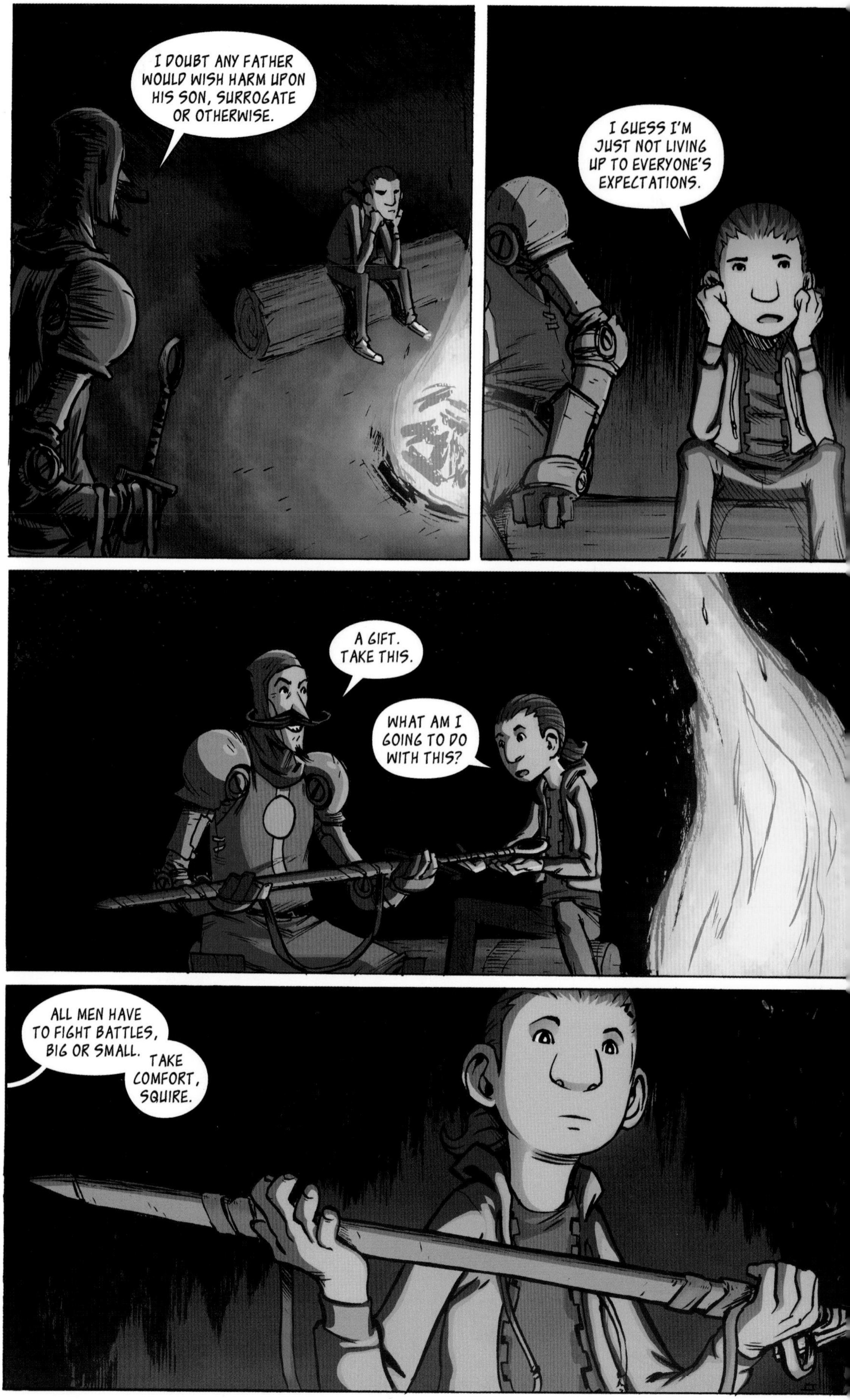
I DOUBT ANY FATHER WOULD WISH HARM UPON HIS SON, SURROGATE OR OTHERWISE.
I GUESS I'M JUST NOT LIVING UP TO EVERYONE'S EXPECTATIONS.
A GIFT. TAKE THIS.
WHAT AM I GOING TO DO WITH THIS?
ALL MEN HAVE TO FIGHT BATTLES, BIG OR SMALL.
TAKE COMFORT, SQUIRE.

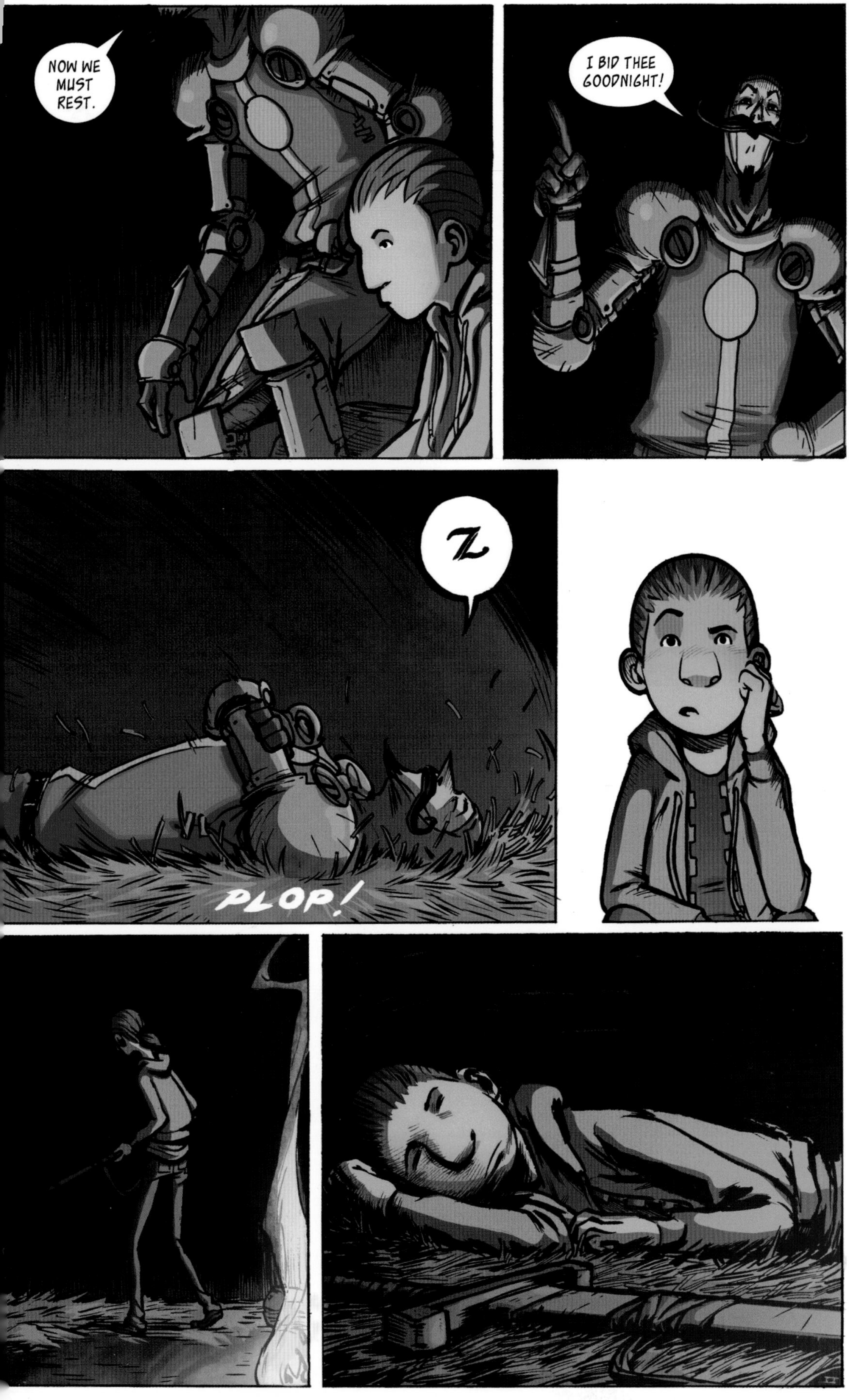
NOW WE MUST REST.
I BID THEE GOODNIGHT!
Z
PLOP!

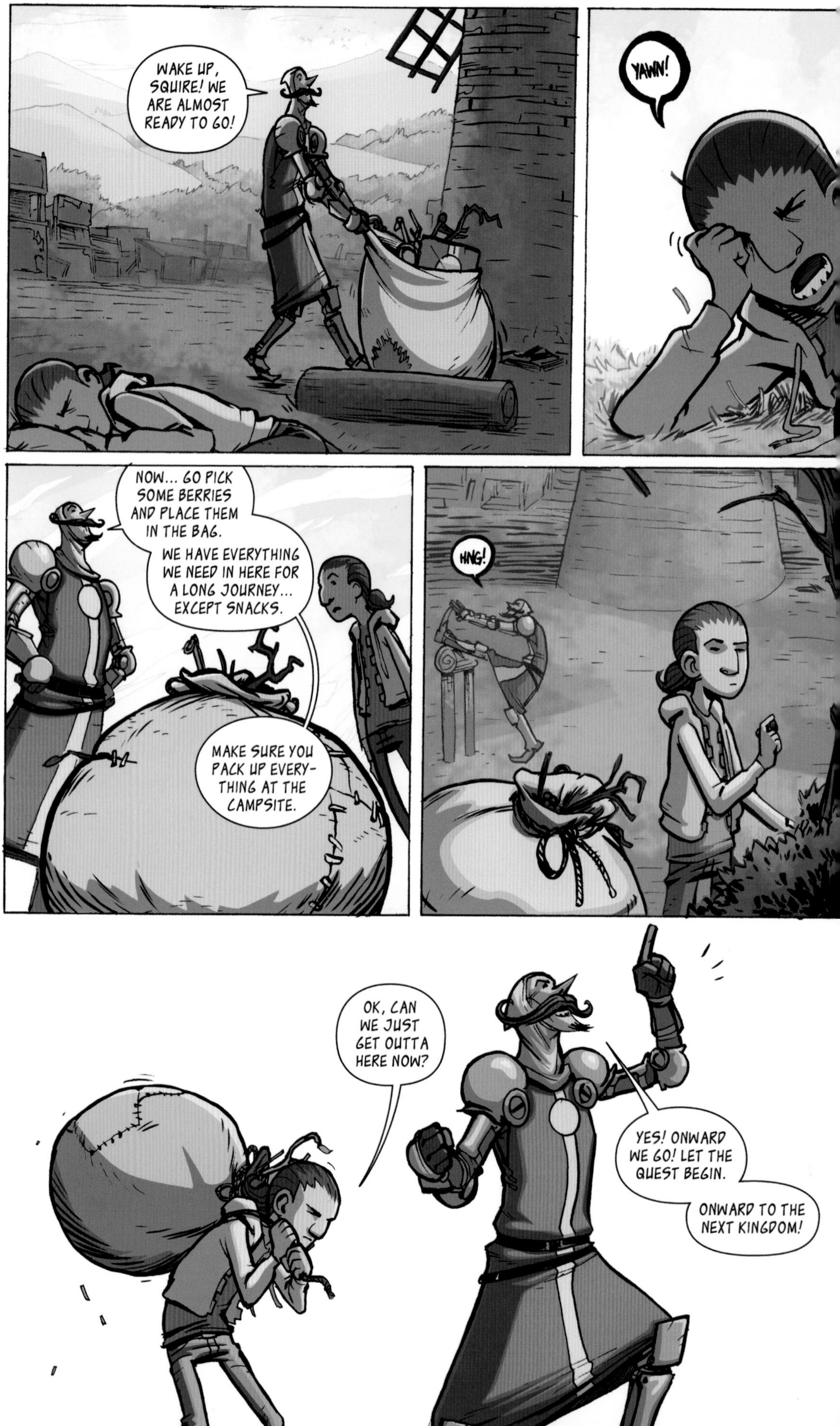
WAKE UP, SQUIRE! WE ARE ALMOST READY TO GO!
YAWN!
NOW... GO PICK SOME BERRIES AND PLACE THEM IN THE BAG.
WE HAVE EVERYTHING WE NEED IN HERE FOR A LONG JOURNEY... EXCEPT SNACKS.
MAKE SURE YOU PACK UP EVERY-THING AT THE CAMPSITE.
HNG!
OK, CAN WE JUST GET OUTTA HERE NOW?
YES! ONWARD WE GO! LET THE QUEST BEGIN.
ONWARD TO THE NEXT KINGDOM!

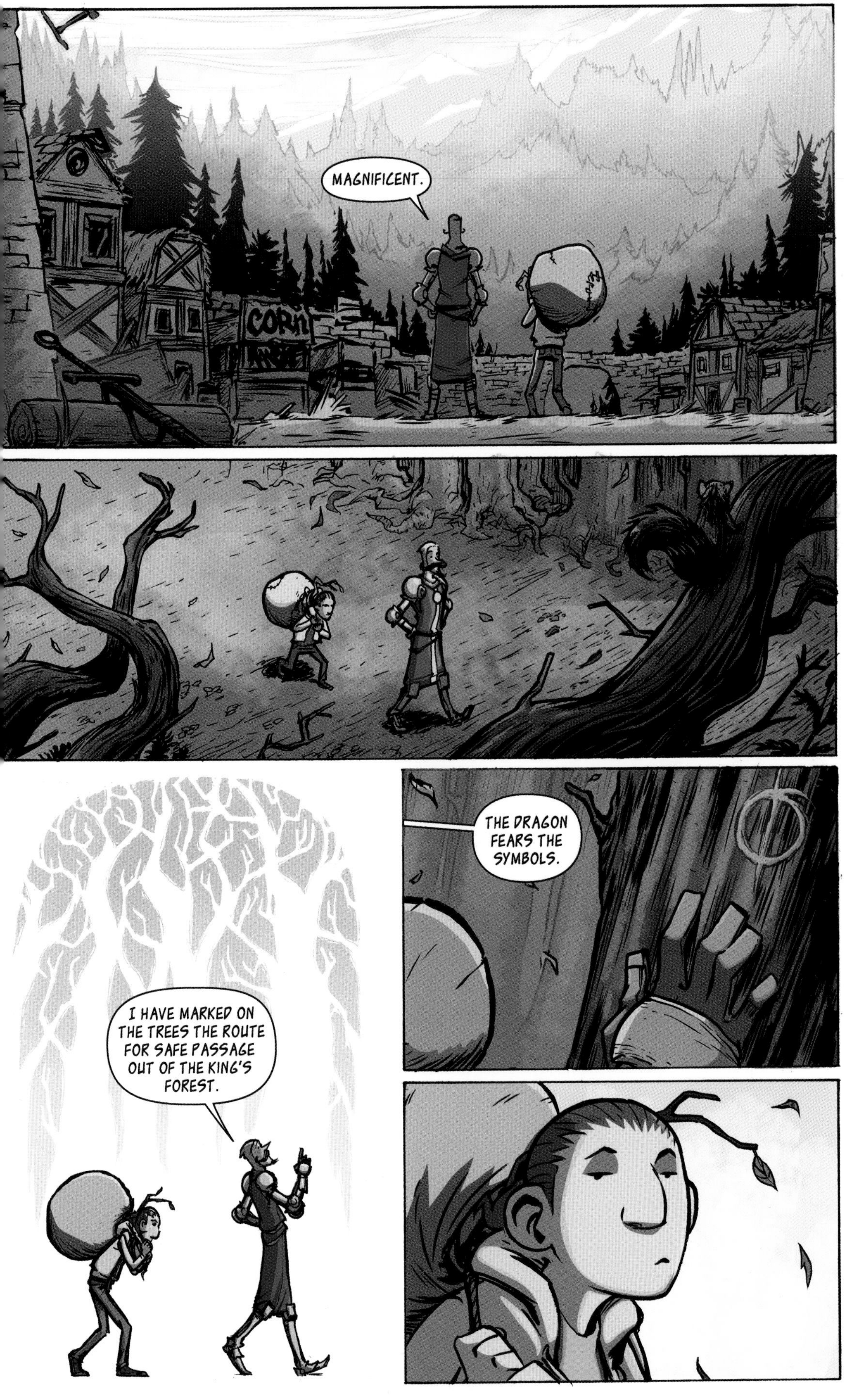

MAGNIFICENT.
CORN
THE DRAGON FEARS THE SYMBOLS.
I HAVE MARKED ON THE TREES THE ROUTE FOR SAFE PASSAGE OUT OF THE KING'S FOREST.

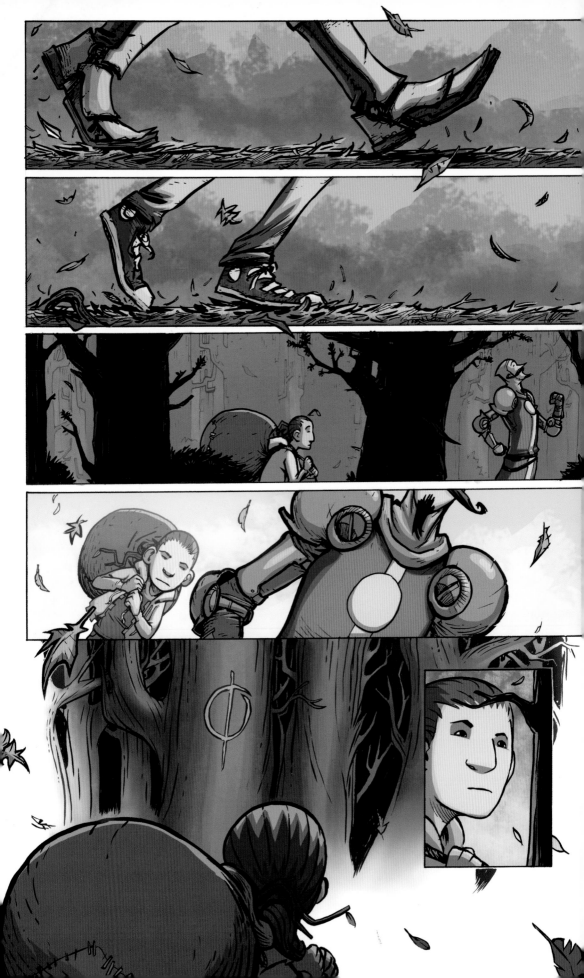

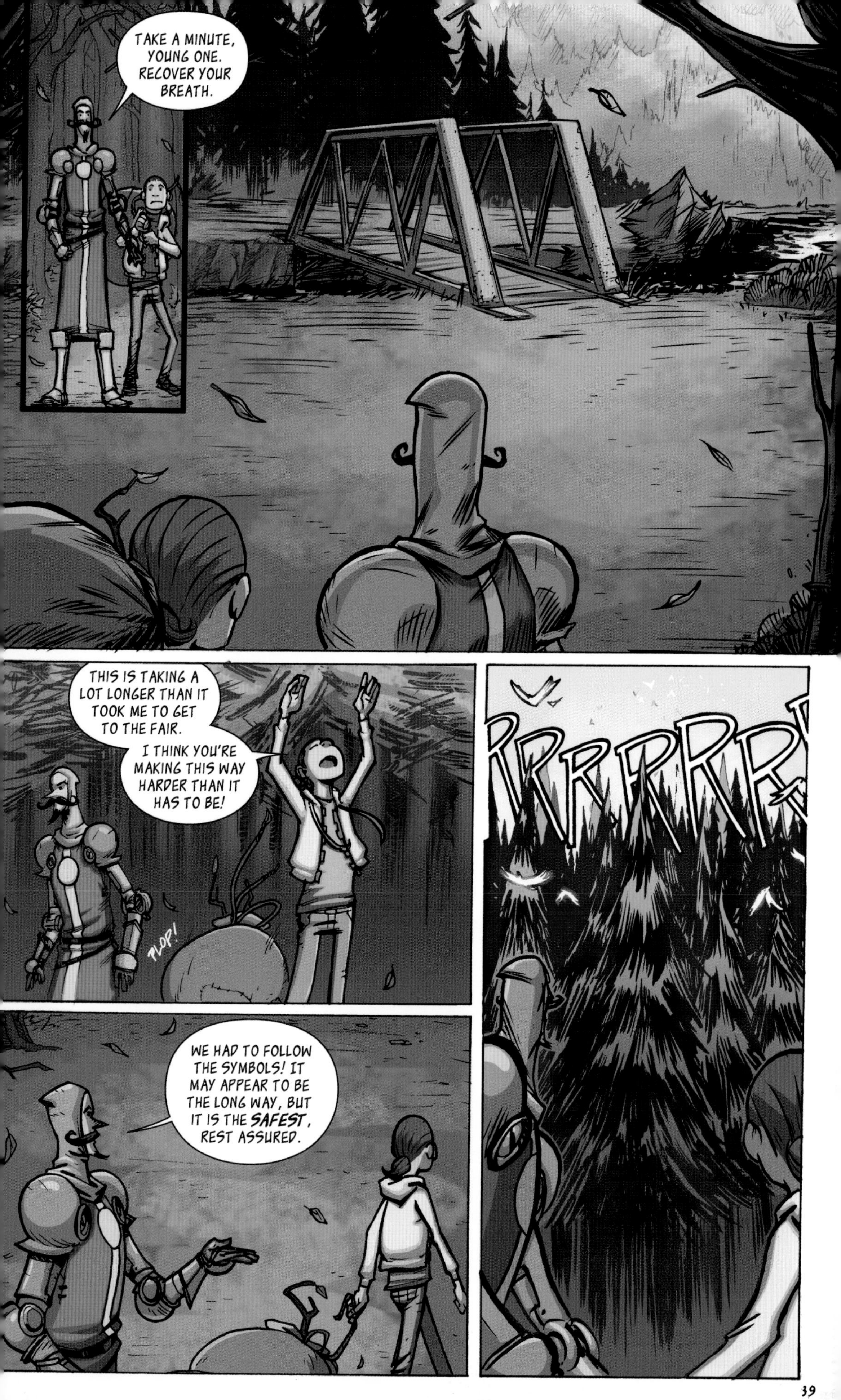

TAKE A MINUTE, YOUNG ONE. RECOVER YOUR BREATH.
THIS IS TAKING A LOT LONGER THAN IT TOOK ME TO GET TO THE FAIR.
I THINK YOU'RE MAKING THIS WAY HARDER THAN IT HAS TO BE!
PLOP!
WE HAD TO FOLLOW THE SYMBOLS! IT MAY APPEAR TO BE THE LONG WAY, BUT IT IS THE SAFEST, REST ASSURED.
RRRRRRR

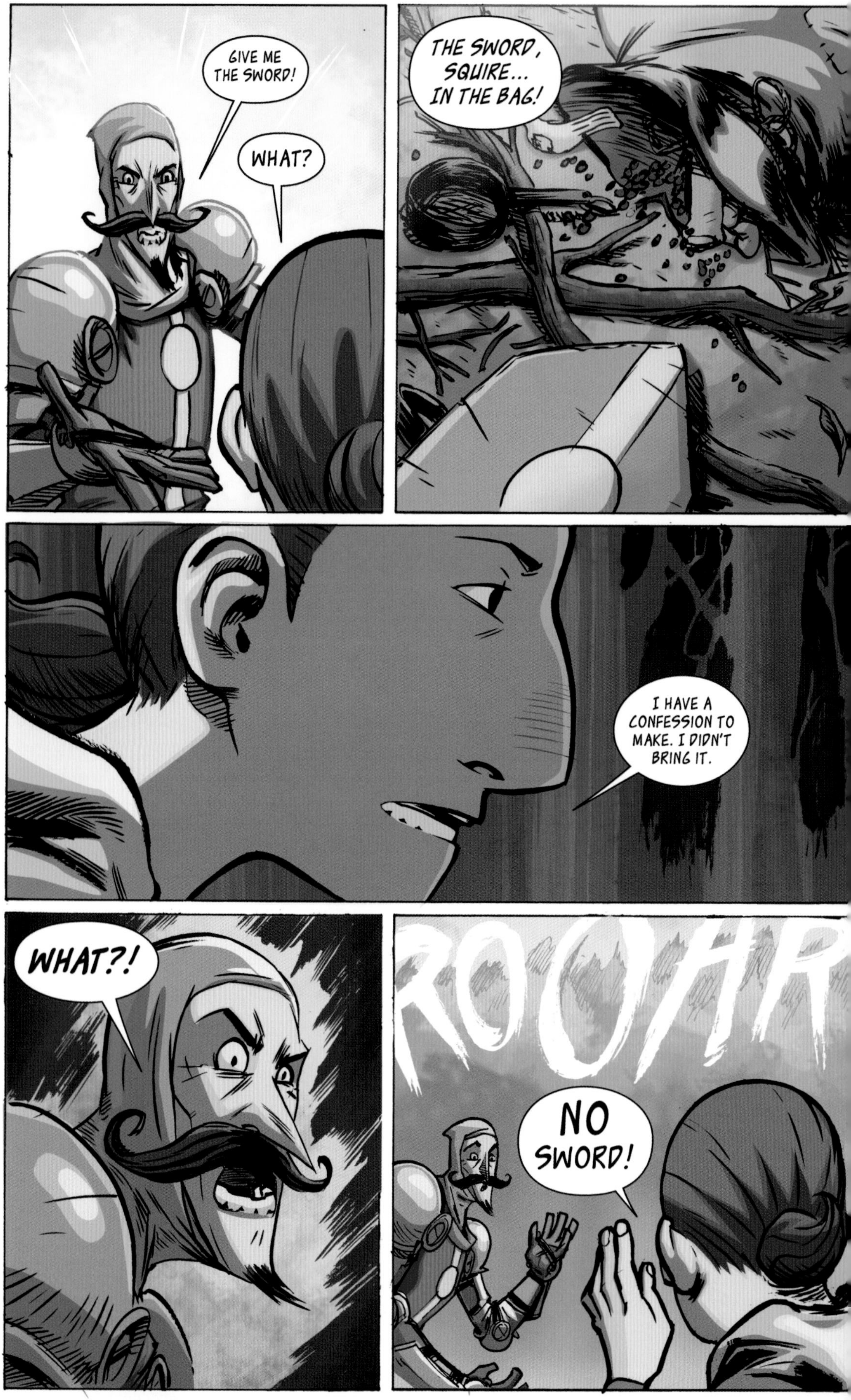
GIVE ME THE SWORD!
WHAT?
THE SWORD, SQUIRE... IN THE BAG!
I HAVE A CONFESSION TO MAKE. I DIDN'T BRING IT.
WHAT?!
ROOAHR
NO SWORD!

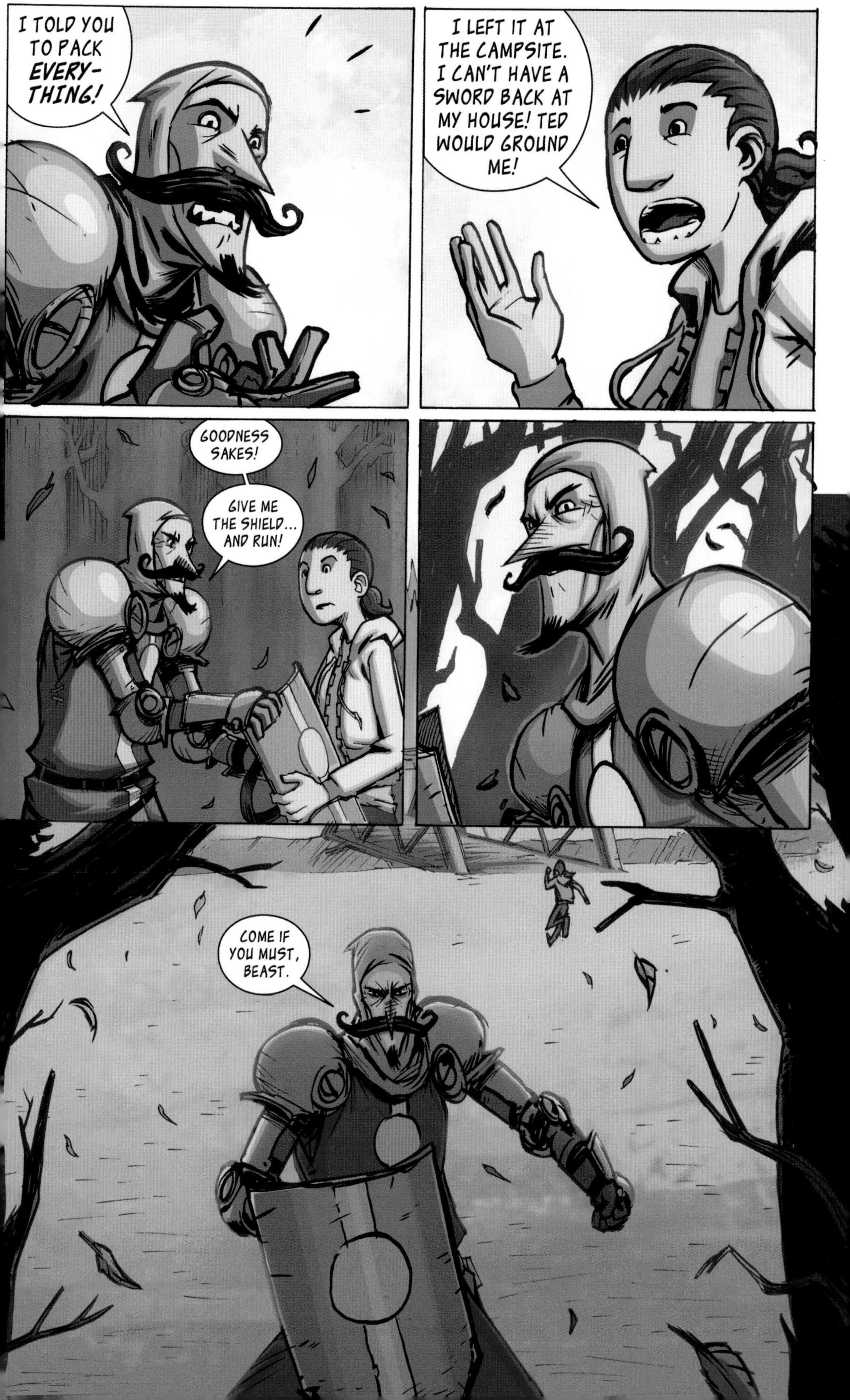
I TOLD YOU TO PACK EVERY-THING!
I LEFT IT AT THE CAMPSITE. I CAN'T HAVE A SWORD BACK AT MY HOUSE! TED WOULD GROUND ME!
GOODNESS SAKES!
GIVE ME THE SHIELD... AND RUN!
COME IF YOU MUST, BEAST.

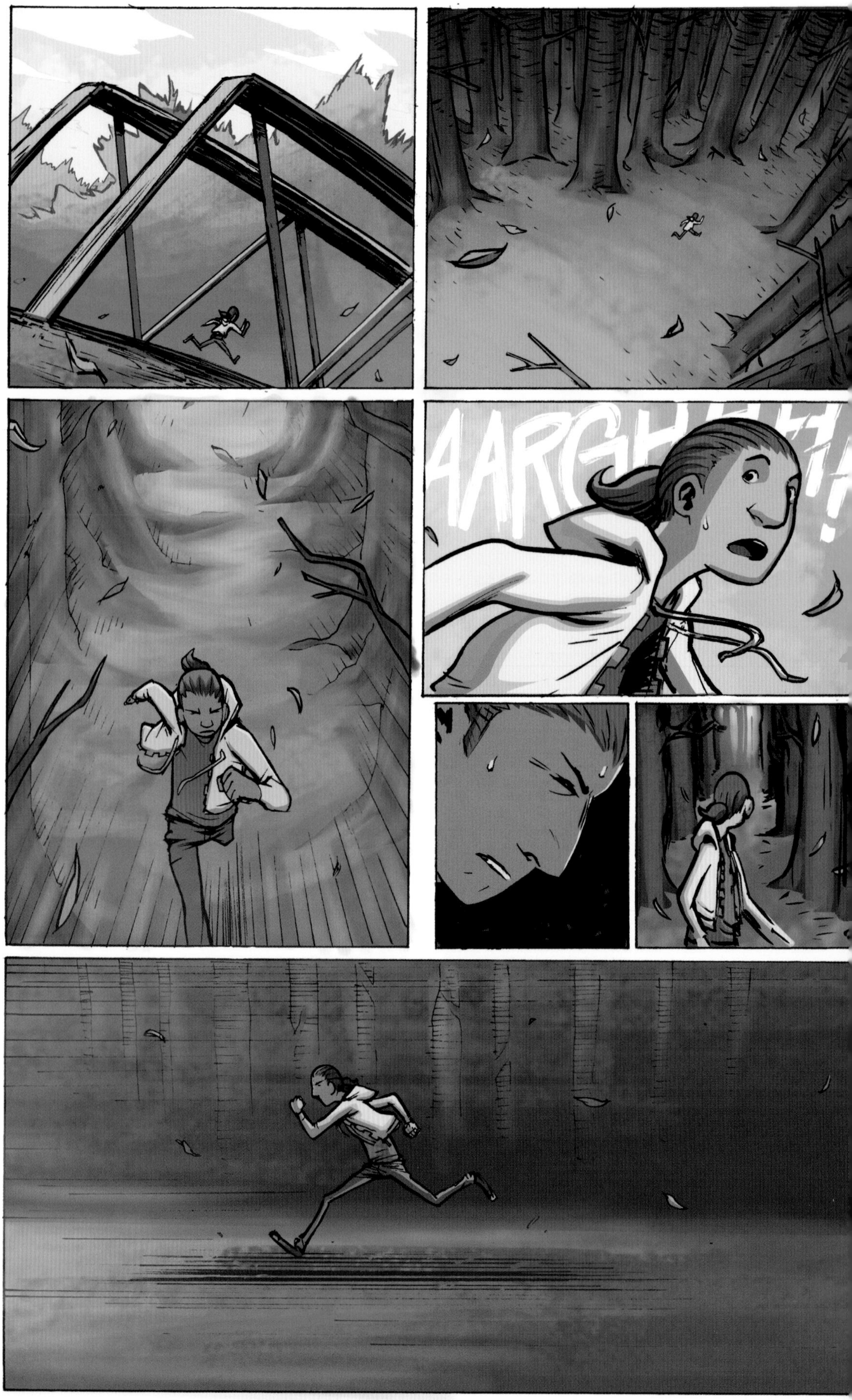
AARGH

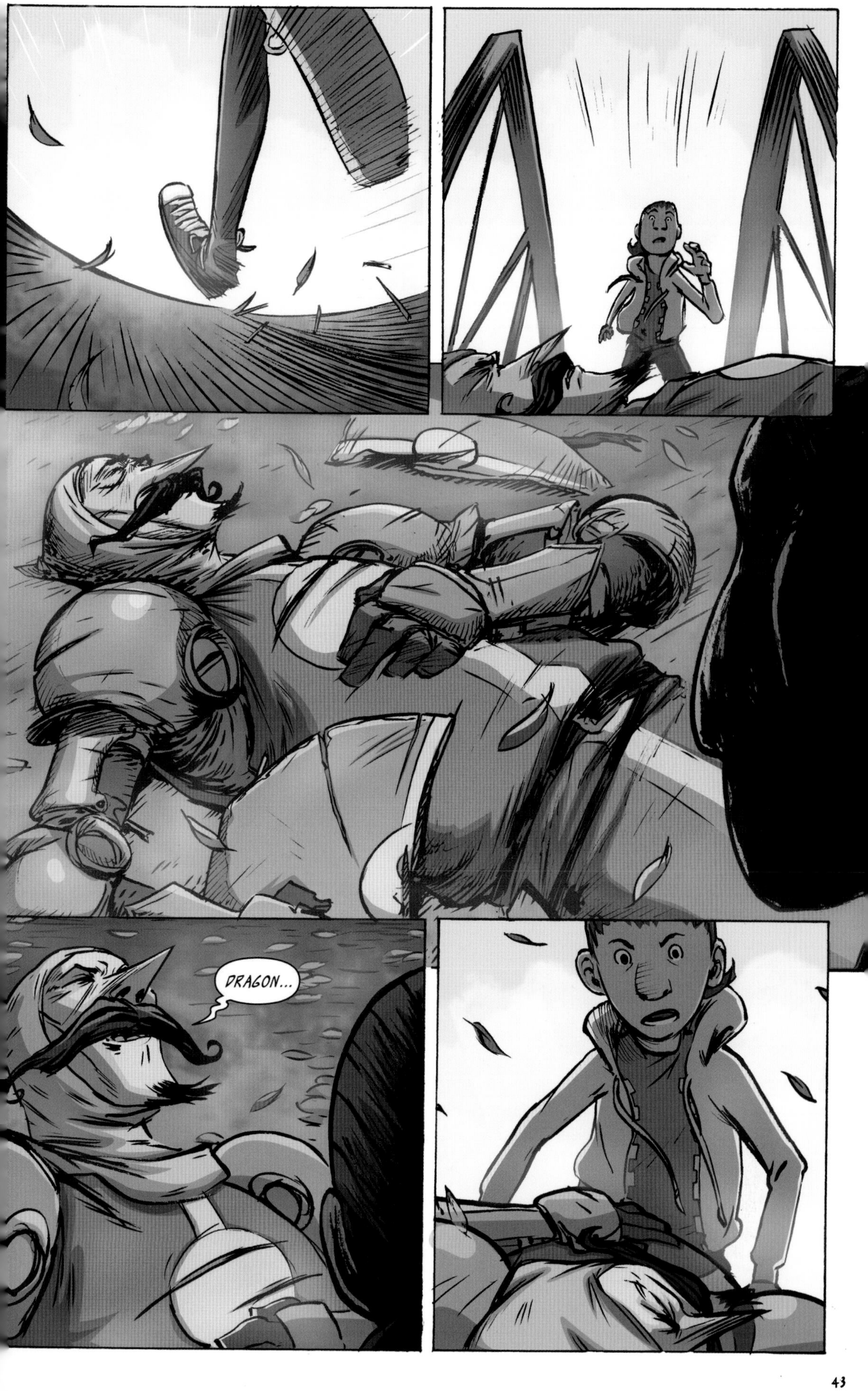
DRAGON...

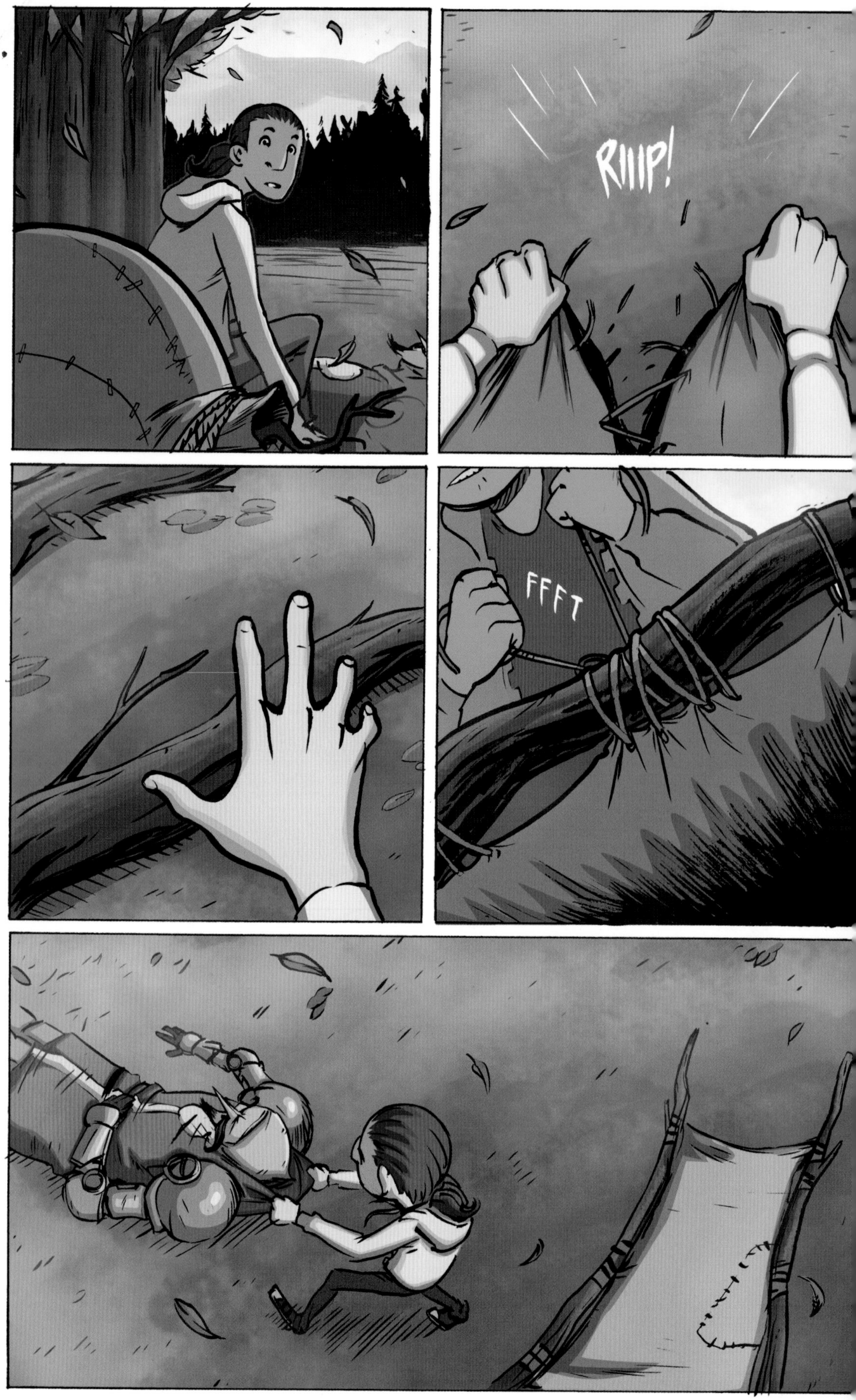
RIIIP!
FFFT

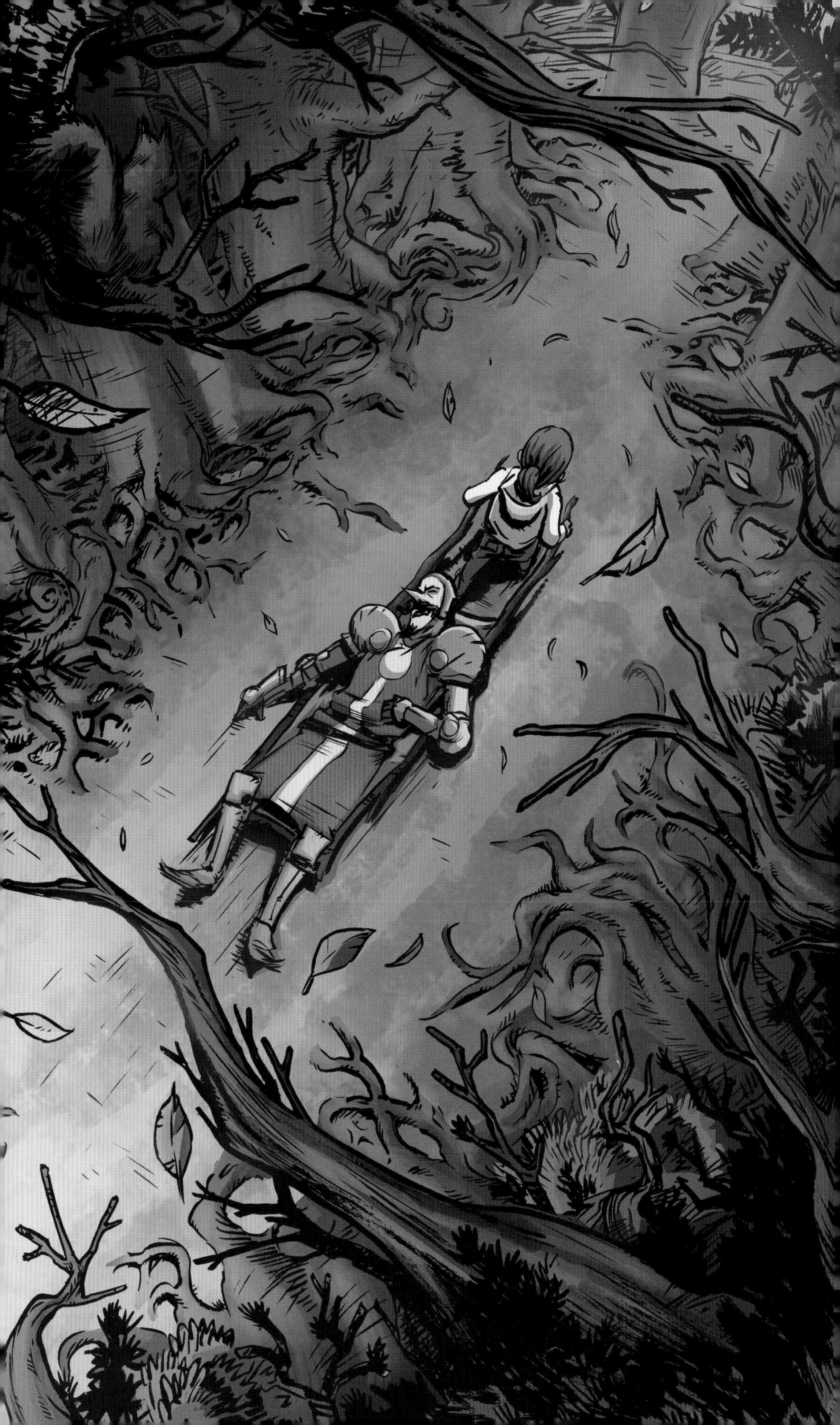

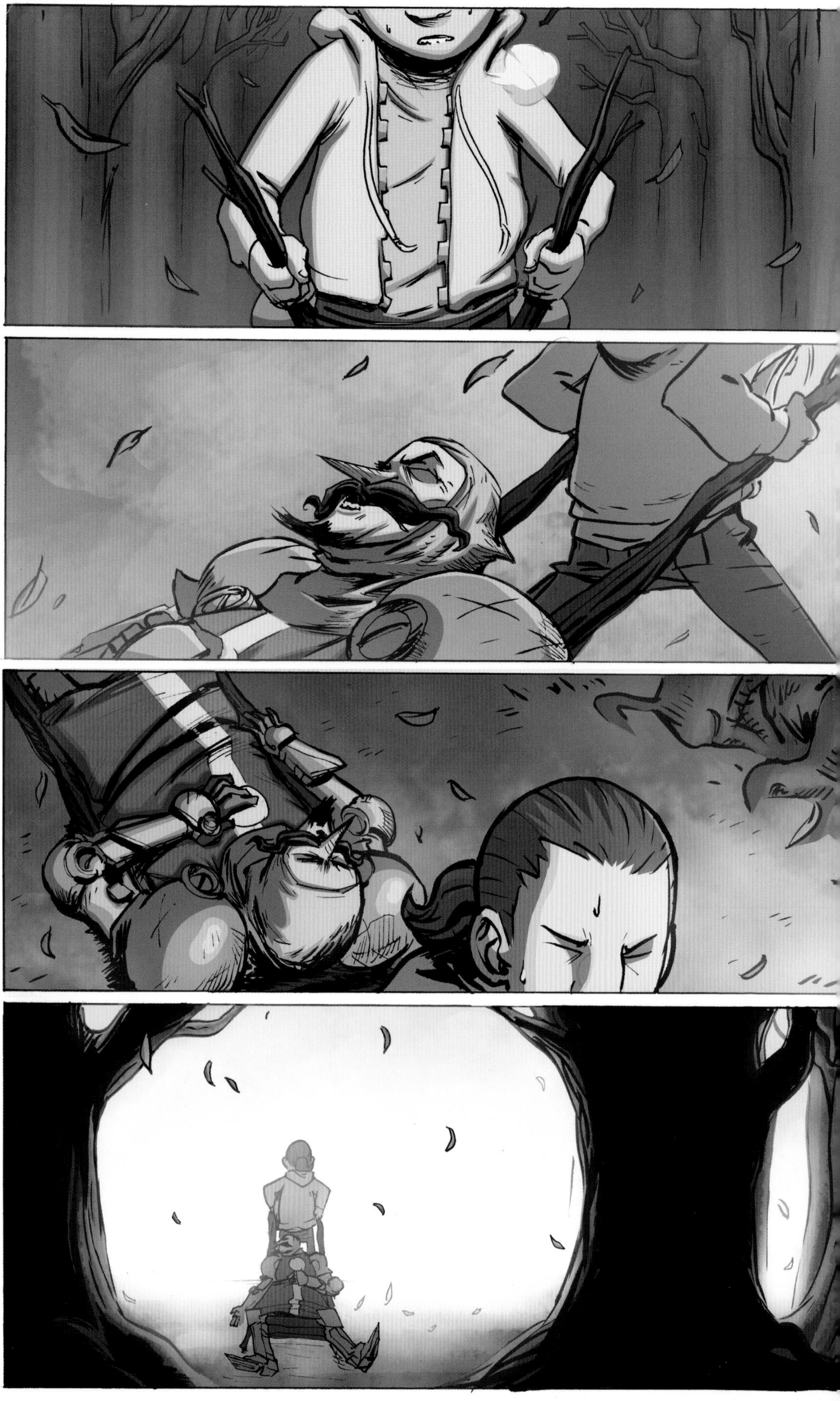

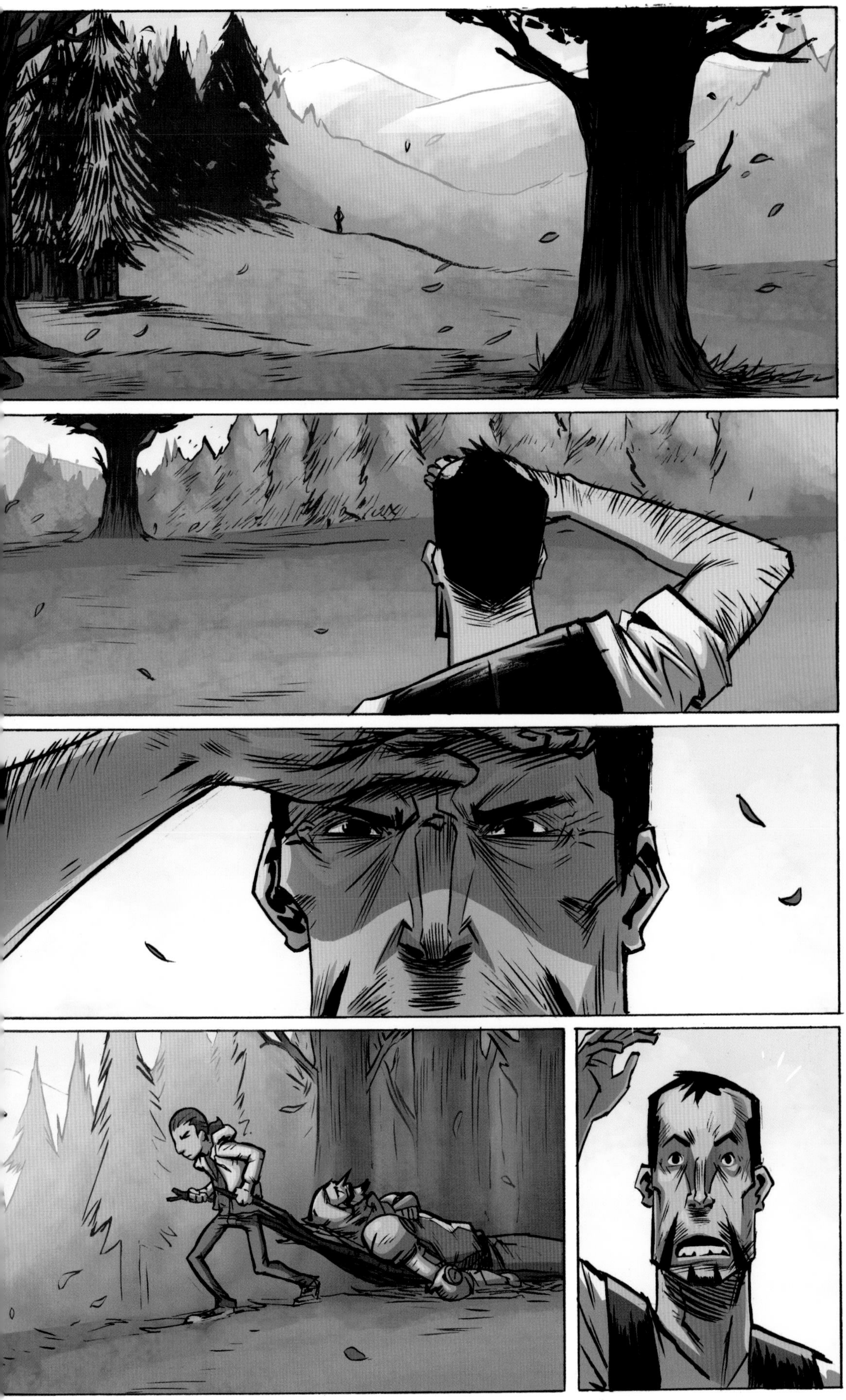

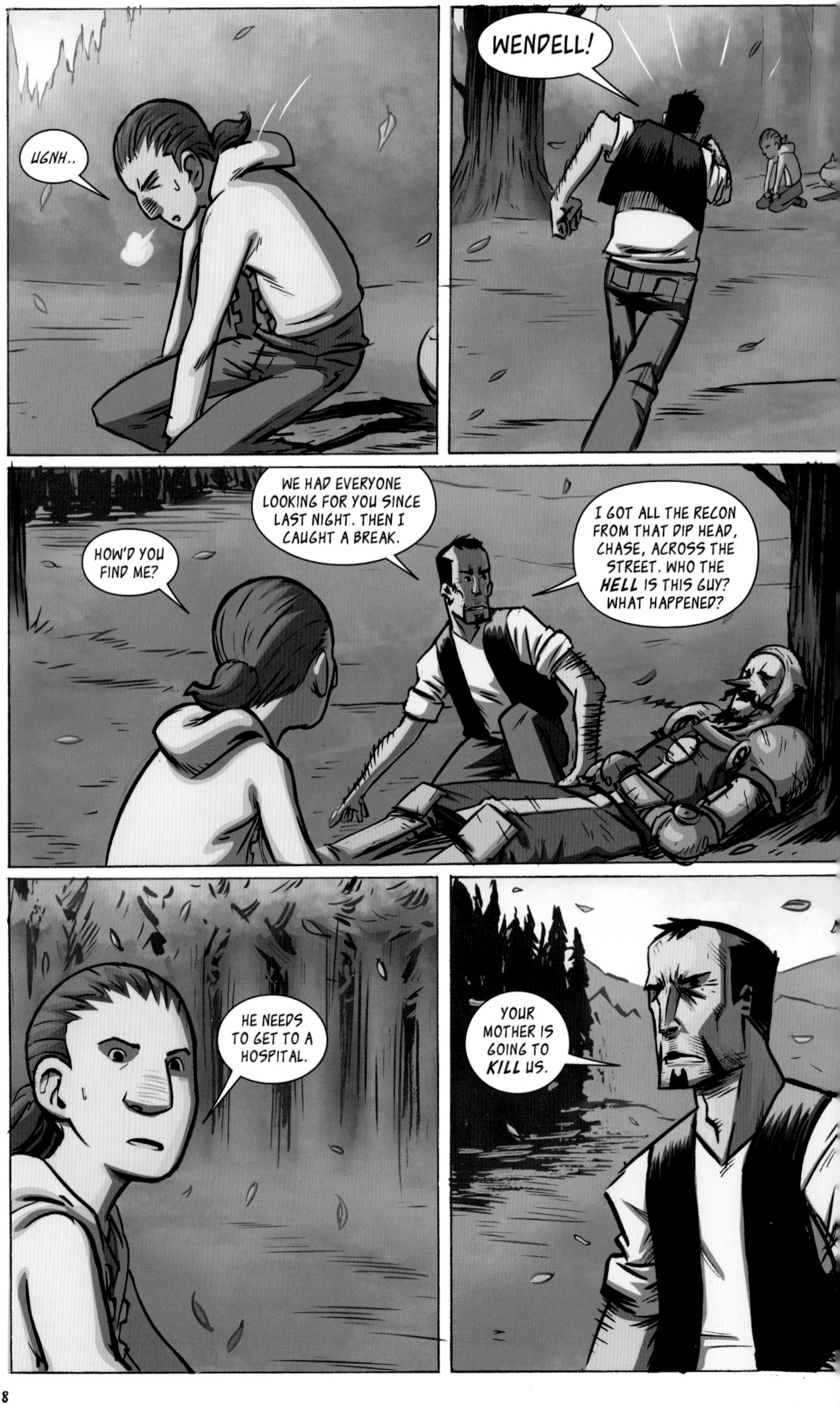
UGNH..
WENDELL!
HOW'D YOU FIND ME?
WE HAD EVERYONE LOOKING FOR YOU SINCE LAST NIGHT. THEN I CAUGHT A BREAK.
I GOT ALL THE RECON FROM THAT DIP HEAD, CHASE, ACROSS THE STREET. WHO THE HELL IS THIS GUY? WHAT HAPPENED?
HE NEEDS TO GET TO A HOSPITAL.
YOUR MOTHER IS GOING TO KILL US.

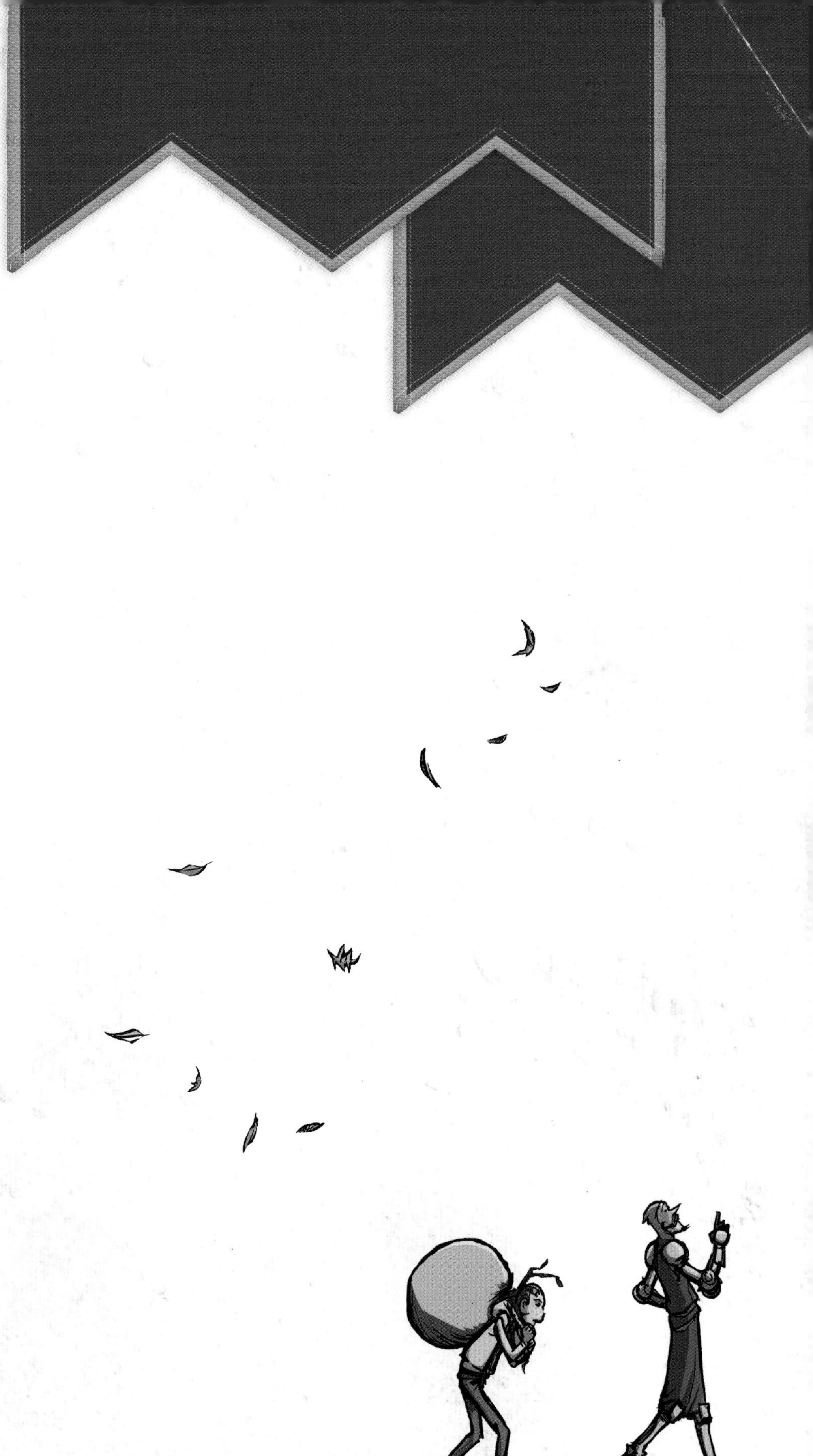

Chapter | Three

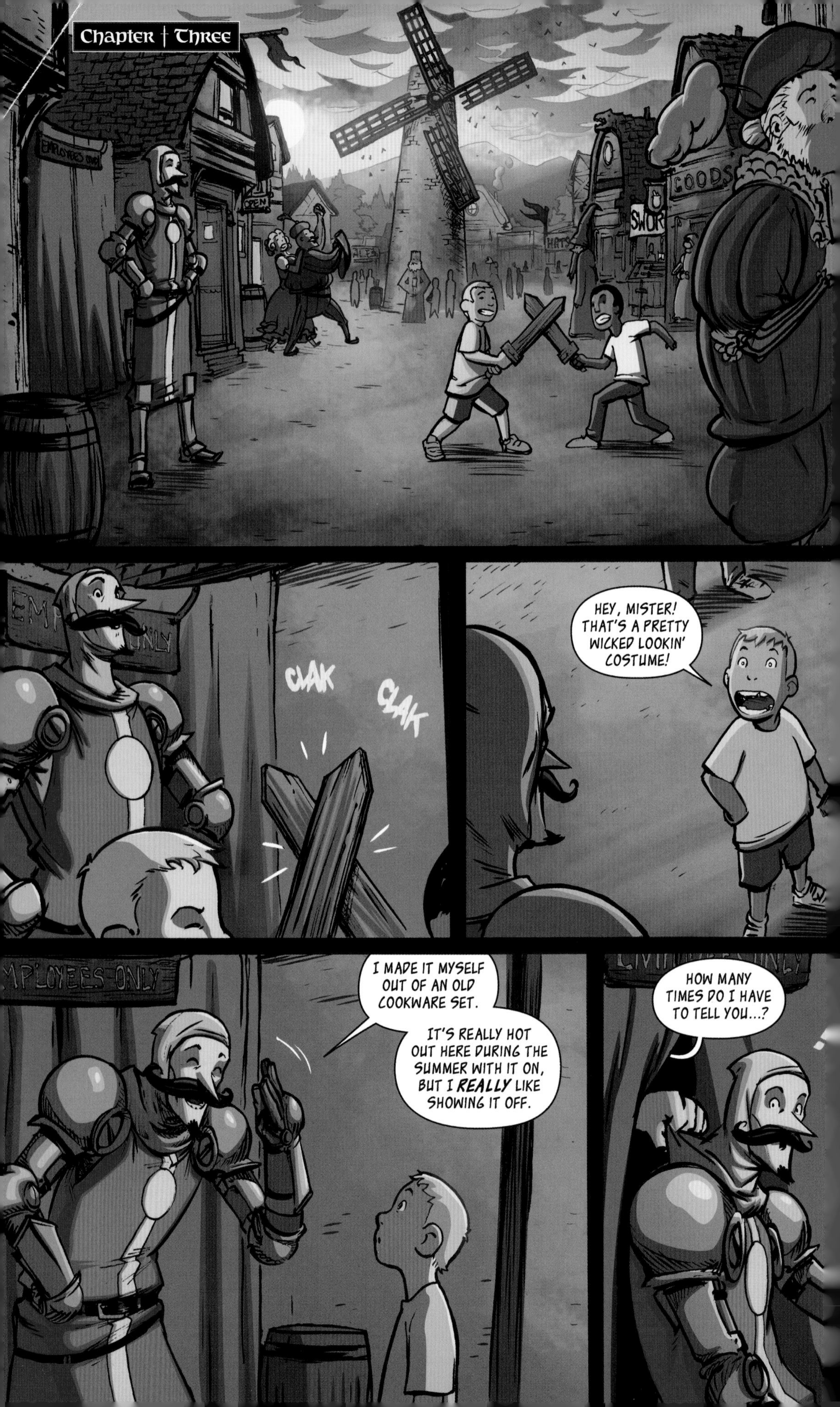
EMPLOYEES ONLY
OPEN
SWORDS
HATS
GOODS
CLAK
CLAK
HEY, MISTER! THAT'S A PRETTY WICKED LOOKIN' COSTUME!
EMPLOYEES ONLY
I MADE IT MYSELF OUT OF AN OLD COOKWARE SET.
IT'S REALLY HOT OUT HERE DURING THE SUMMER WITH IT ON, BUT I *REALLY* LIKE SHOWING IT OFF.
HOW MANY TIMES DO I HAVE TO TELL YOU...?

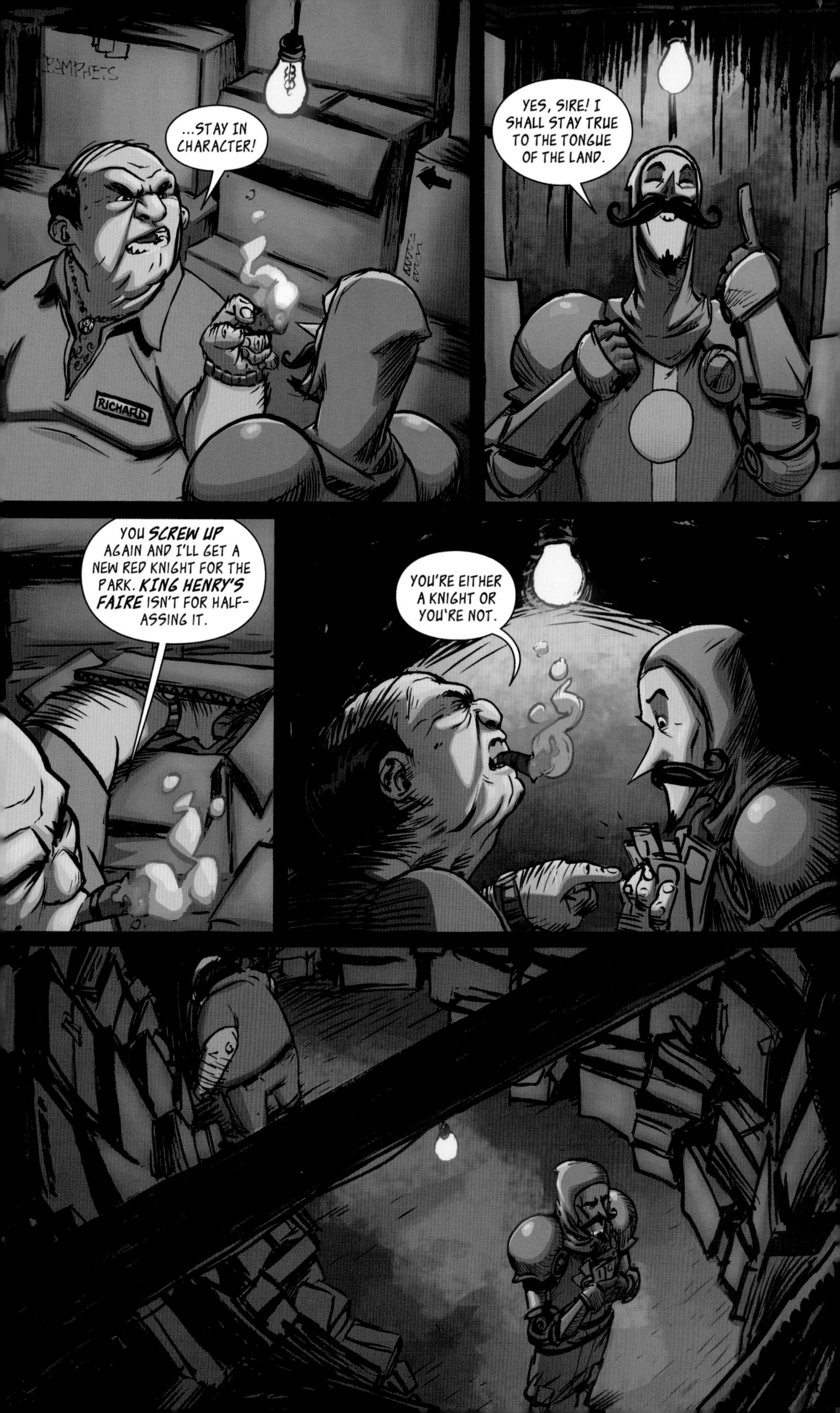

...STAY IN CHARACTER!
YES, SIRE! I SHALL STAY TRUE TO THE TONGUE OF THE LAND.
YOU SCREW UP AGAIN AND I'LL GET A NEW RED KNIGHT FOR THE PARK. KING HENRY'S FAIRE ISN'T FOR HALF-ASSING IT.
YOU'RE EITHER A KNIGHT OR YOU'RE NOT.
RICHARD

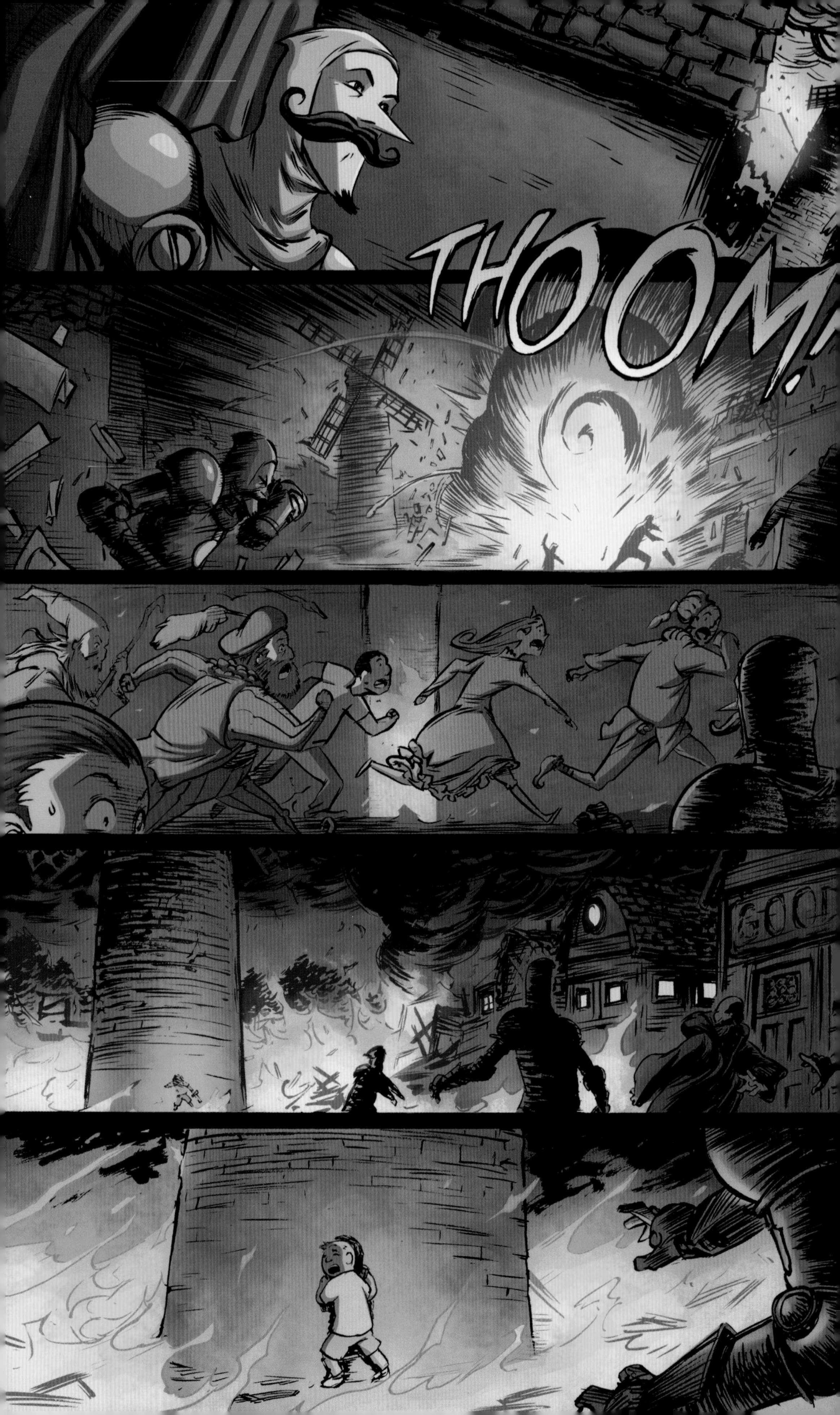
THOOM!!

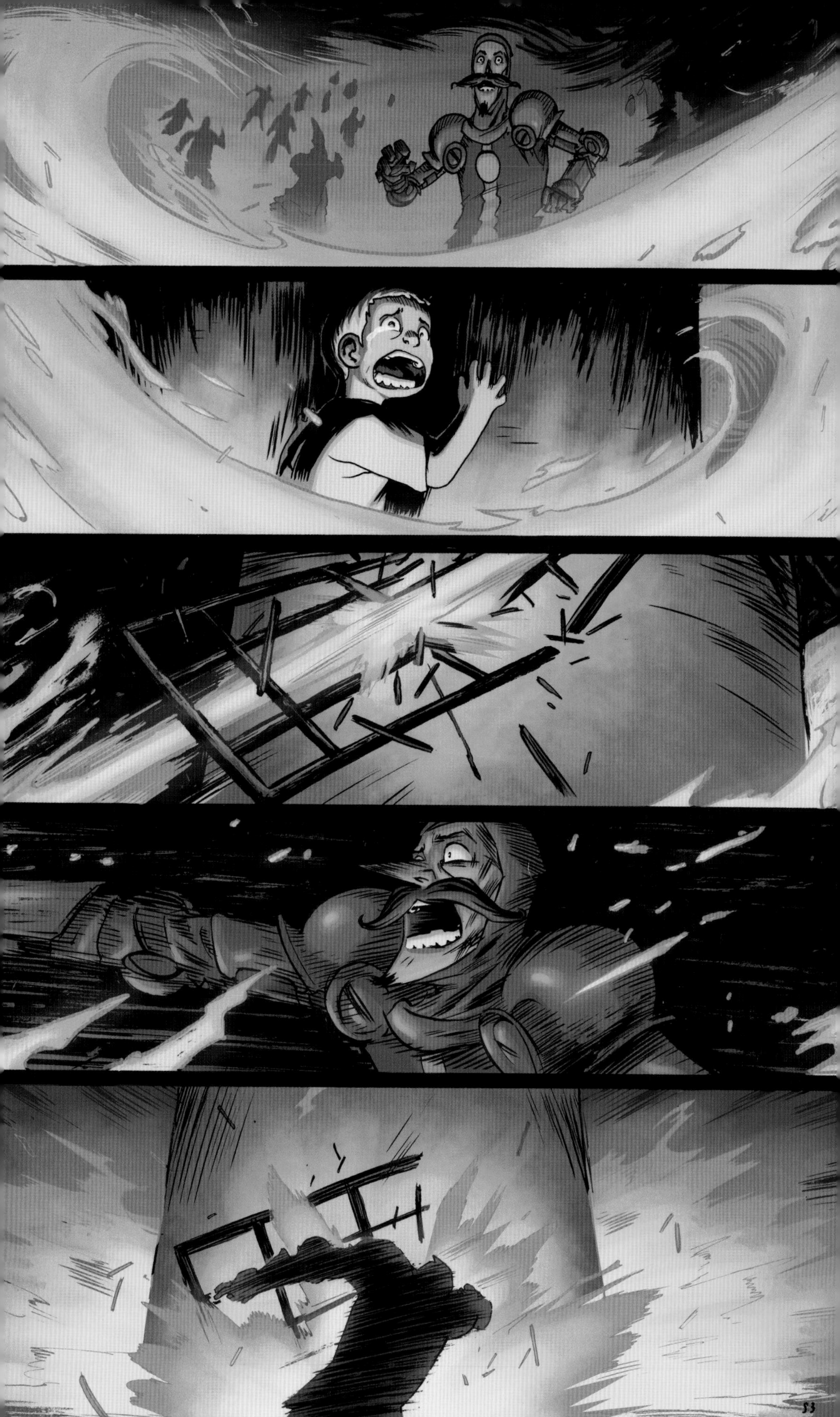

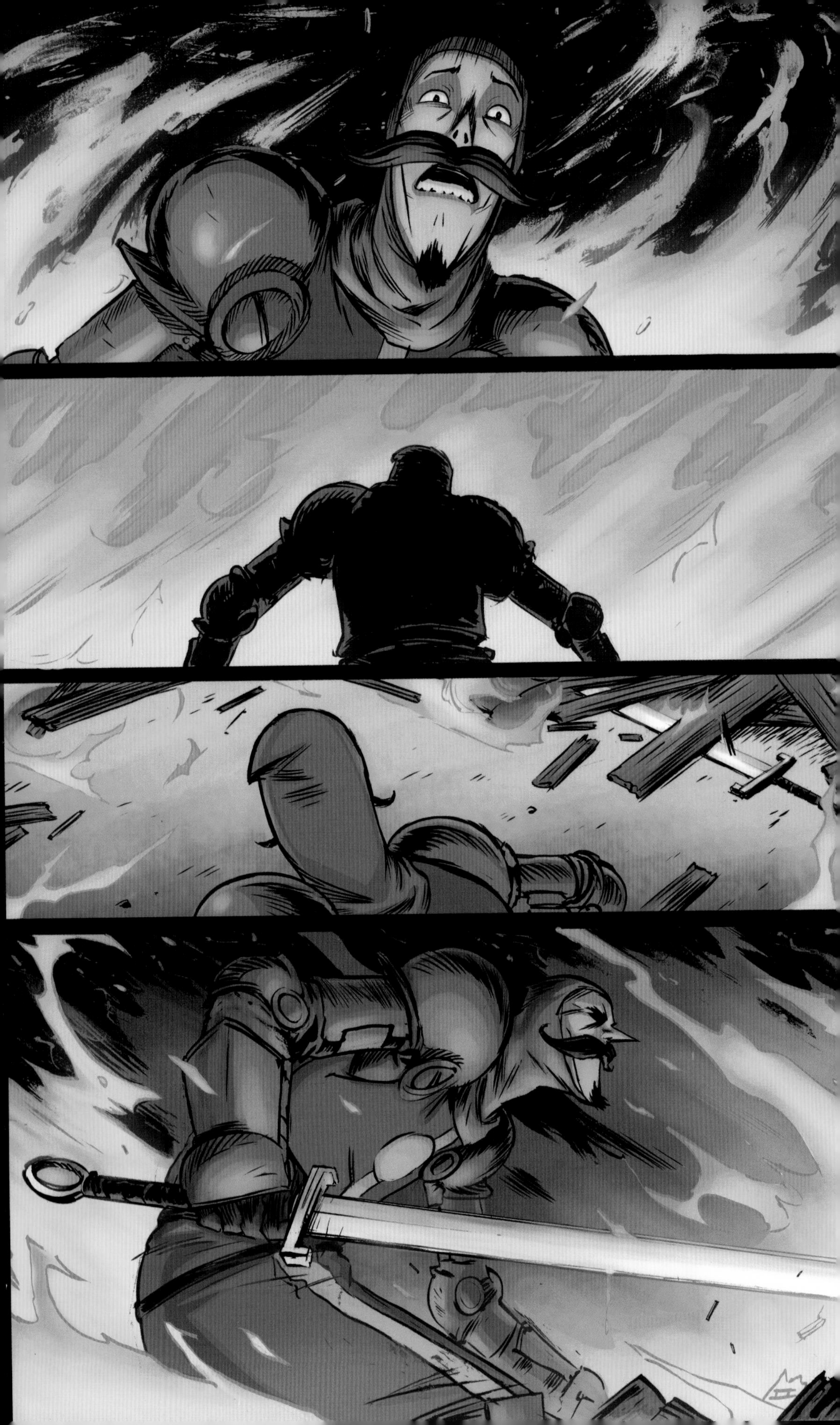

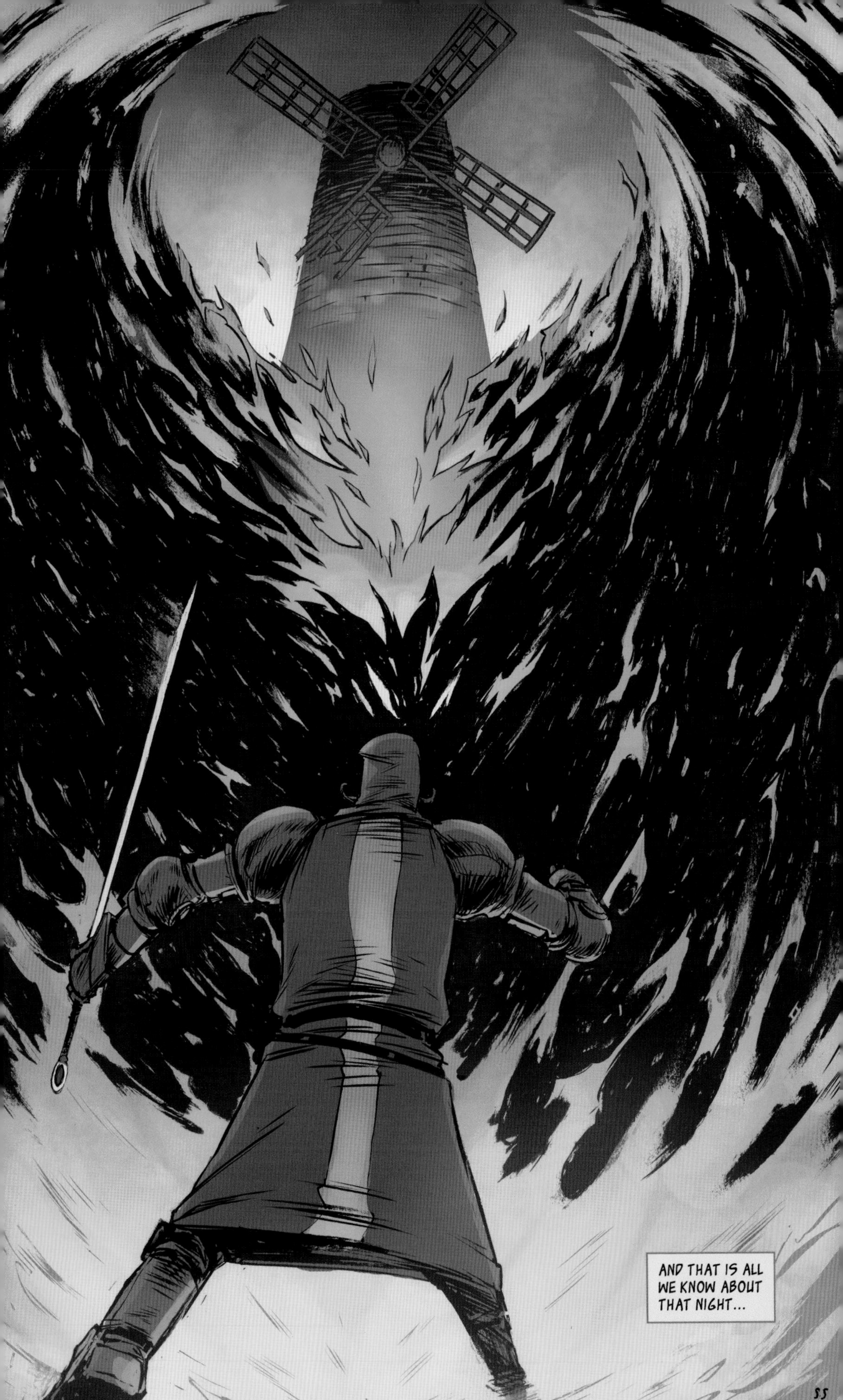
AND THAT IS ALL WE KNOW ABOUT THAT NIGHT...

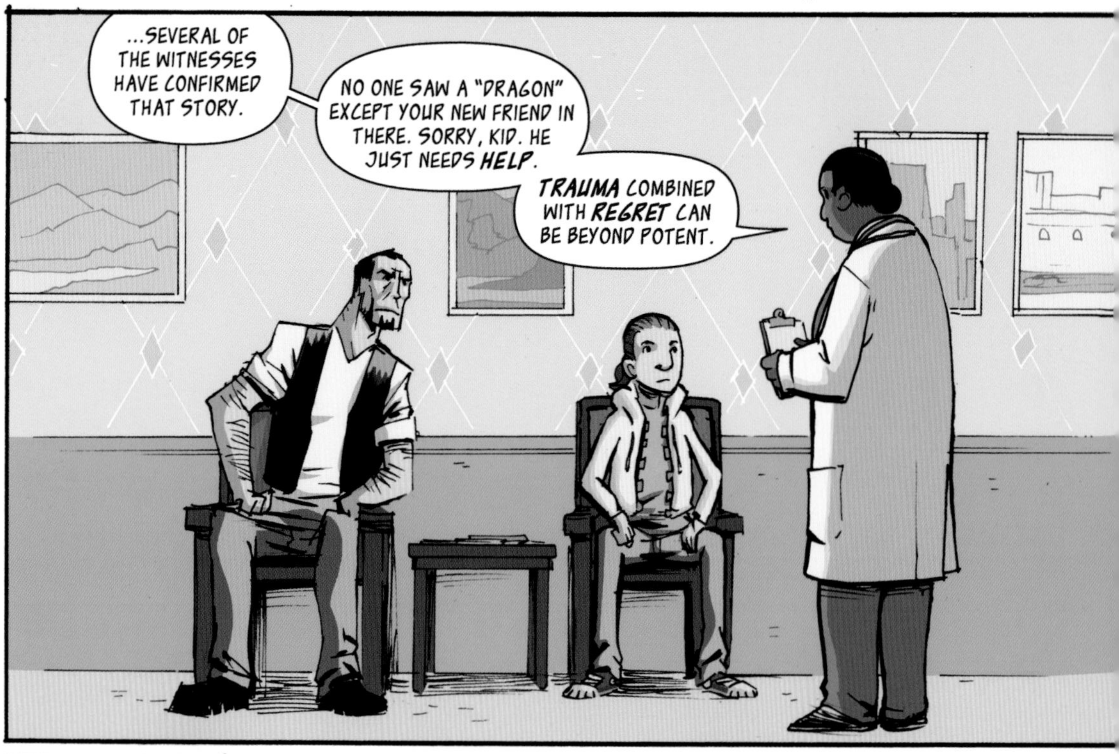
...SEVERAL OF THE WITNESSES HAVE CONFIRMED THAT STORY.
NO ONE SAW A "DRAGON" EXCEPT YOUR NEW FRIEND IN THERE. SORRY, KID. HE JUST NEEDS HELP.
TRAUMA COMBINED WITH REGRET CAN BE BEYOND POTENT.

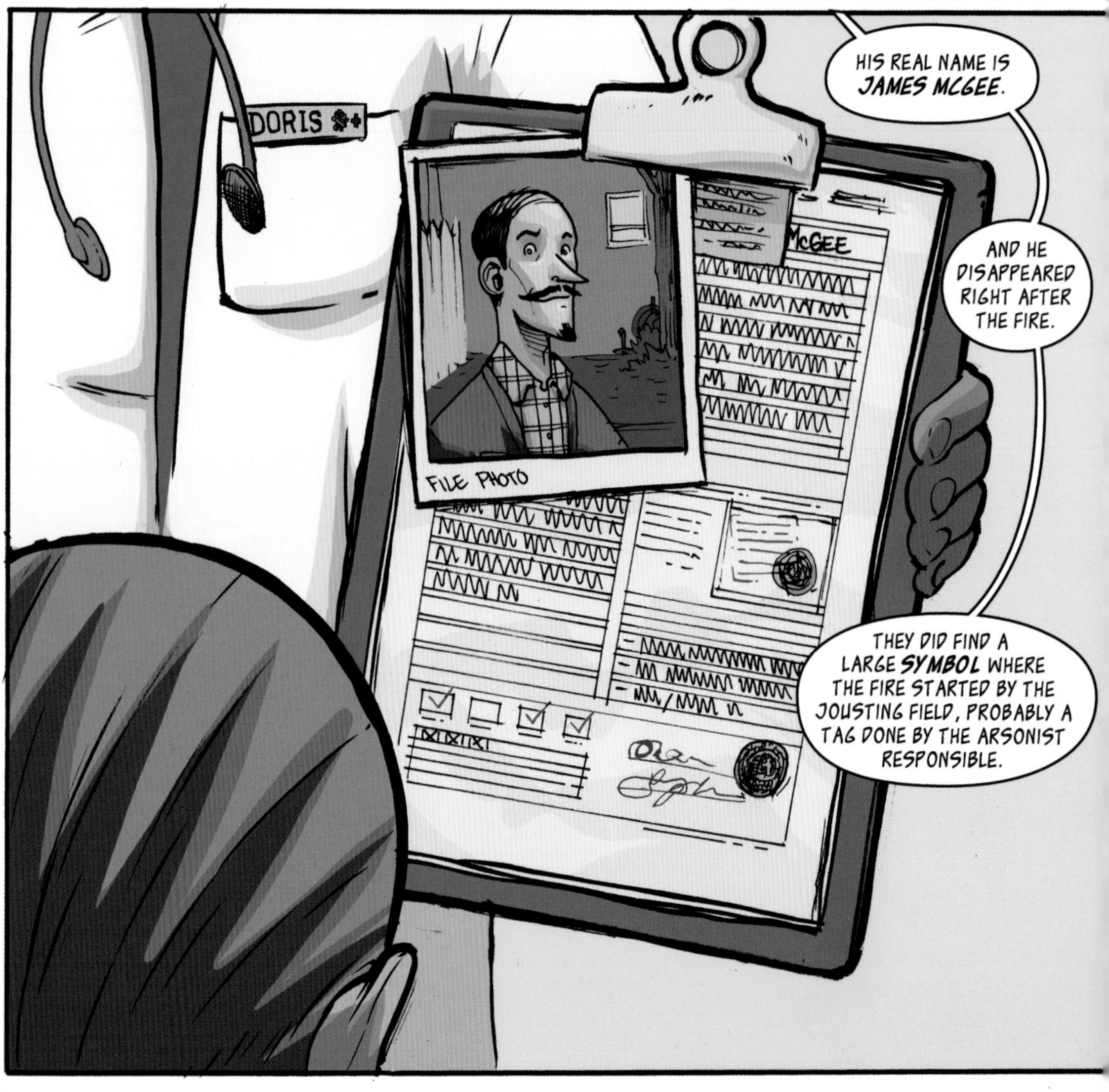
DORIS
HIS REAL NAME IS JAMES MCGEE.
McGEE
FILE PHOTO
AND HE DISAPPEARED RIGHT AFTER THE FIRE.
THEY DID FIND A LARGE SYMBOL WHERE THE FIRE STARTED BY THE JOUSTING FIELD, PROBABLY A TAG DONE BY THE ARSONIST RESPONSIBLE.

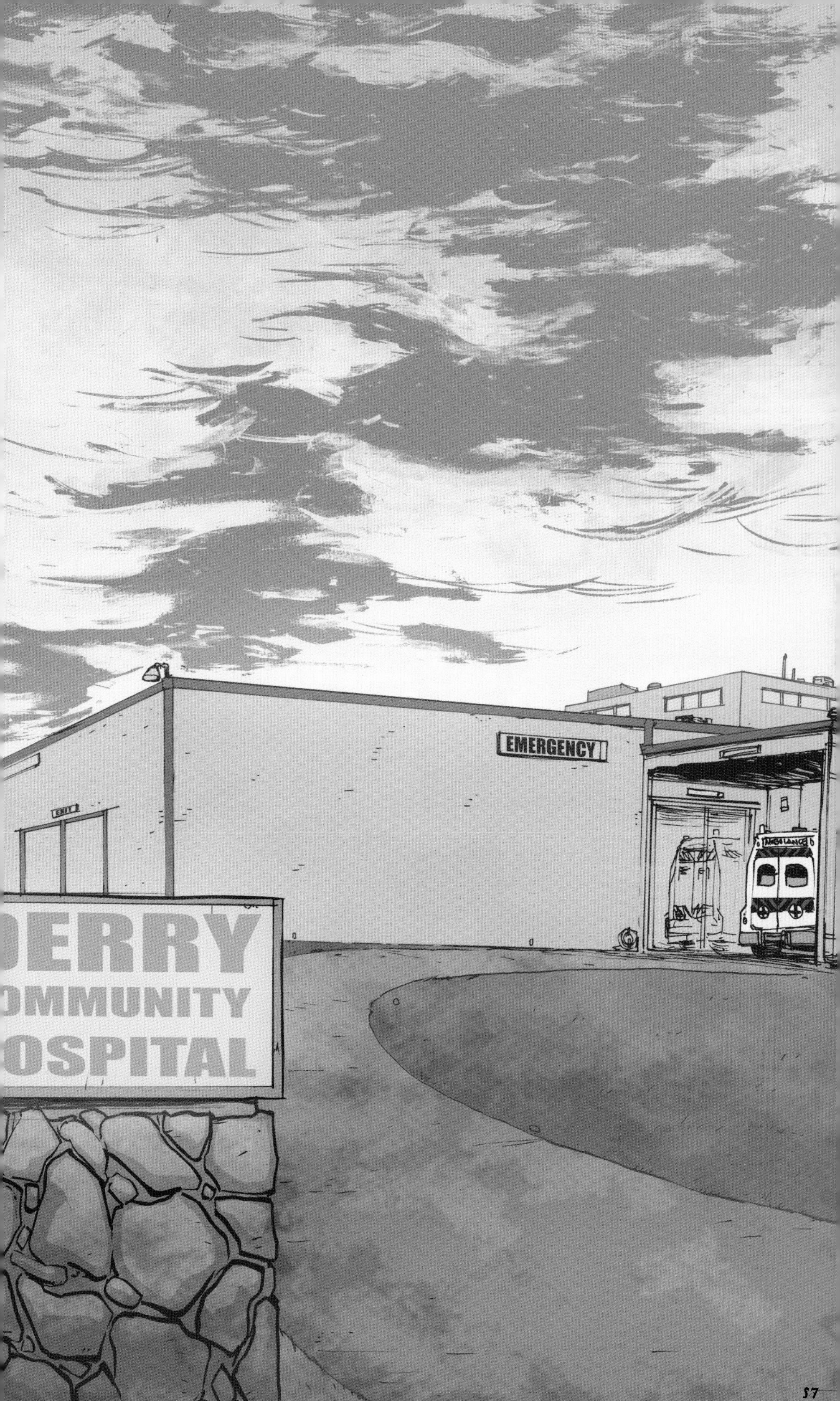
EMERGENCY
EXIT
AMBULANCE
ERRY
OMMUNITY
OSPITAL

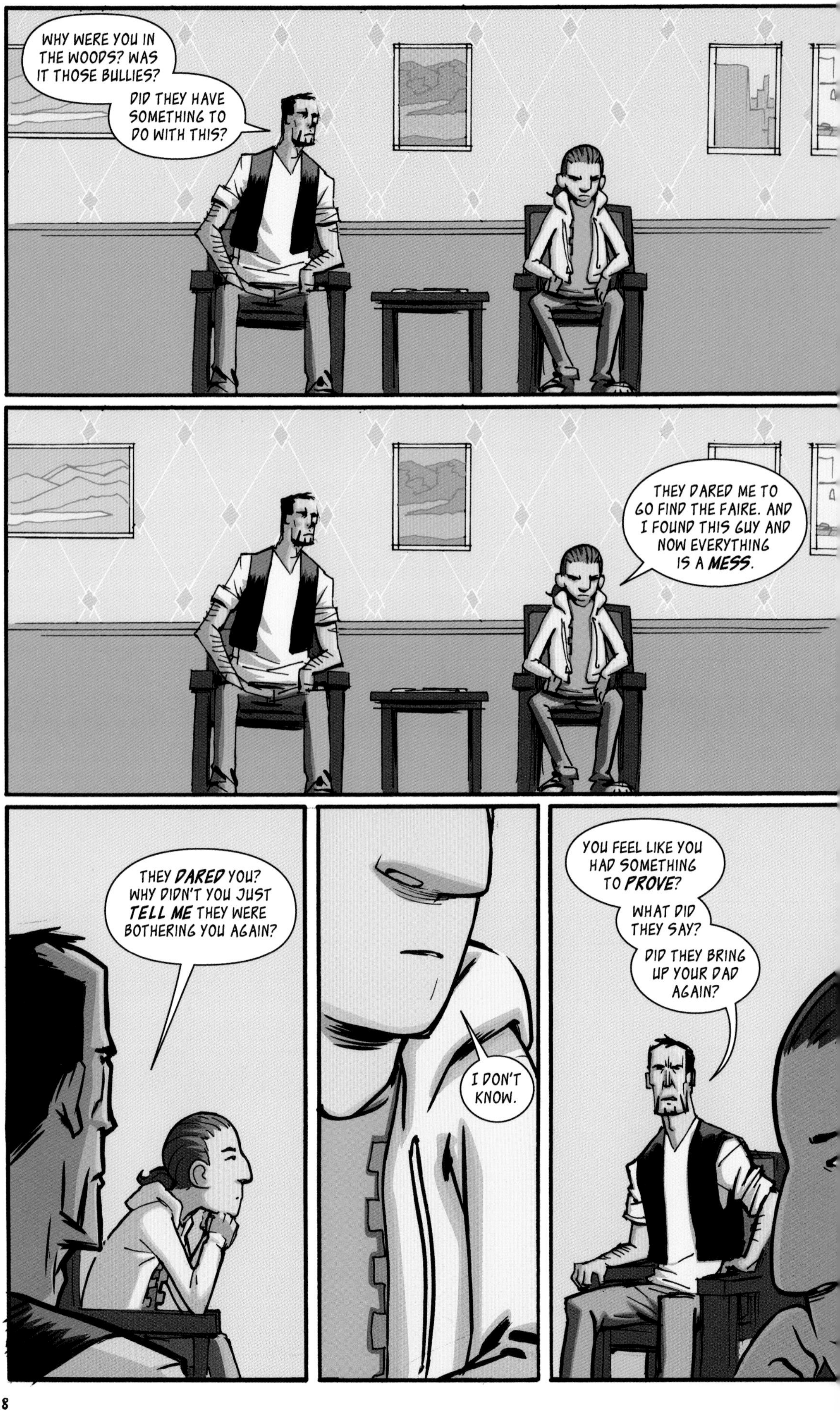
WHY WERE YOU IN THE WOODS? WAS IT THOSE BULLIES?
DID THEY HAVE SOMETHING TO DO WITH THIS?
THEY DARED ME TO GO FIND THE FAIRE. AND I FOUND THIS GUY AND NOW EVERYTHING IS A MESS.
THEY DARED YOU? WHY DIDN'T YOU JUST TELL ME THEY WERE BOTHERING YOU AGAIN?
I DON'T KNOW.
YOU FEEL LIKE YOU HAD SOMETHING TO PROVE?
WHAT DID THEY SAY?
DID THEY BRING UP YOUR DAD AGAIN?

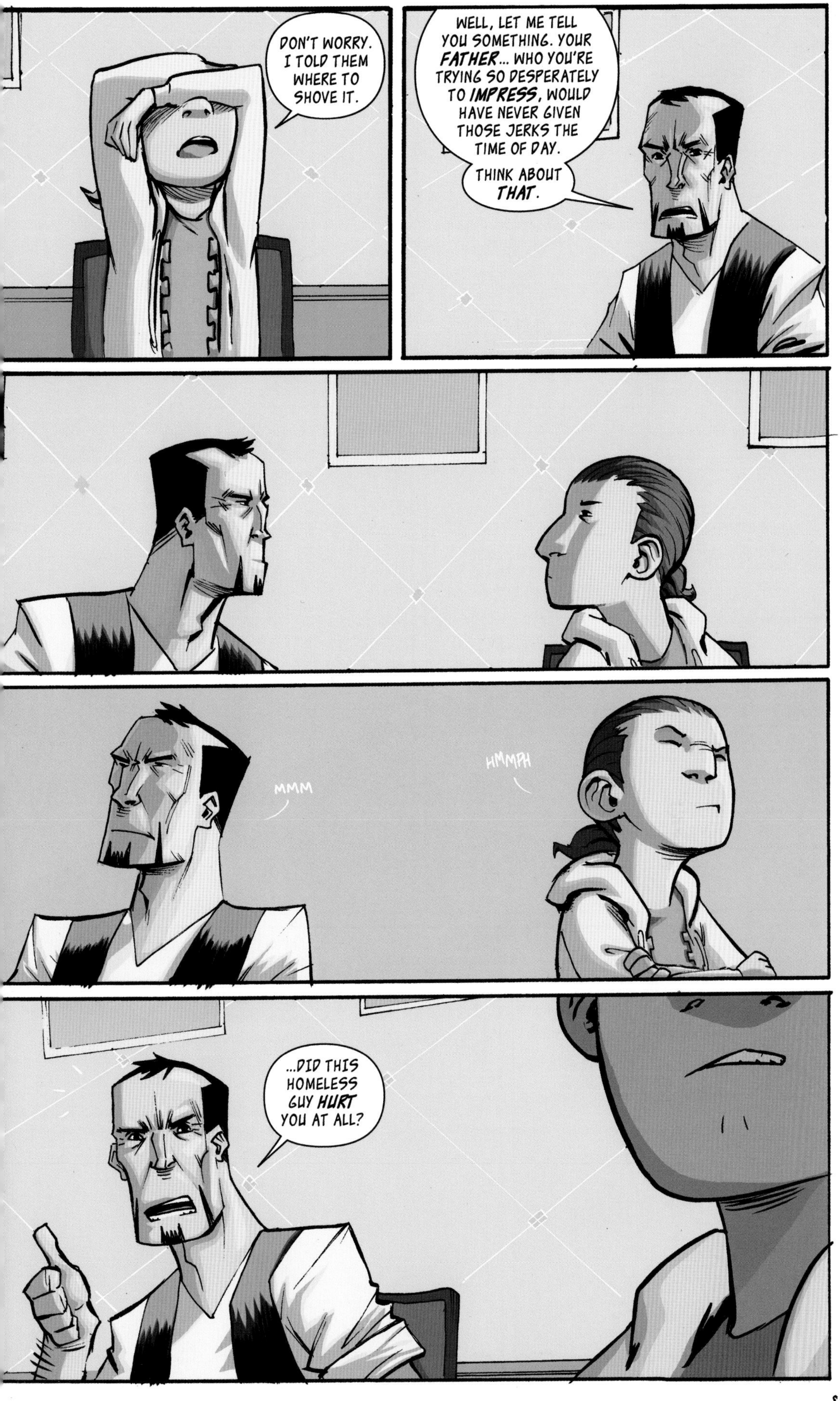
DON'T WORRY. I TOLD THEM WHERE TO SHOVE IT.
WELL, LET ME TELL YOU SOMETHING. YOUR FATHER... WHO YOU'RE TRYING SO DESPERATELY TO IMPRESS, WOULD HAVE NEVER GIVEN THOSE JERKS THE TIME OF DAY.
THINK ABOUT THAT.
MMM
HMMPH
...DID THIS HOMELESS GUY HURT YOU AT ALL?

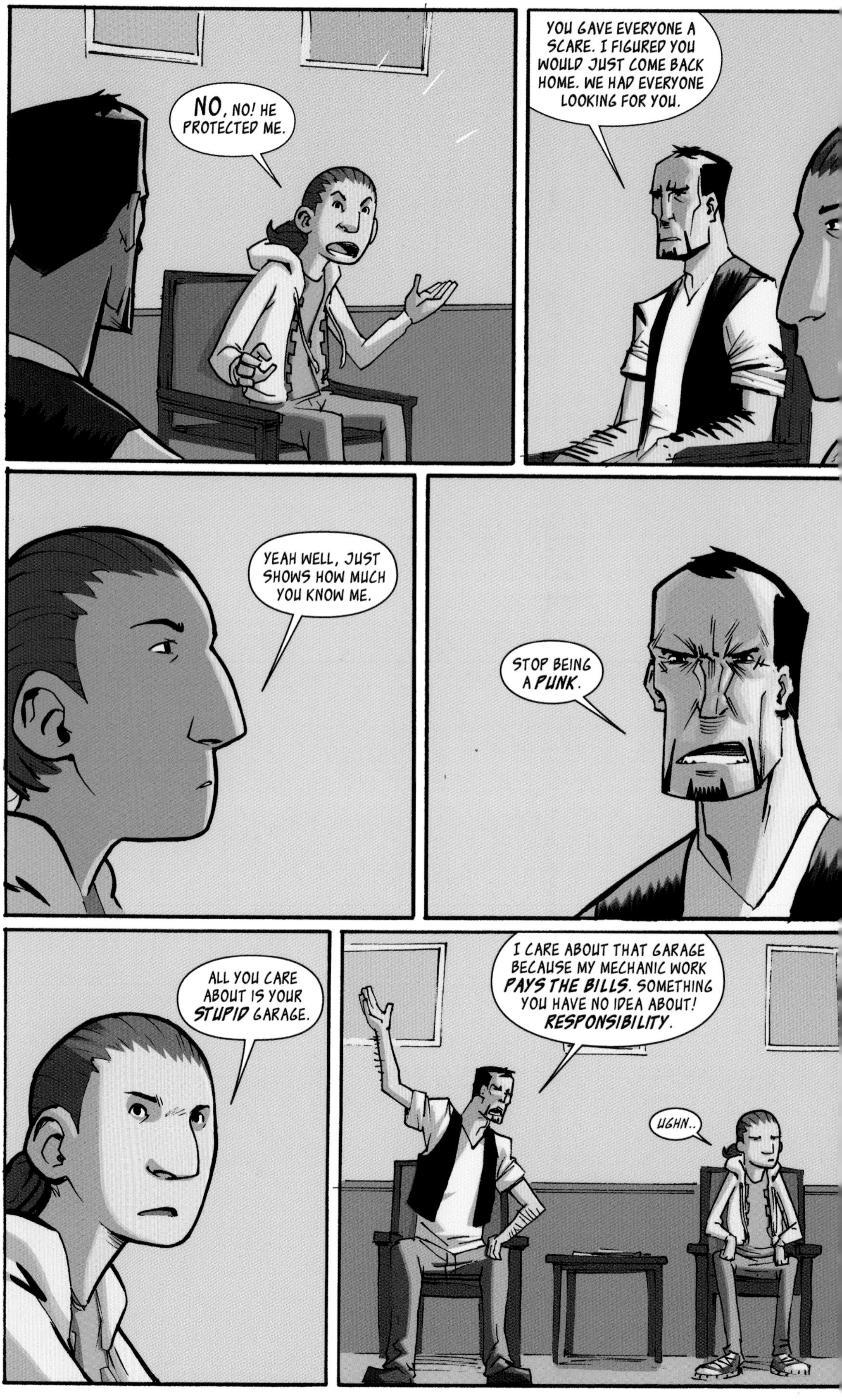
NO, NO! HE PROTECTED ME.
YOU GAVE EVERYONE A SCARE. I FIGURED YOU WOULD JUST COME BACK HOME. WE HAD EVERYONE LOOKING FOR YOU.
YEAH WELL, JUST SHOWS HOW MUCH YOU KNOW ME.
STOP BEING A PUNK.
ALL YOU CARE ABOUT IS YOUR STUPID GARAGE.
I CARE ABOUT THAT GARAGE BECAUSE MY MECHANIC WORK PAYS THE BILLS. SOMETHING YOU HAVE NO IDEA ABOUT! RESPONSIBILITY.
UGHN..

HE'S AWAKE IF YOU WANT TO TALK TO HIM.

I'D LIKE A WORD WITH HIM. COME ON, WENDELL.

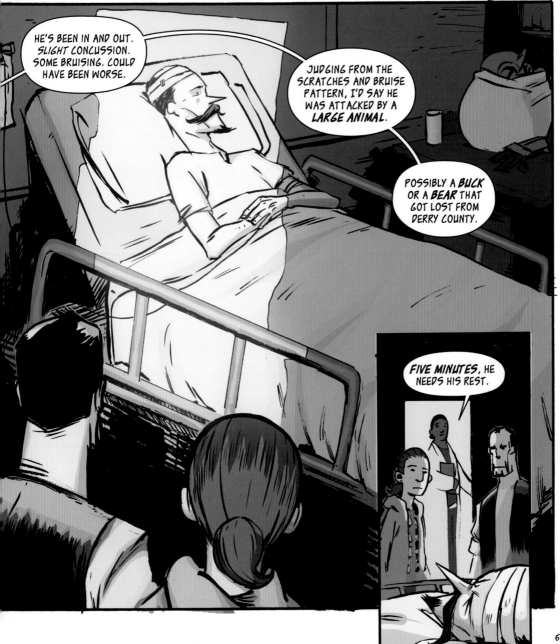

HE'S BEEN IN AND OUT. SLIGHT CONCUSSION. SOME BRUISING. COULD HAVE BEEN WORSE.

JUDGING FROM THE SCRATCHES AND BRUISE PATTERN, I'D SAY HE WAS ATTACKED BY A *LARGE ANIMAL*.

POSSIBLY A *BUCK* OR A *BEAR* THAT GOT LOST FROM DERRY COUNTY.

FIVE MINUTES, HE NEEDS HIS REST.

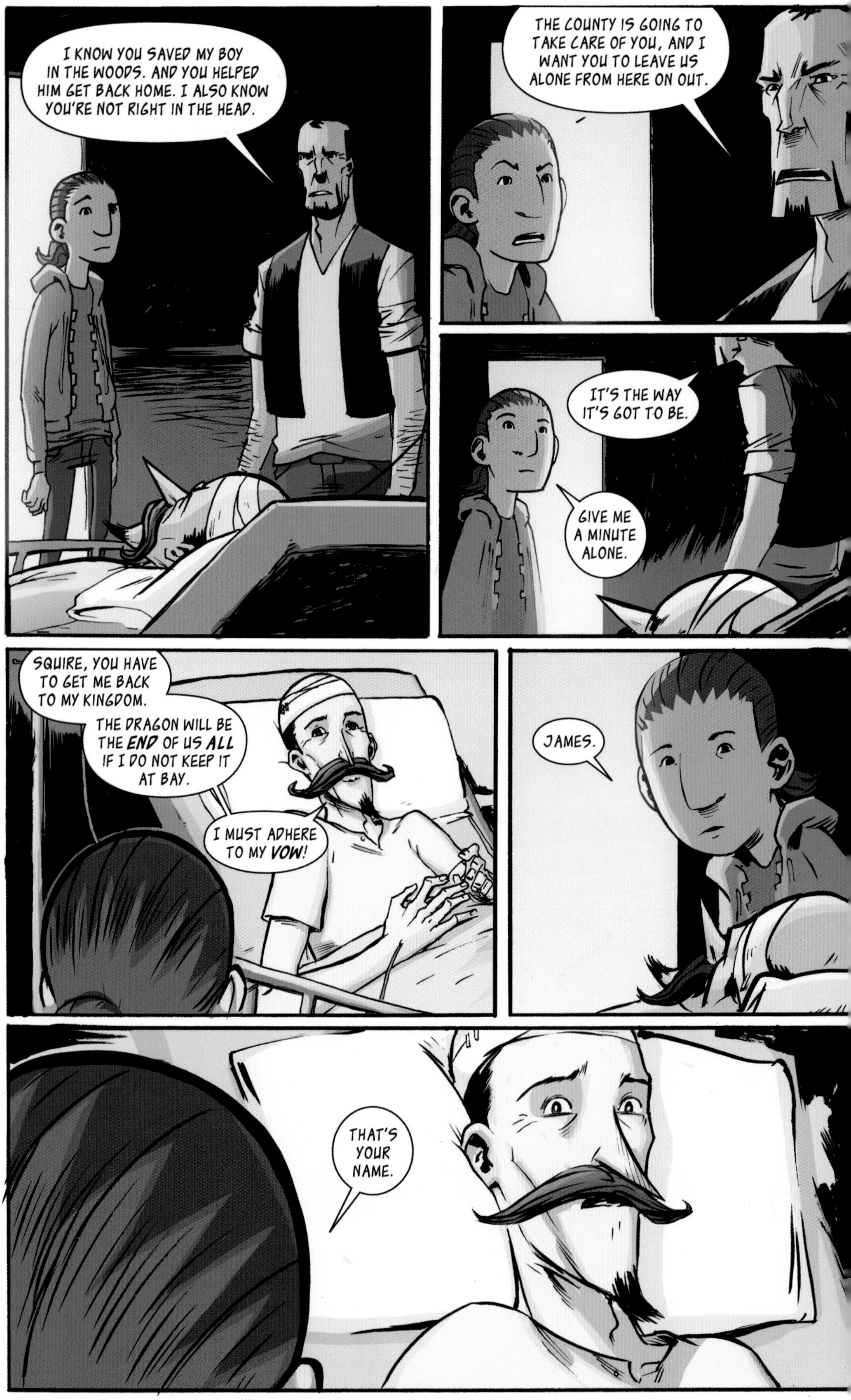
I KNOW YOU SAVED MY BOY IN THE WOODS. AND YOU HELPED HIM GET BACK HOME. I ALSO KNOW YOU'RE NOT RIGHT IN THE HEAD.
THE COUNTY IS GOING TO TAKE CARE OF YOU, AND I WANT YOU TO LEAVE US ALONE FROM HERE ON OUT.
IT'S THE WAY IT'S GOT TO BE.
GIVE ME A MINUTE ALONE.
SQUIRE, YOU HAVE TO GET ME BACK TO MY KINGDOM.
THE DRAGON WILL BE THE **END** OF US **ALL** IF I DO NOT KEEP IT AT BAY.
I MUST ADHERE TO MY **VOW**!
JAMES.
THAT'S YOUR NAME.

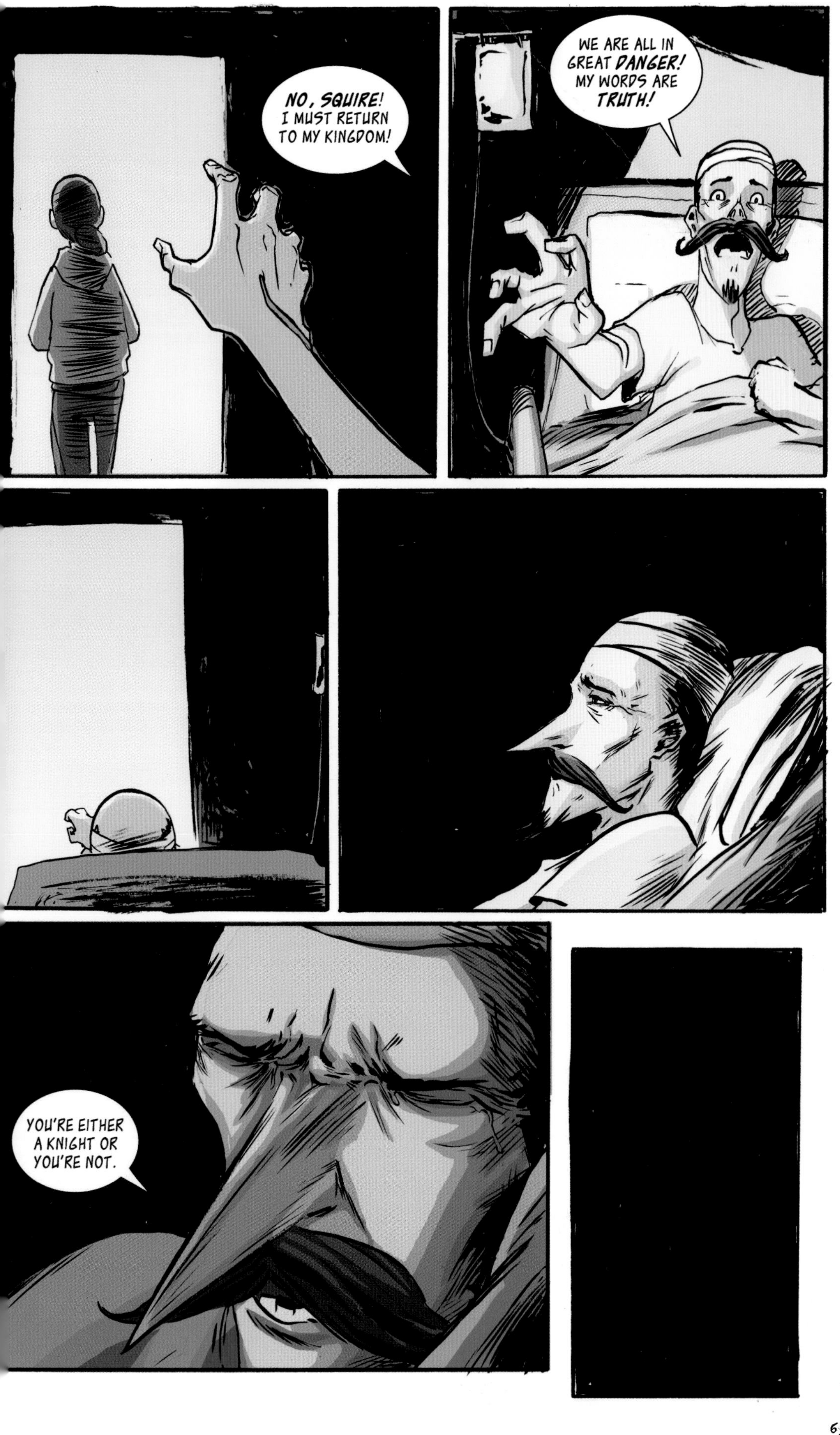
NO, SQUIRE! I MUST RETURN TO MY KINGDOM!
WE ARE ALL IN GREAT DANGER! MY WORDS ARE TRUTH!
YOU'RE EITHER A KNIGHT OR YOU'RE NOT.

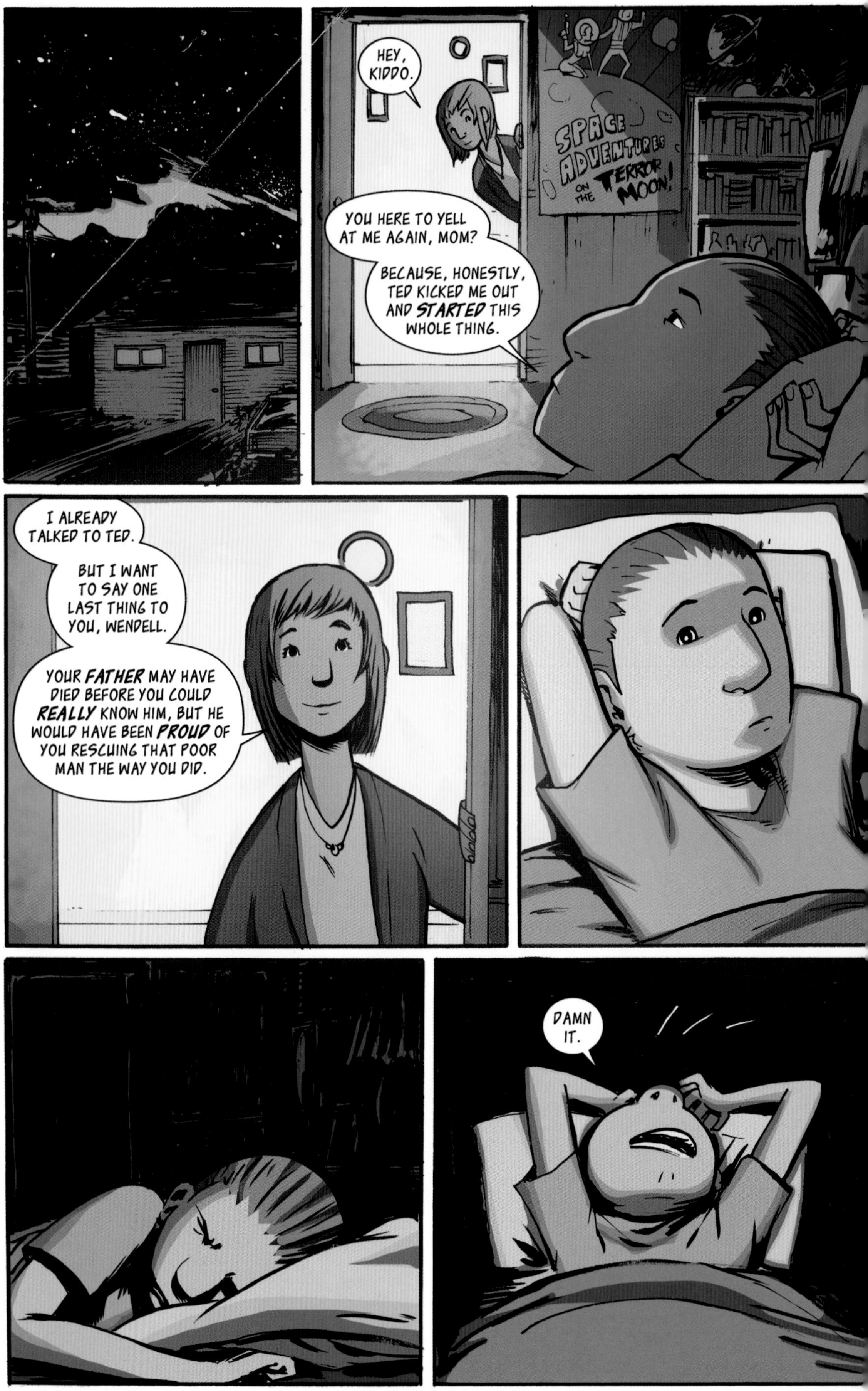
HEY, KIDDO.
YOU HERE TO YELL AT ME AGAIN, MOM?
BECAUSE, HONESTLY, TED KICKED ME OUT AND STARTED THIS WHOLE THING.
SPACE ADVENTURES ON THE TERROR MOON!
I ALREADY TALKED TO TED.
BUT I WANT TO SAY ONE LAST THING TO YOU, WENDELL.
YOUR FATHER MAY HAVE DIED BEFORE YOU COULD REALLY KNOW HIM, BUT HE WOULD HAVE BEEN PROUD OF YOU RESCUING THAT POOR MAN THE WAY YOU DID.
DAMN IT.

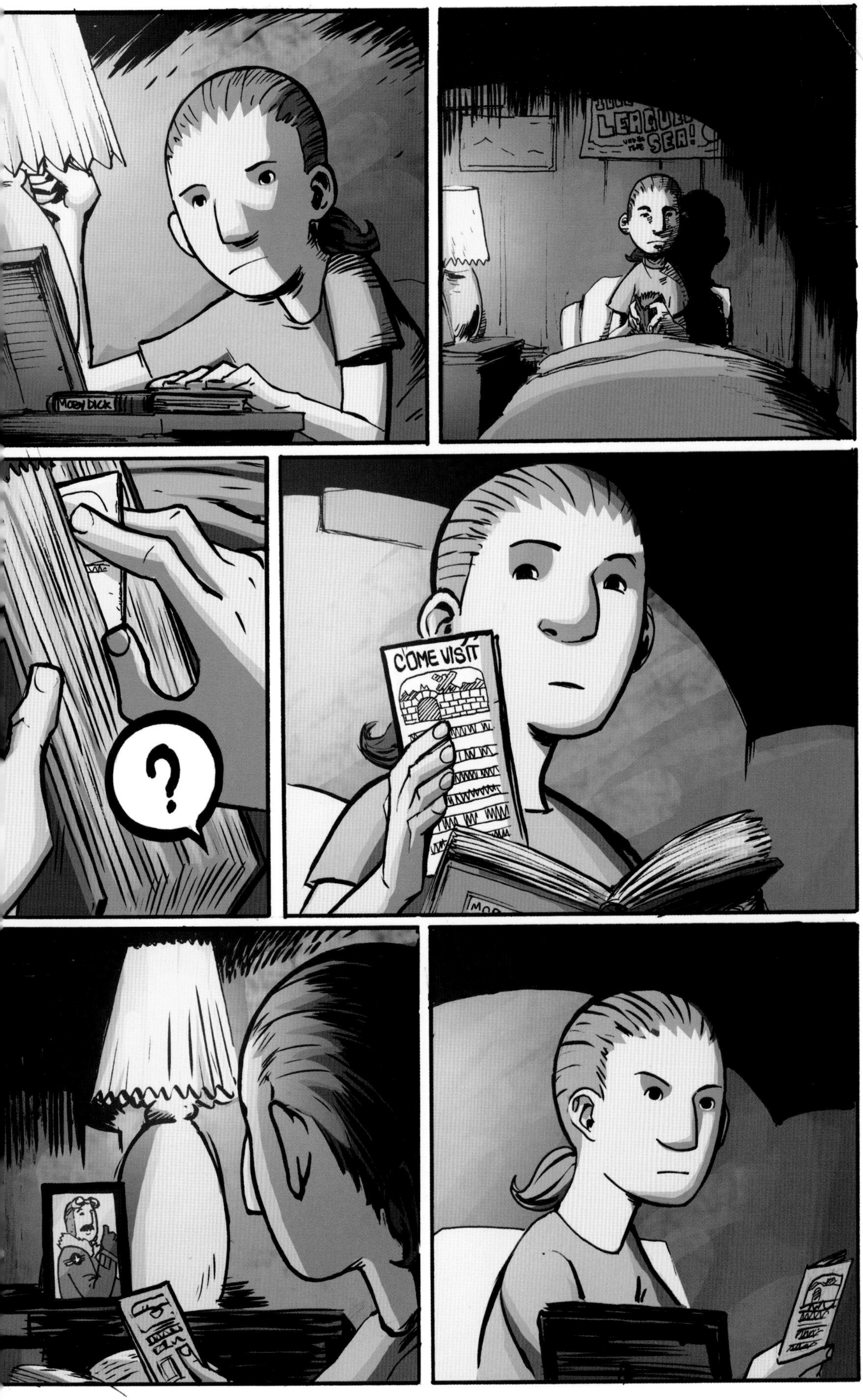
MOBY DICK
LEAGUE
UNDER THE
SEA!
?
COME VISIT

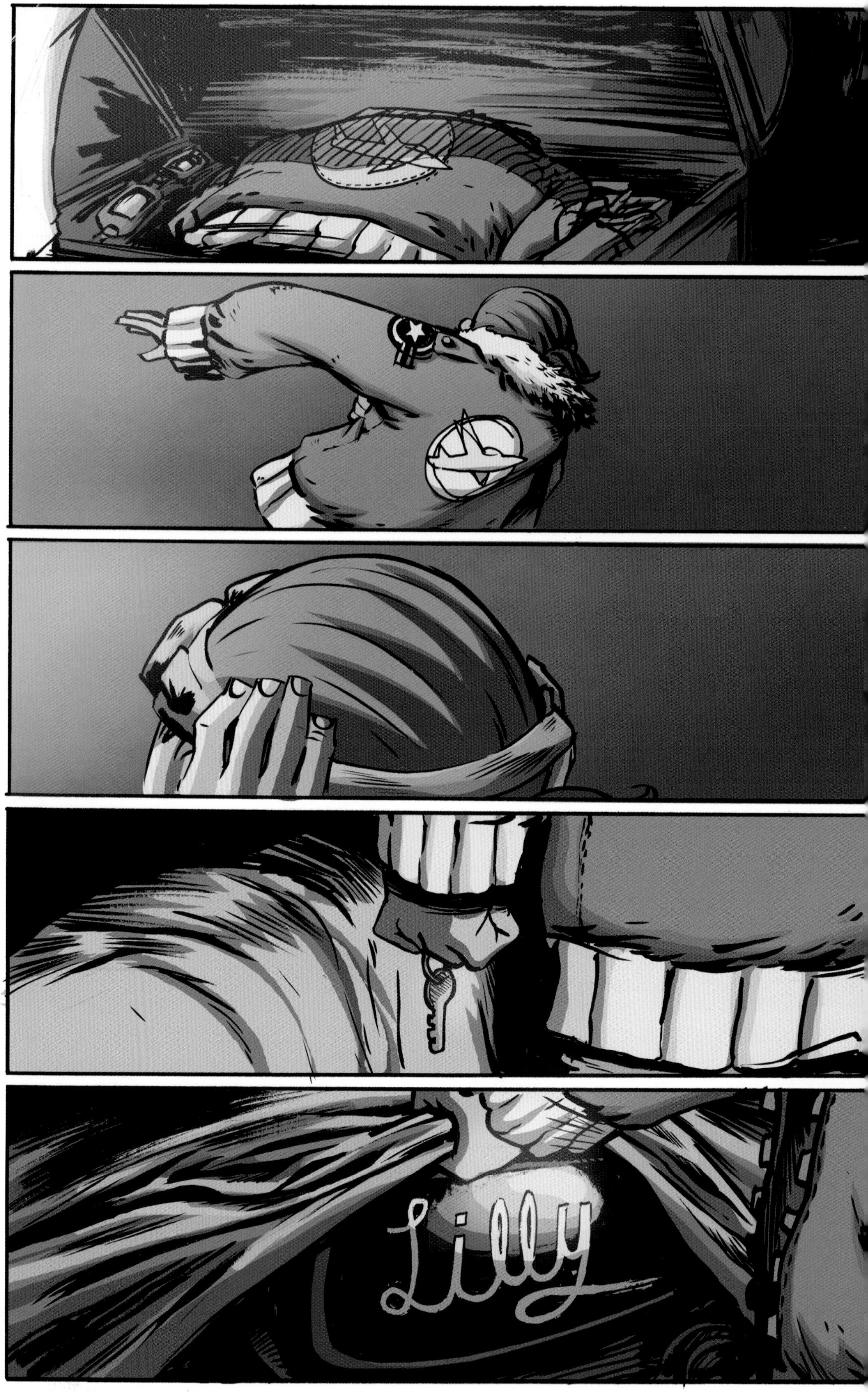
Lilly

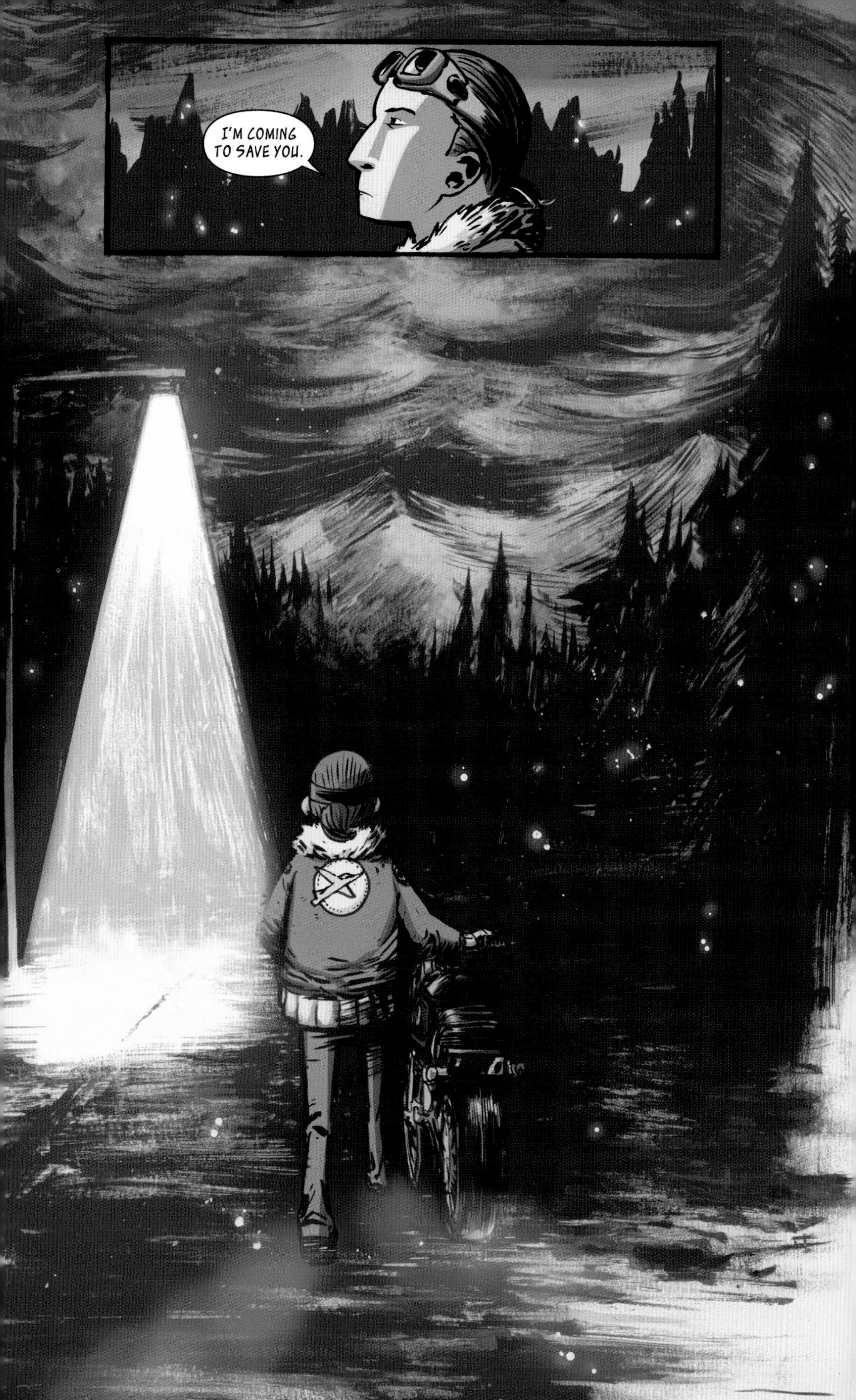
I'M COMING TO SAVE YOU.

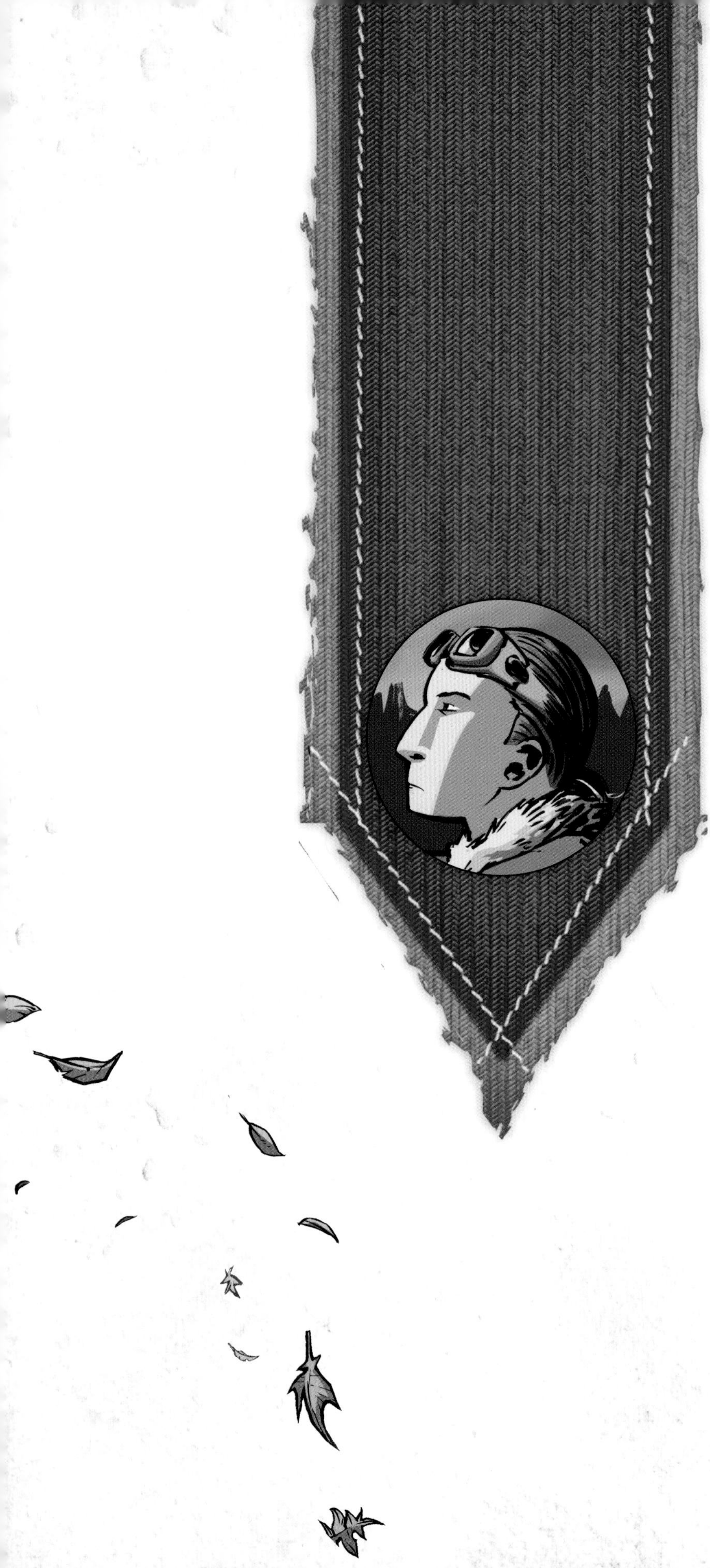

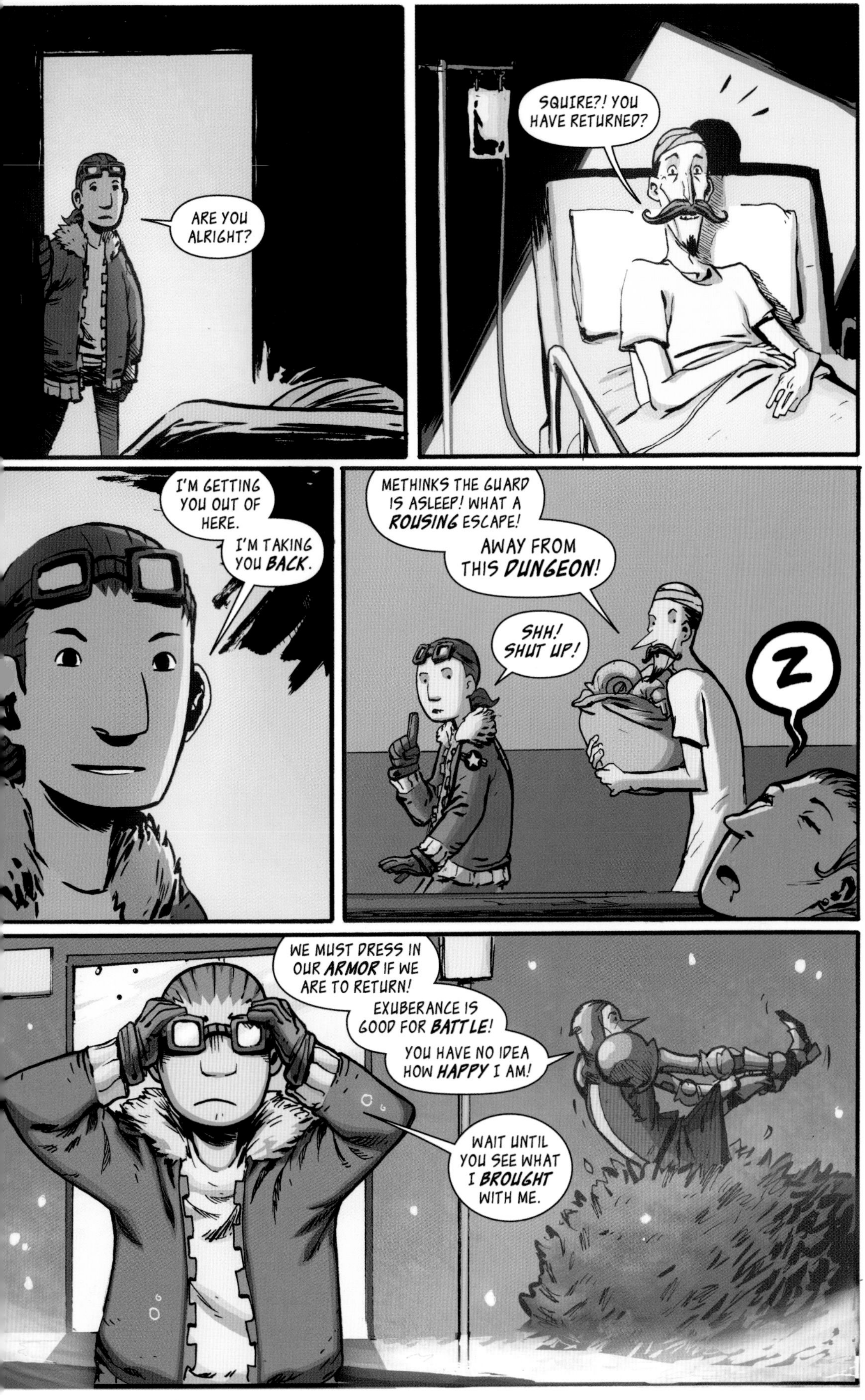
ARE YOU ALRIGHT?
SQUIRE?! YOU HAVE RETURNED?
I'M GETTING YOU OUT OF HERE.
I'M TAKING YOU BACK.
METHINKS THE GUARD IS ASLEEP! WHAT A ROUSING ESCAPE!
AWAY FROM THIS DUNGEON!
SHH! SHUT UP!
Z
WE MUST DRESS IN OUR ARMOR IF WE ARE TO RETURN!
EXUBERANCE IS GOOD FOR BATTLE!
YOU HAVE NO IDEA HOW HAPPY I AM!
WAIT UNTIL YOU SEE WHAT I BROUGHT WITH ME.

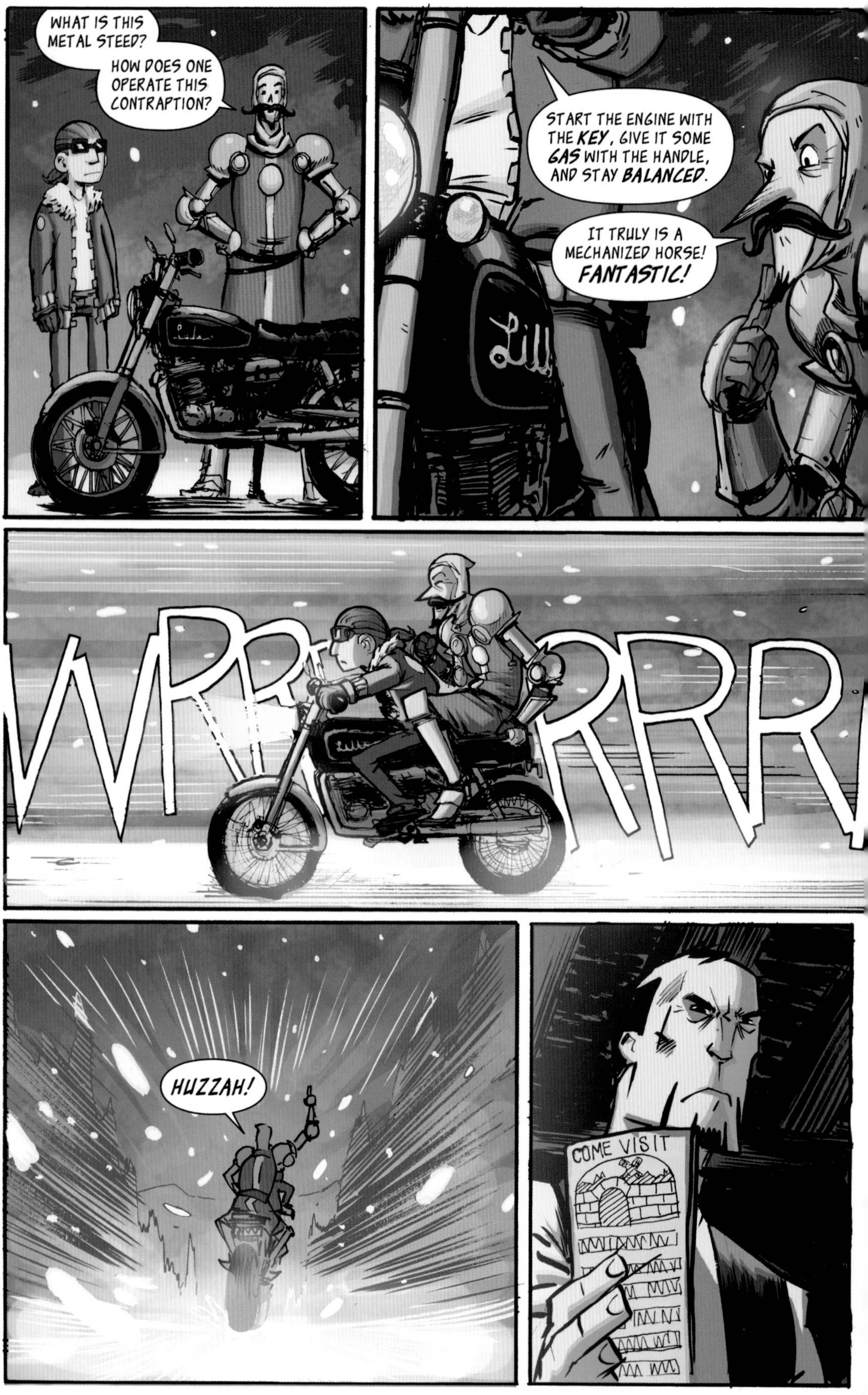

WHAT IS THIS METAL STEED?
HOW DOES ONE OPERATE THIS CONTRAPTION?
START THE ENGINE WITH THE KEY, GIVE IT SOME GAS WITH THE HANDLE, AND STAY BALANCED.
IT TRULY IS A MECHANIZED HORSE! FANTASTIC!
WRRRRRRR
HUZZAH!
COME VISIT

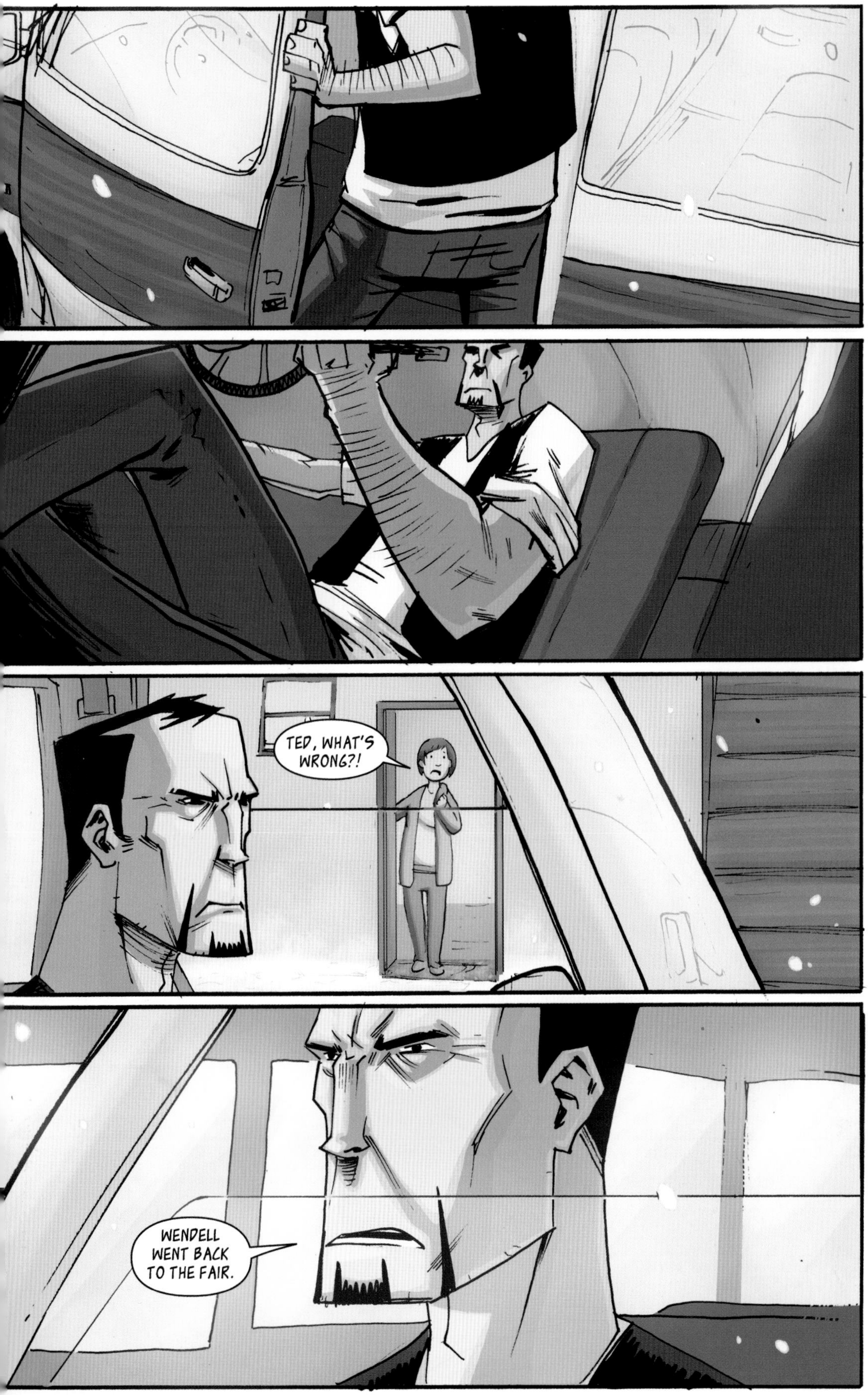
TED, WHAT'S WRONG?!
WENDELL WENT BACK TO THE FAIR.

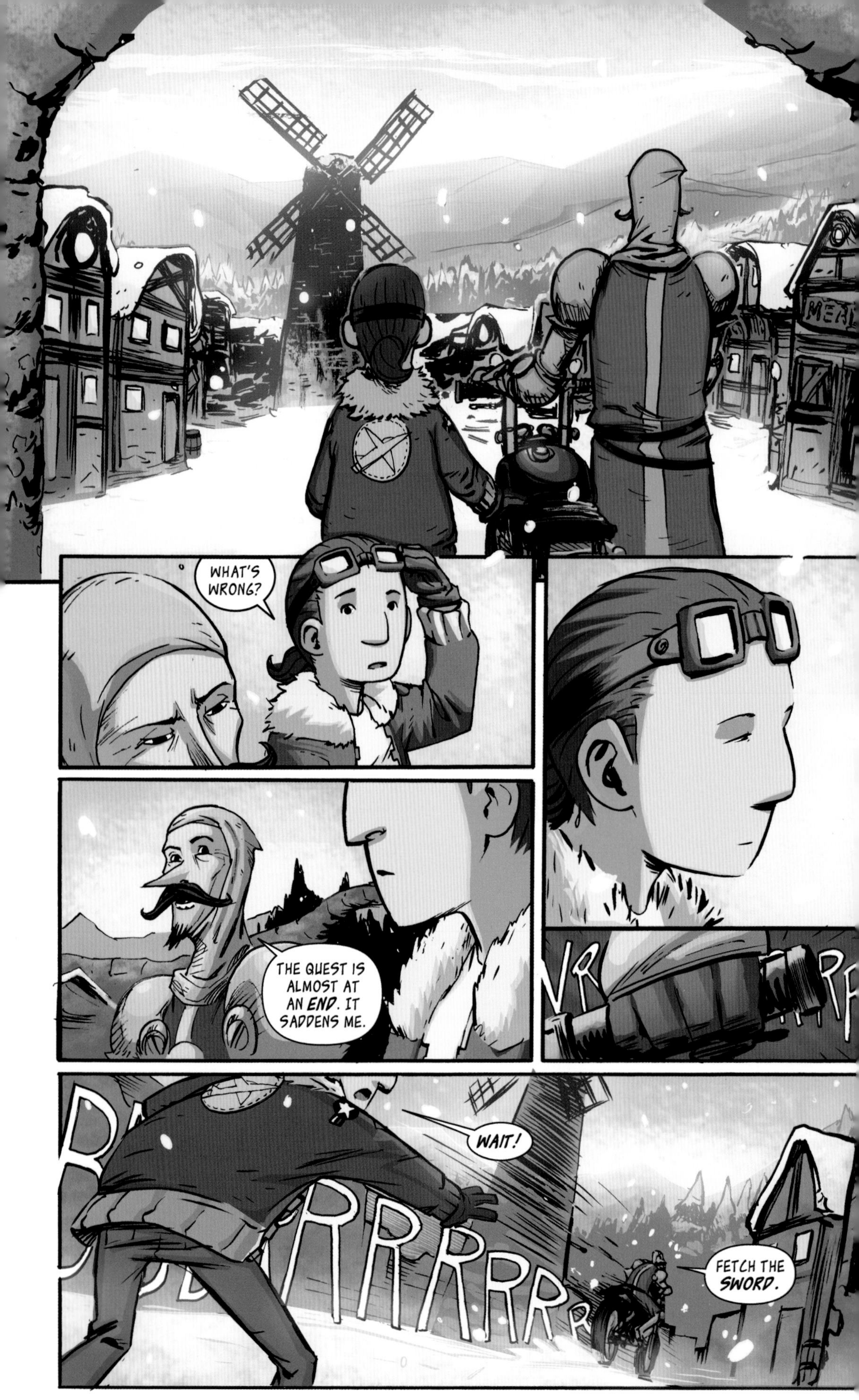
WHAT'S WRONG?
THE QUEST IS ALMOST AT AN *END*. IT SADDENS ME.
WAIT!
FETCH THE *SWORD*.

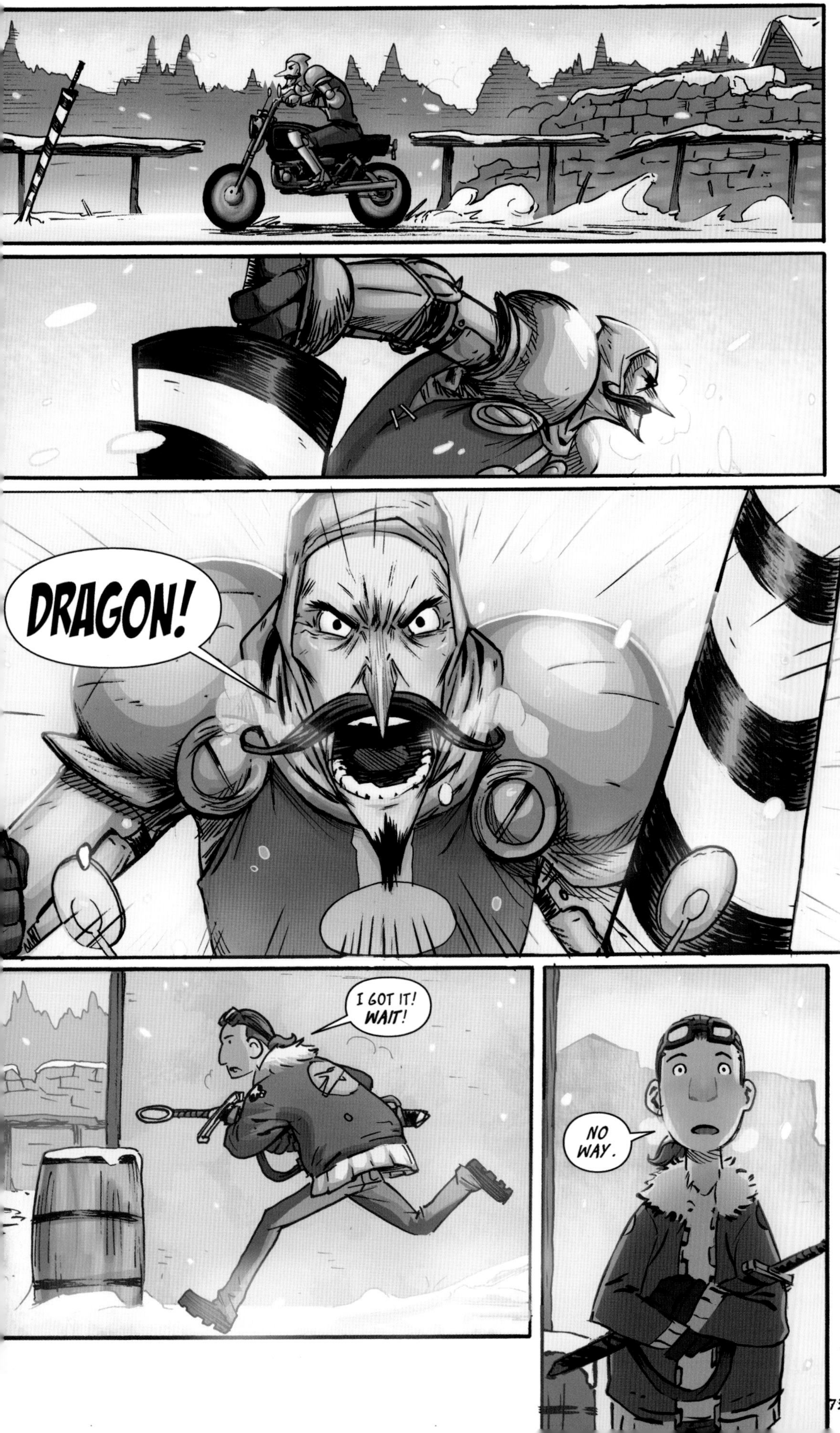
DRAGON!
I GOT IT! WAIT!
NO WAY.

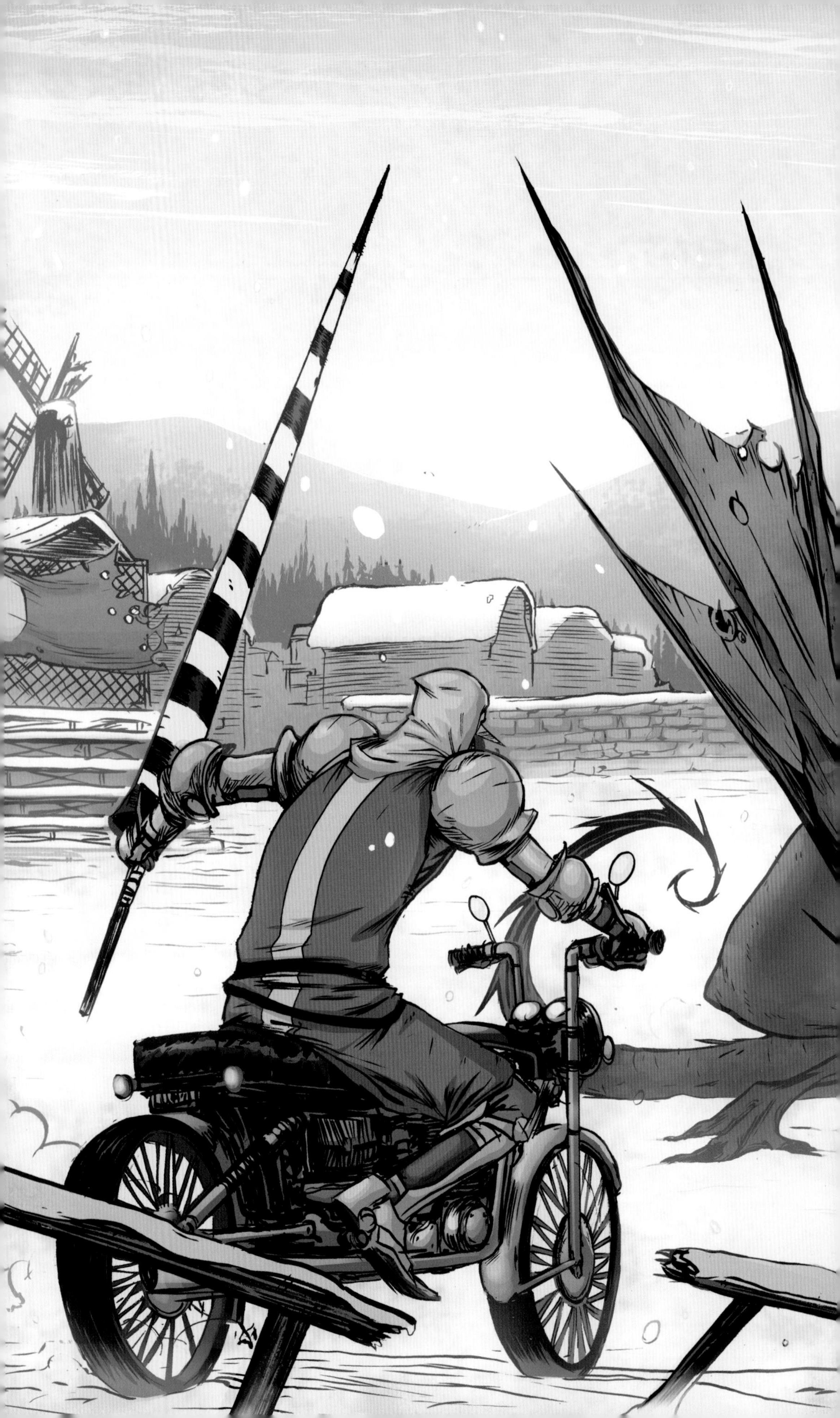

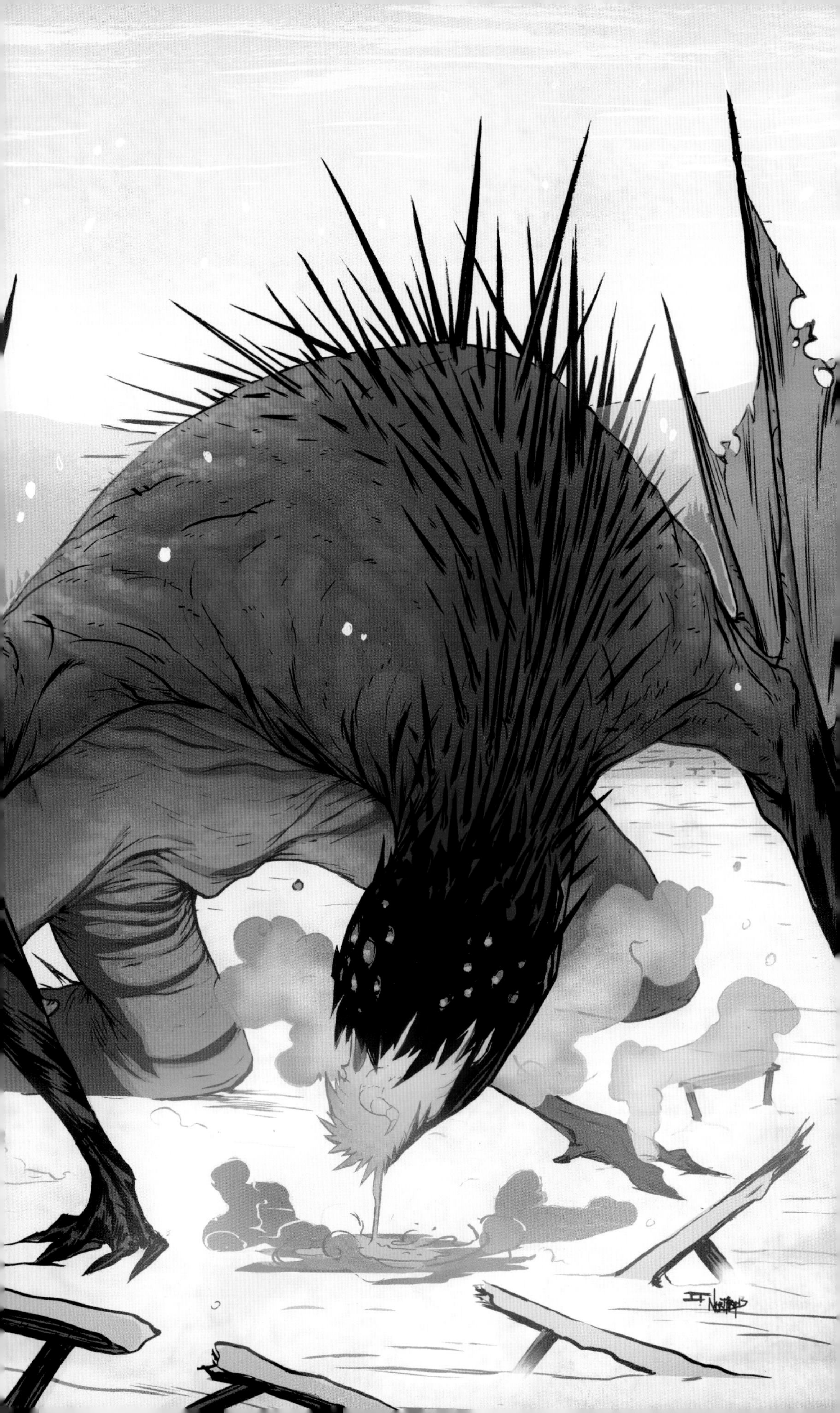

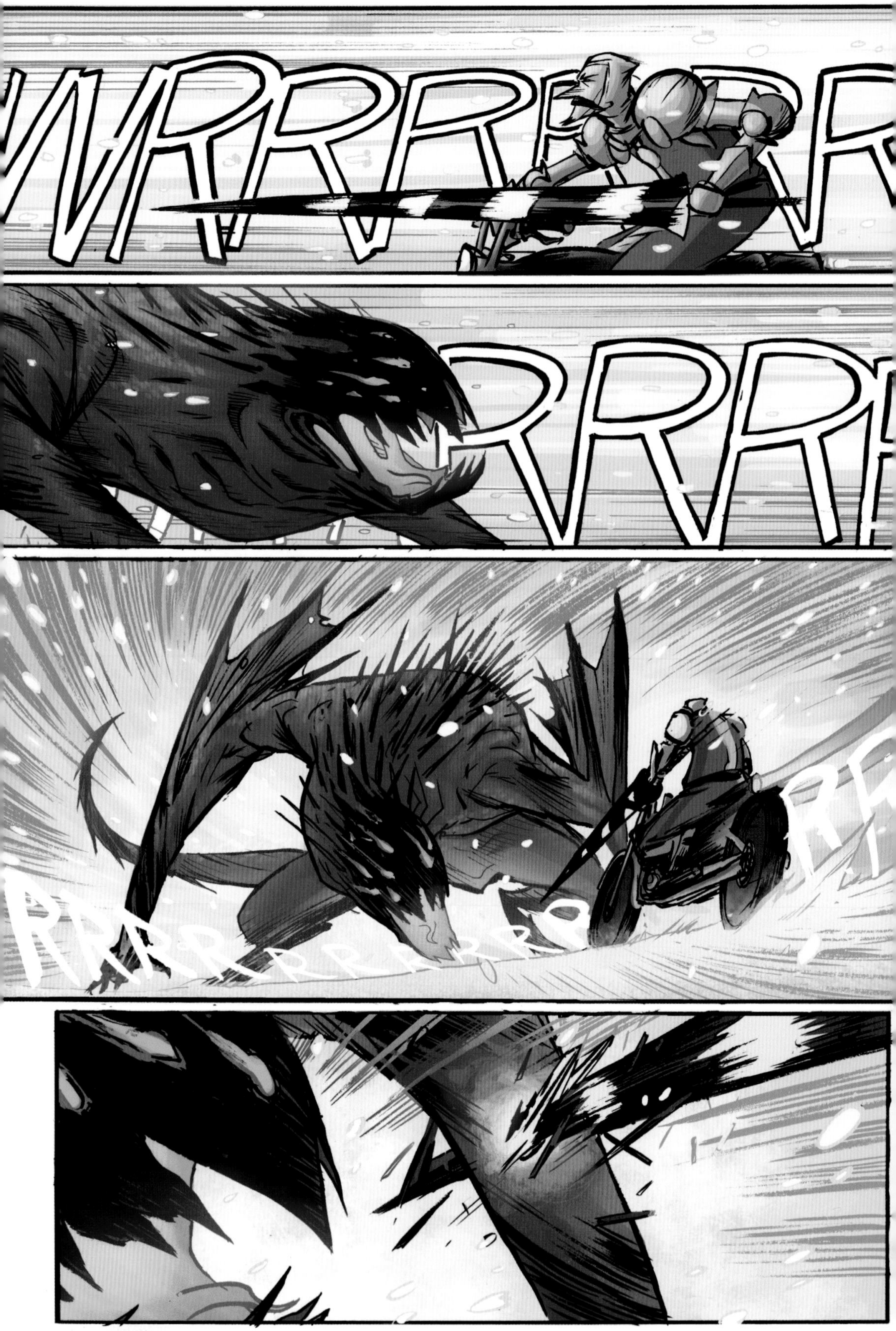
WRRRRRRRR
RRRRR
RRRRRRRRRRRR

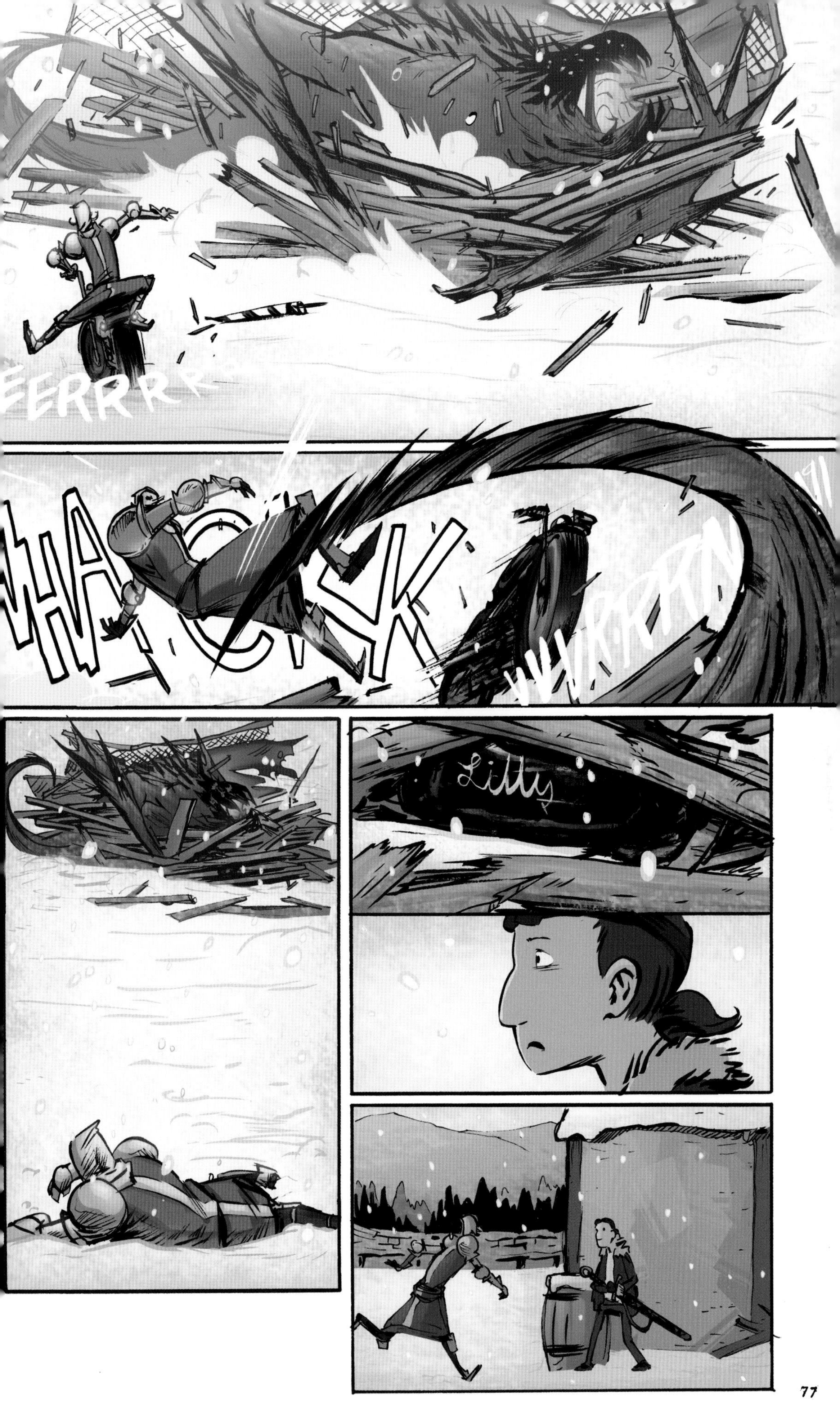
ERRRR
HACK
VVVRRRRN
Lilly

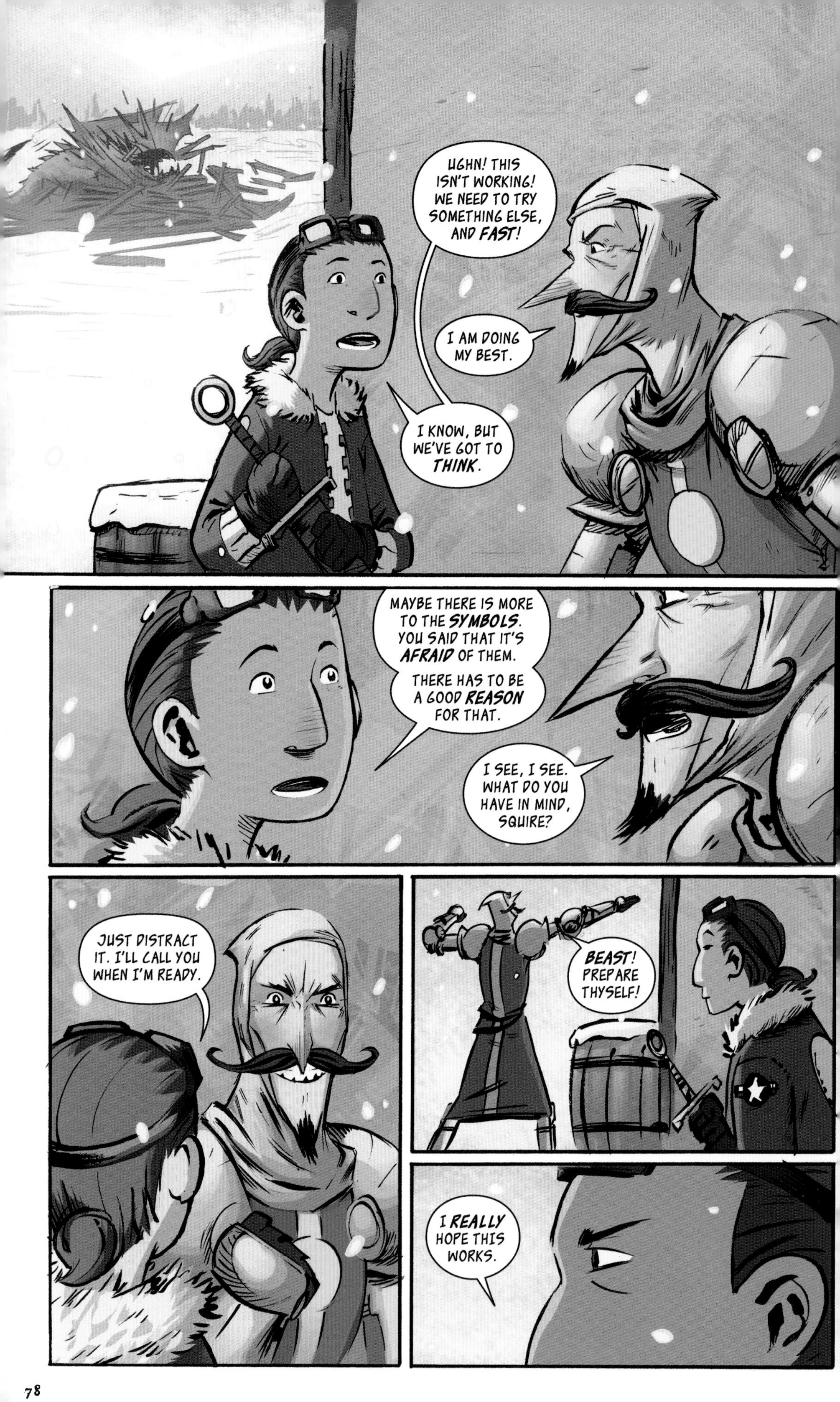
UGHN! THIS ISN'T WORKING! WE NEED TO TRY SOMETHING ELSE, AND FAST!
I AM DOING MY BEST.
I KNOW, BUT WE'VE GOT TO THINK.
MAYBE THERE IS MORE TO THE SYMBOLS. YOU SAID THAT IT'S AFRAID OF THEM.
THERE HAS TO BE A GOOD REASON FOR THAT.
I SEE, I SEE. WHAT DO YOU HAVE IN MIND, SQUIRE?
JUST DISTRACT IT. I'LL CALL YOU WHEN I'M READY.
BEAST! PREPARE THYSELF!
I REALLY HOPE THIS WORKS.

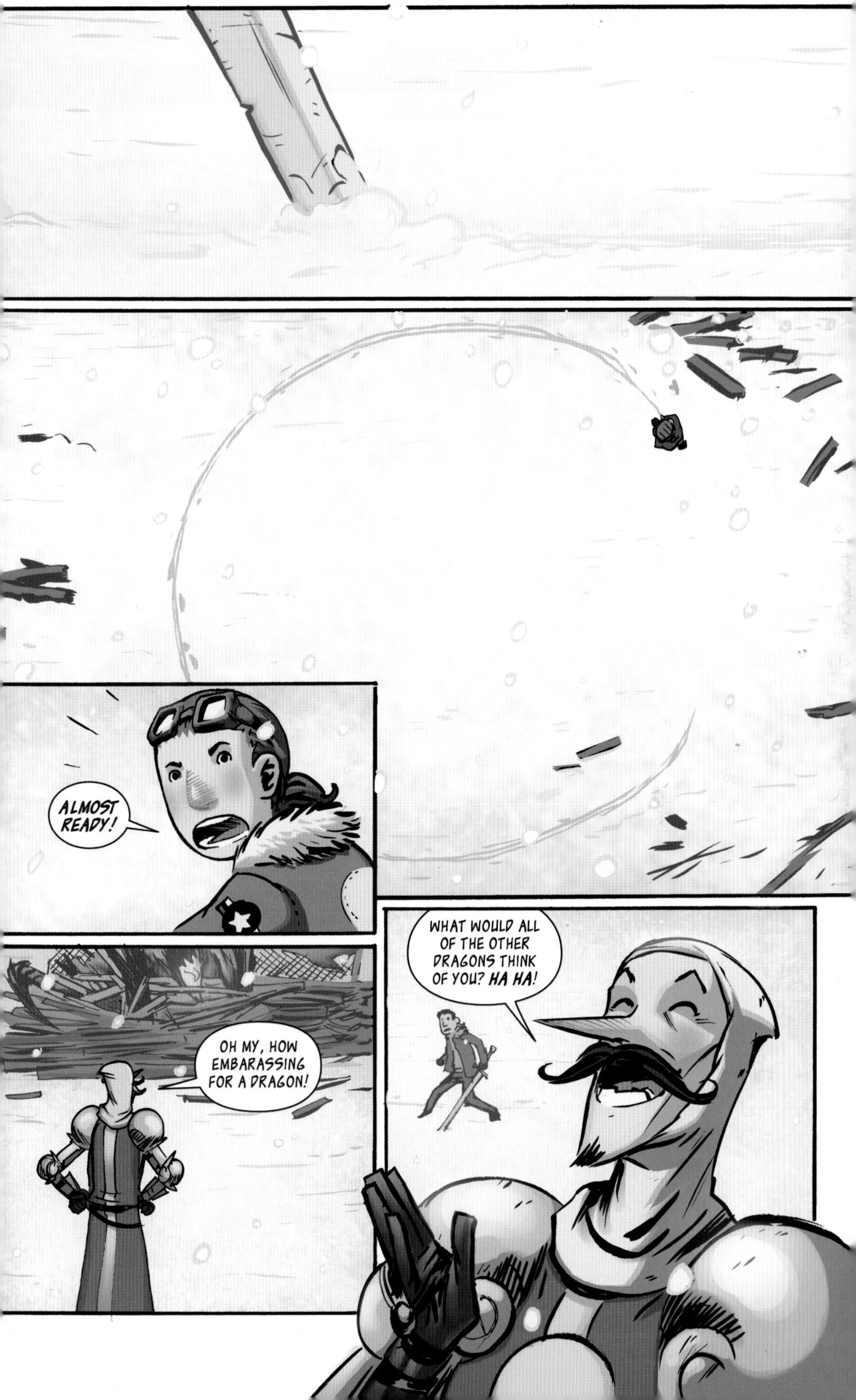
ALMOST READY!
OH MY, HOW EMBARASSING FOR A DRAGON!
WHAT WOULD ALL OF THE OTHER DRAGONS THINK OF YOU? HA HA!

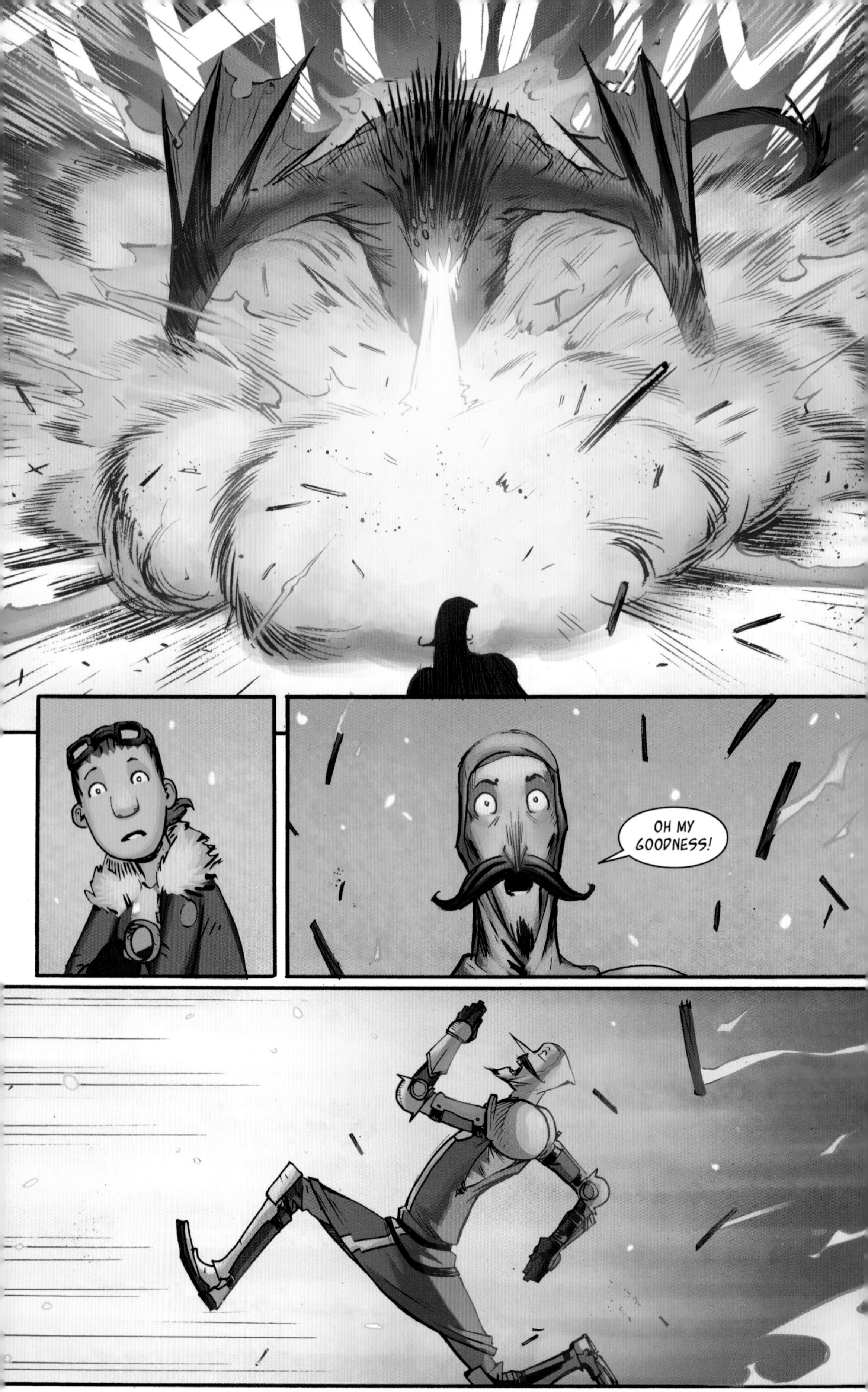
OH MY
GOODNESS!

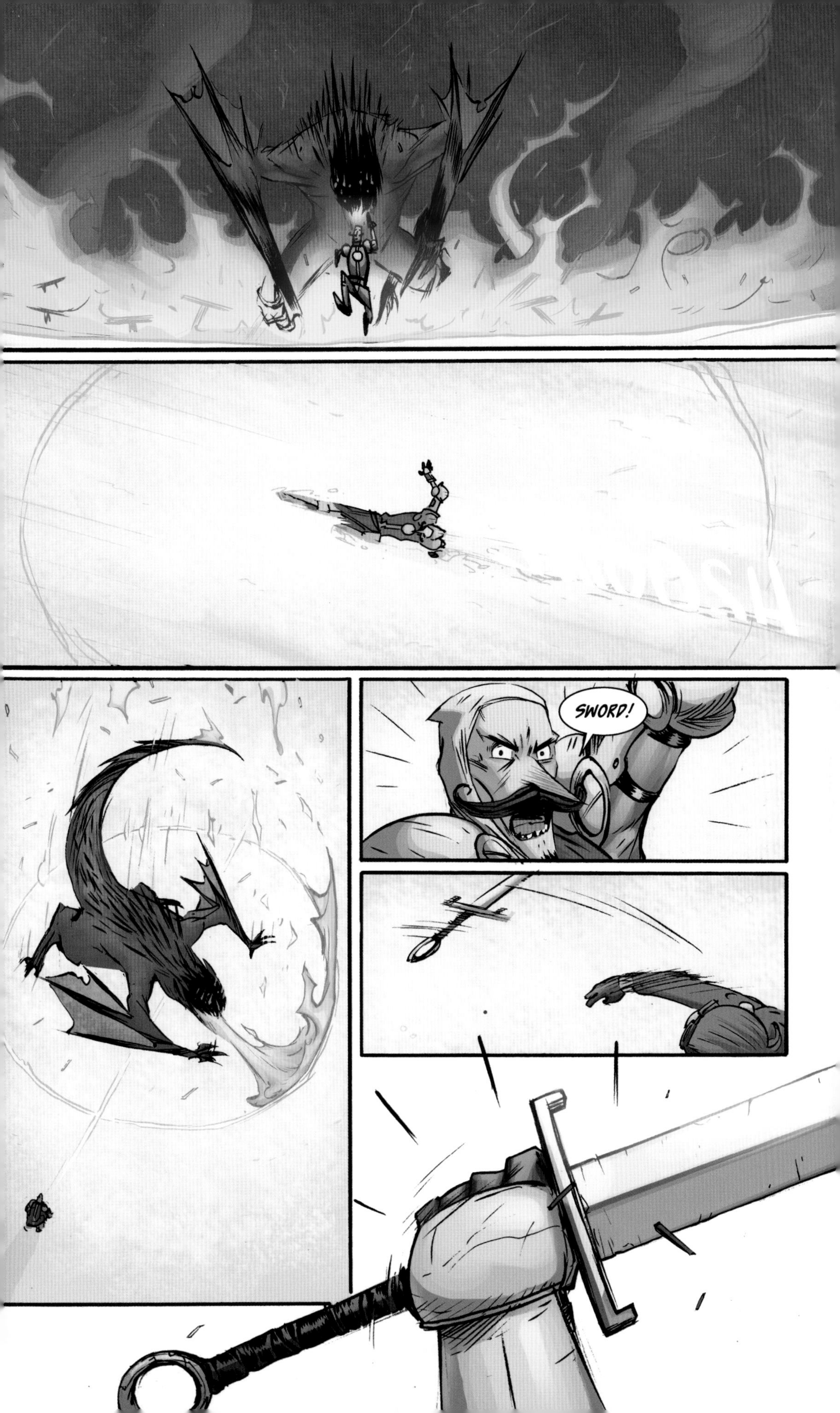
SWORD!

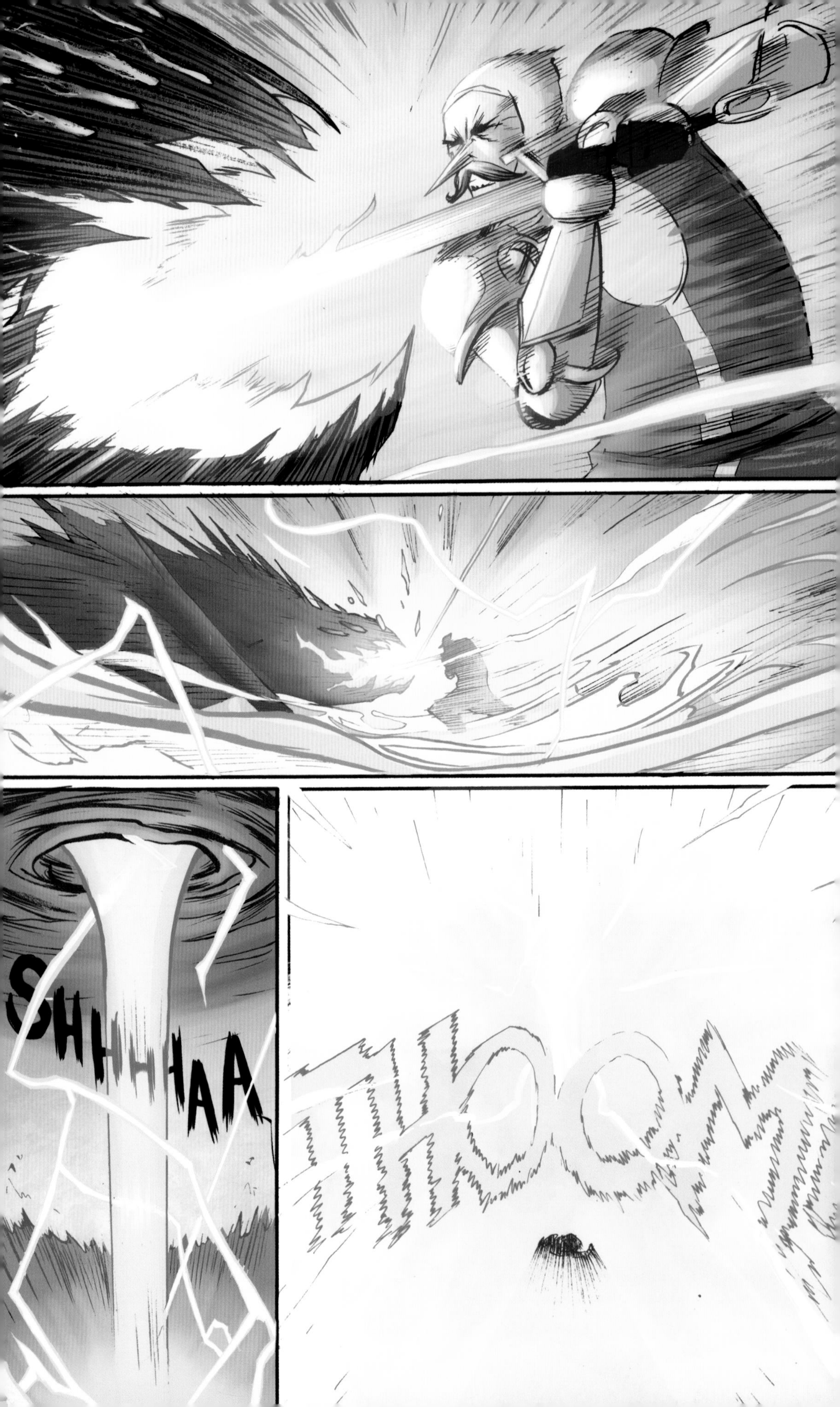
SHHHAA
THOOM

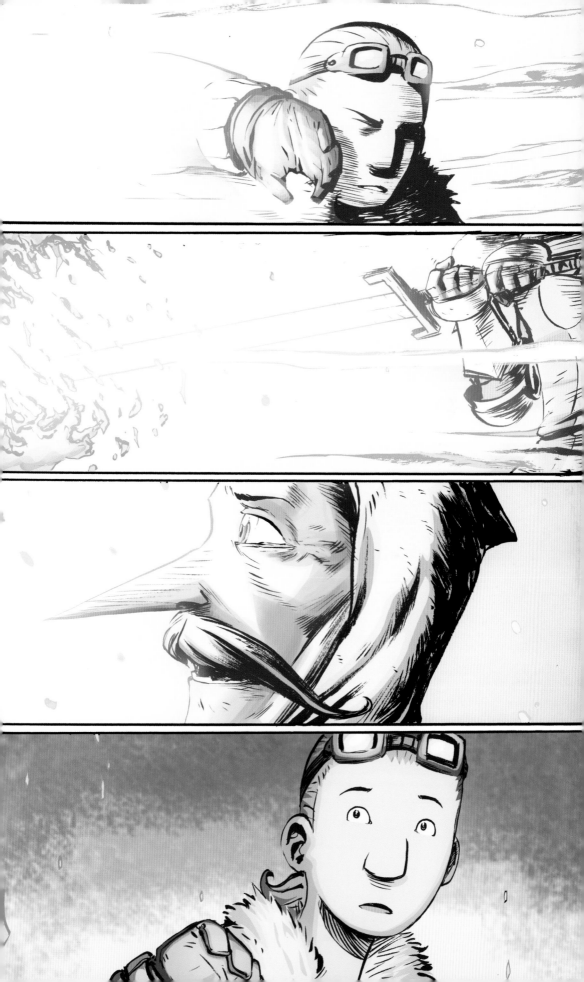

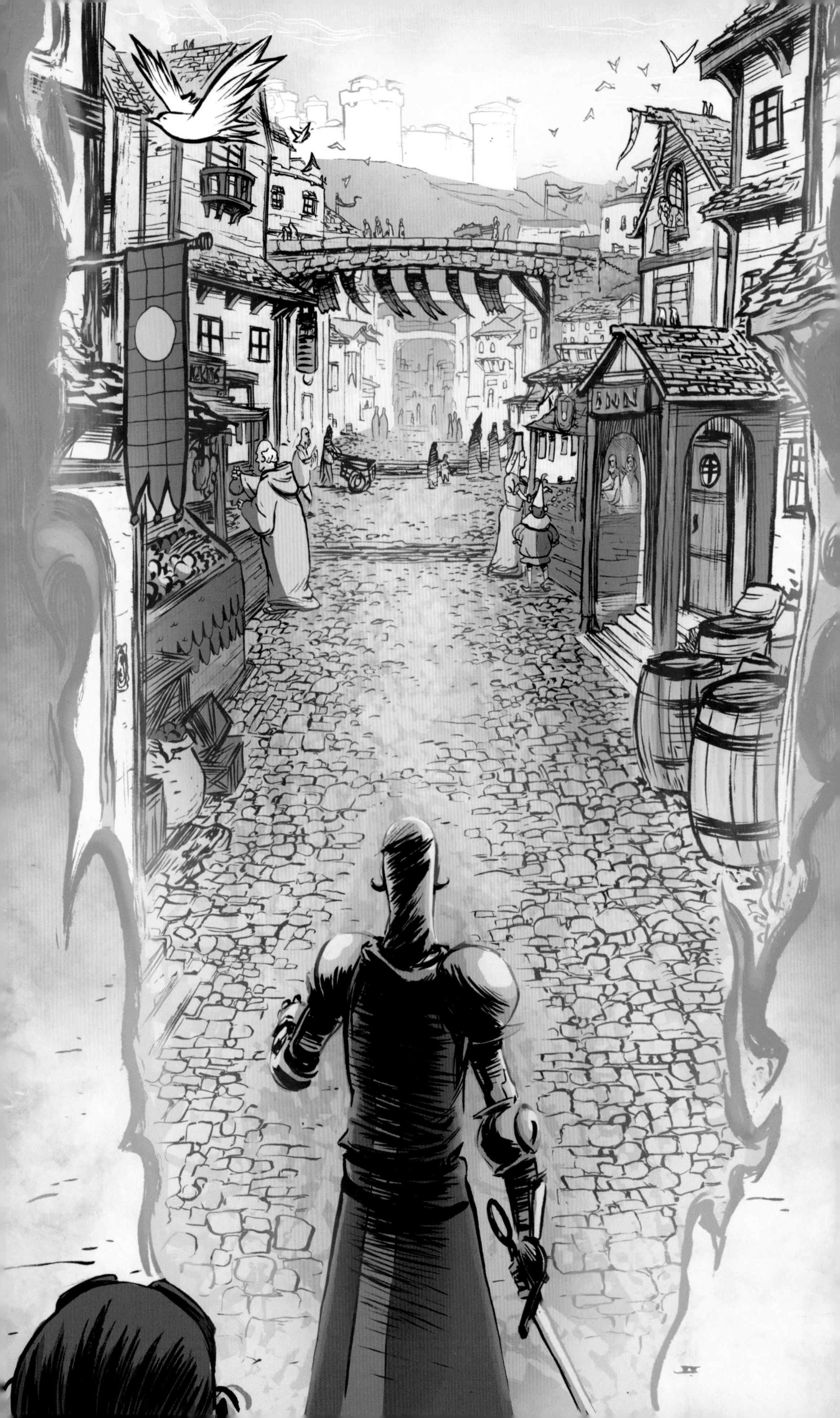
INN

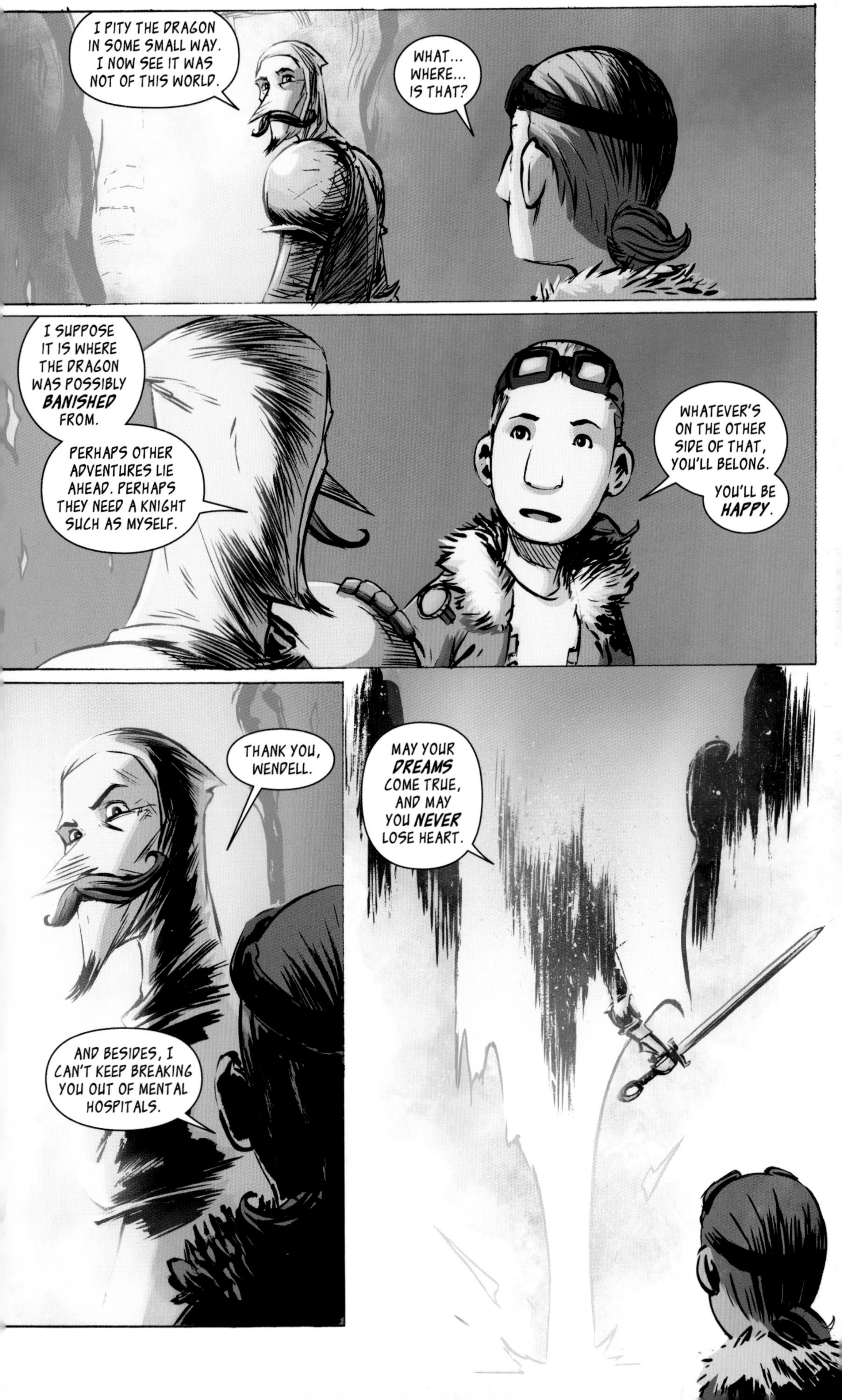
I PITY THE DRAGON IN SOME SMALL WAY. I NOW SEE IT WAS NOT OF THIS WORLD.
WHAT... WHERE... IS THAT?
I SUPPOSE IT IS WHERE THE DRAGON WAS POSSIBLY BANISHED FROM.
PERHAPS OTHER ADVENTURES LIE AHEAD. PERHAPS THEY NEED A KNIGHT SUCH AS MYSELF.
WHATEVER'S ON THE OTHER SIDE OF THAT, YOU'LL BELONG.
YOU'LL BE HAPPY.
THANK YOU, WENDELL.
AND BESIDES, I CAN'T KEEP BREAKING YOU OUT OF MENTAL HOSPITALS.
MAY YOUR DREAMS COME TRUE, AND MAY YOU NEVER LOSE HEART.

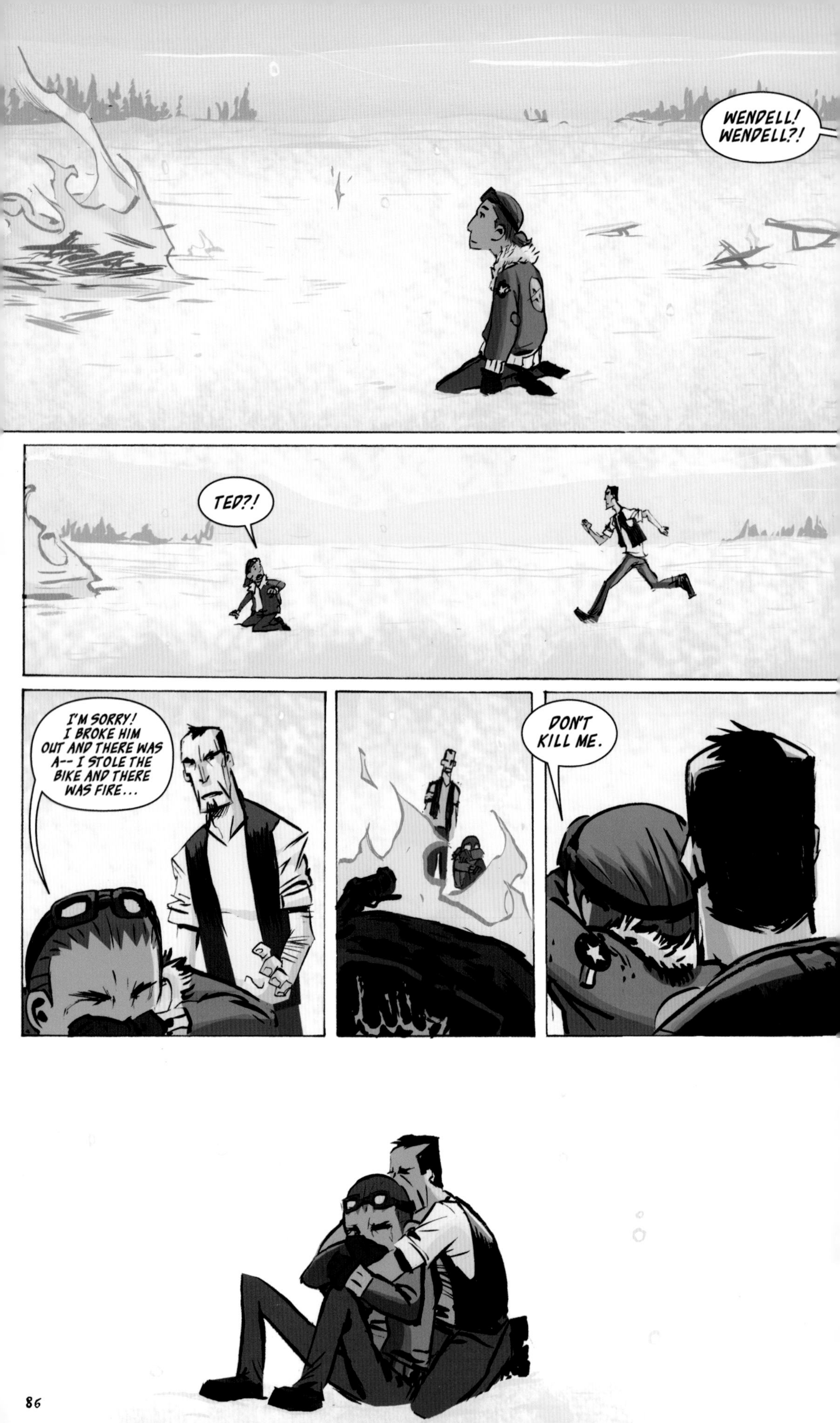
WENDELL! WENDELL?!
TED?!
I'M SORRY! I BROKE HIM OUT AND THERE WAS A-- I STOLE THE BIKE AND THERE WAS FIRE...
DON'T KILL ME.

TWO MONTHS LATER

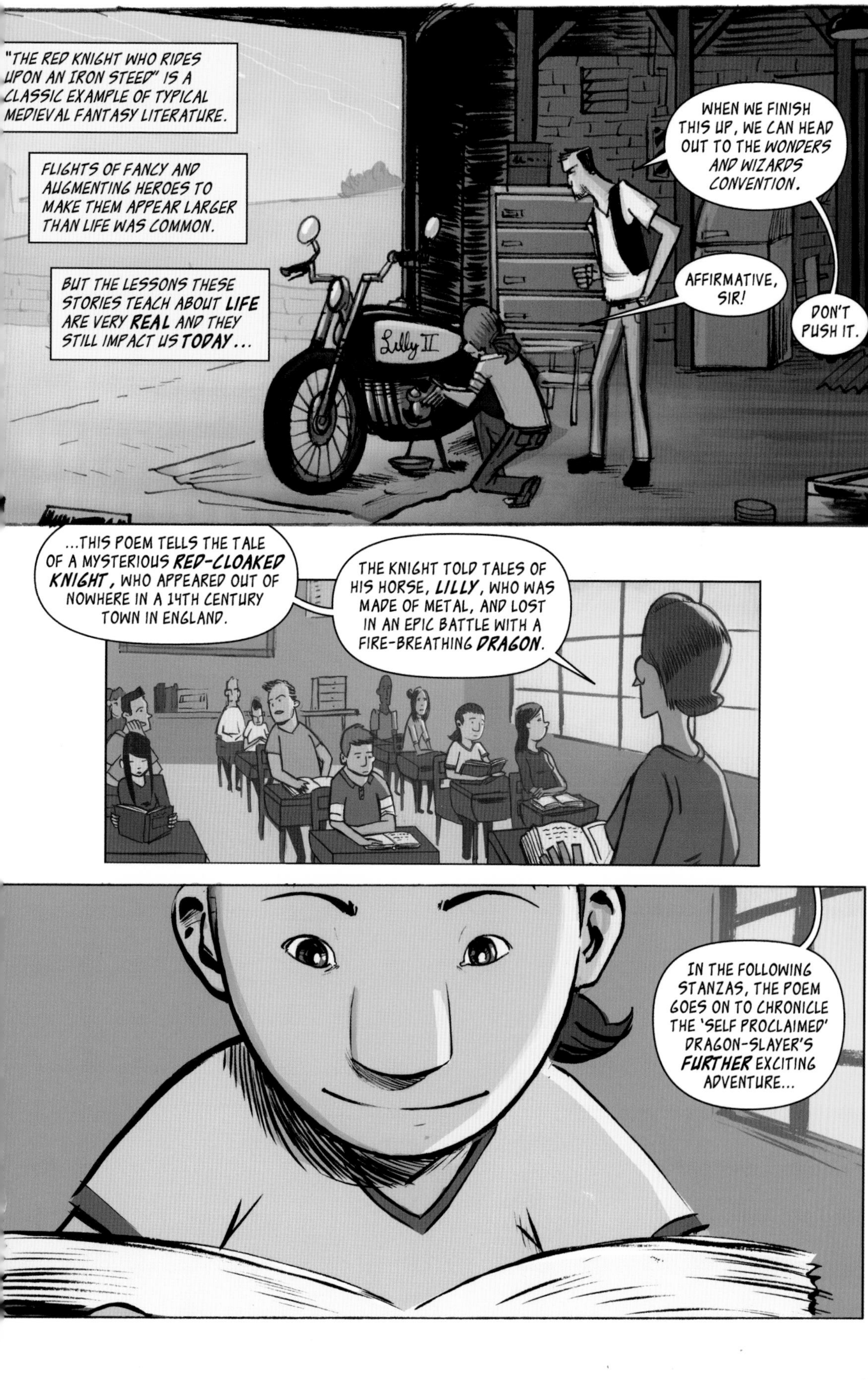
"THE RED KNIGHT WHO RIDES UPON AN IRON STEED" IS A CLASSIC EXAMPLE OF TYPICAL MEDIEVAL FANTASY LITERATURE.
FLIGHTS OF FANCY AND AUGMENTING HEROES TO MAKE THEM APPEAR LARGER THAN LIFE WAS COMMON.
BUT THE LESSONS THESE STORIES TEACH ABOUT LIFE ARE VERY REAL AND THEY STILL IMPACT US TODAY...
WHEN WE FINISH THIS UP, WE CAN HEAD OUT TO THE WONDERS AND WIZARDS CONVENTION.
AFFIRMATIVE, SIR!
DON'T PUSH IT.
Lilly II
...THIS POEM TELLS THE TALE OF A MYSTERIOUS RED-CLOAKED KNIGHT, WHO APPEARED OUT OF NOWHERE IN A 14TH CENTURY TOWN IN ENGLAND.
THE KNIGHT TOLD TALES OF HIS HORSE, LILLY, WHO WAS MADE OF METAL, AND LOST IN AN EPIC BATTLE WITH A FIRE-BREATHING DRAGON.
IN THE FOLLOWING STANZAS, THE POEM GOES ON TO CHRONICLE THE 'SELF PROCLAIMED' DRAGON-SLAYER'S FURTHER EXCITING ADVENTURE...

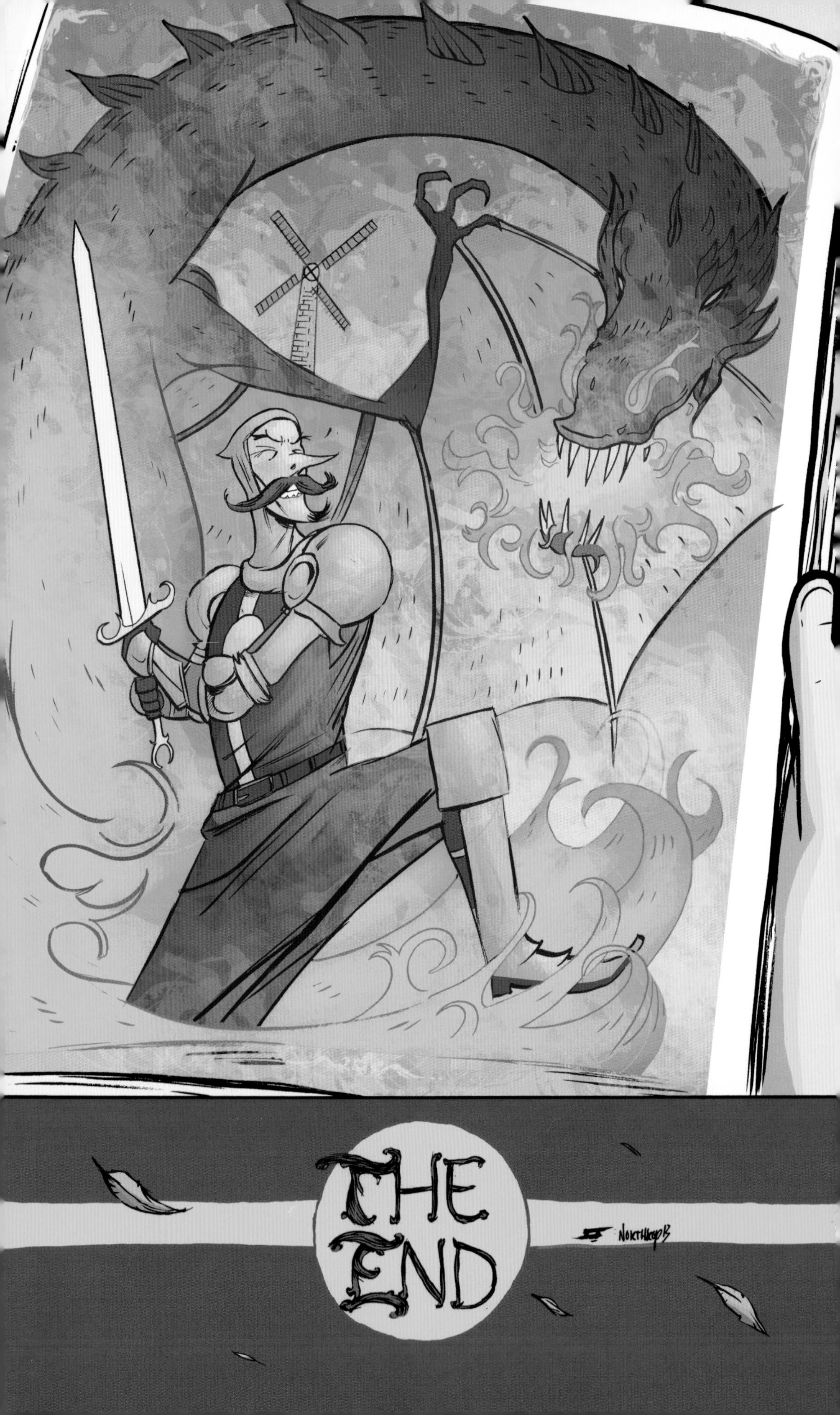
THE END

SHORT STORIES

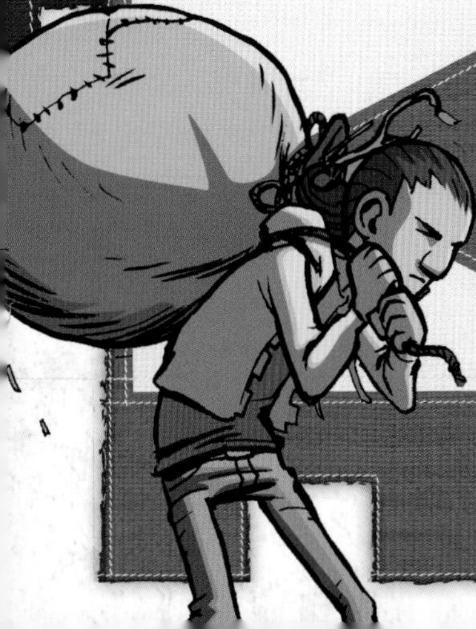

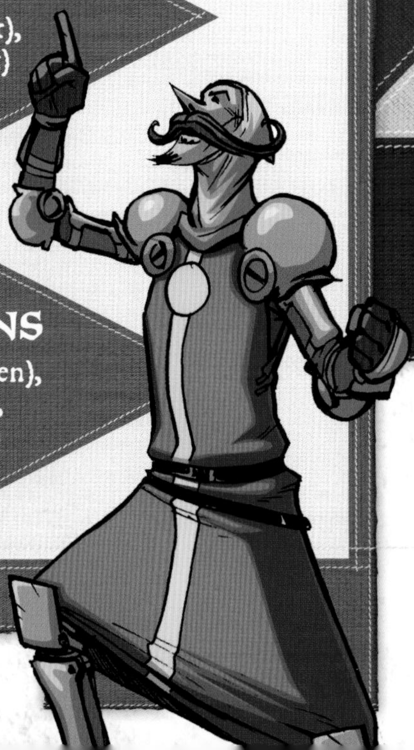

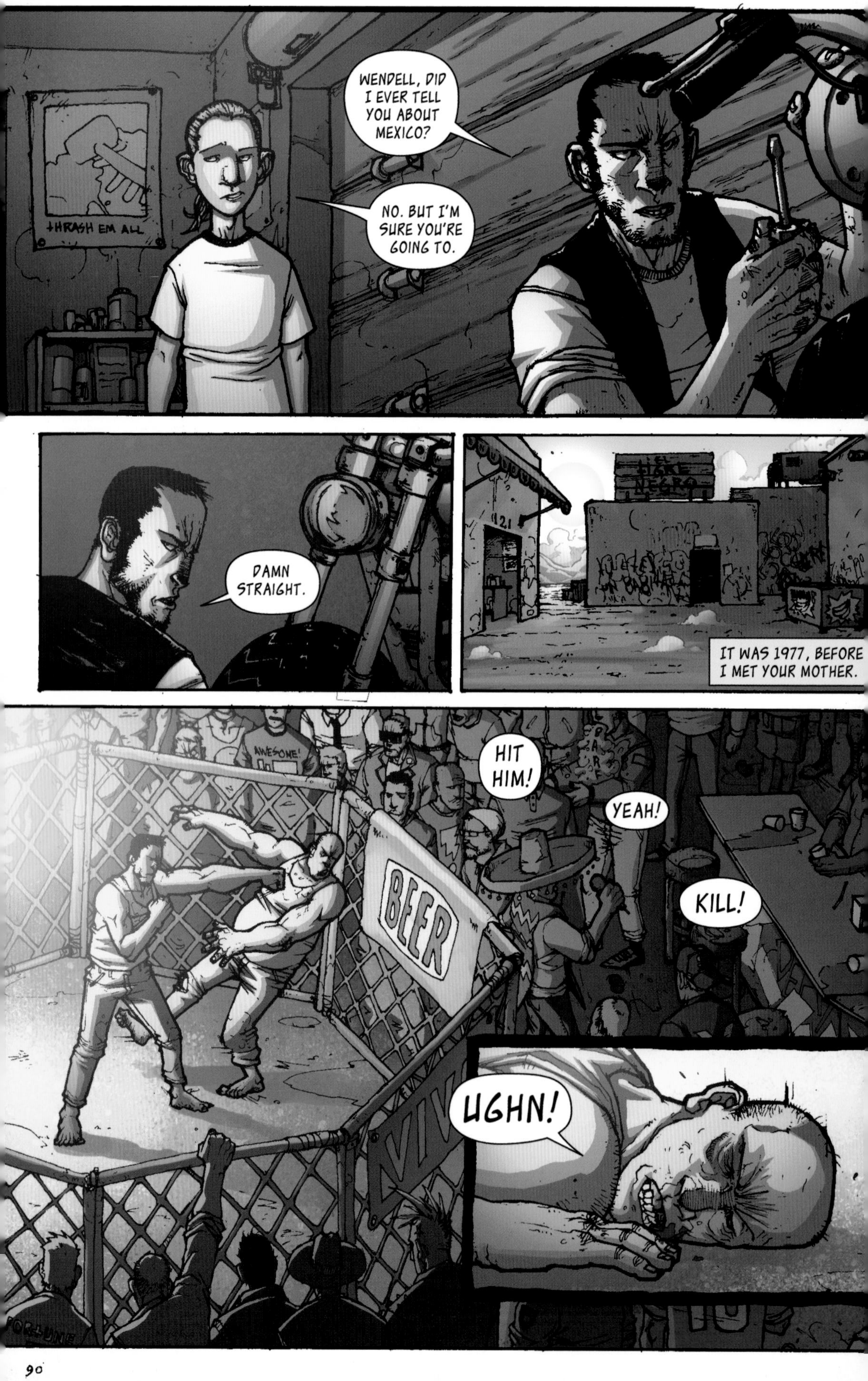
THRASH EM ALL
WENDELL, DID I EVER TELL YOU ABOUT MEXICO?
NO. BUT I'M SURE YOU'RE GOING TO.
DAMN STRAIGHT.
IT WAS 1977, BEFORE I MET YOUR MOTHER.
AWESOME!
HIT HIM!
YEAH!
BEER
KILL!
UGHN!

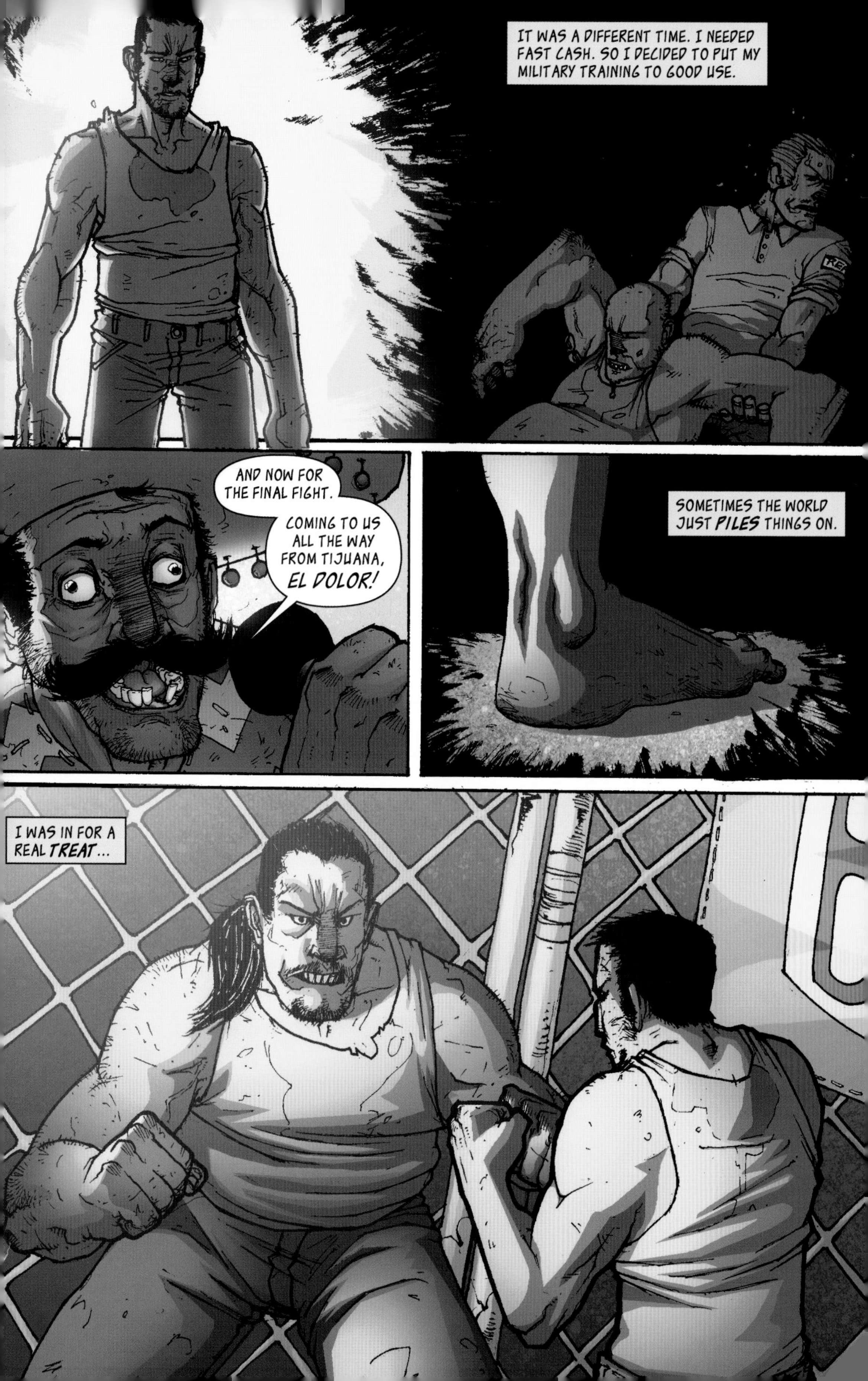
IT WAS A DIFFERENT TIME. I NEEDED FAST CASH. SO I DECIDED TO PUT MY MILITARY TRAINING TO GOOD USE.
AND NOW FOR THE FINAL FIGHT.
COMING TO US ALL THE WAY FROM TIJUANA, EL DOLOR!
SOMETIMES THE WORLD JUST PILES THINGS ON.
I WAS IN FOR A REAL TREAT...

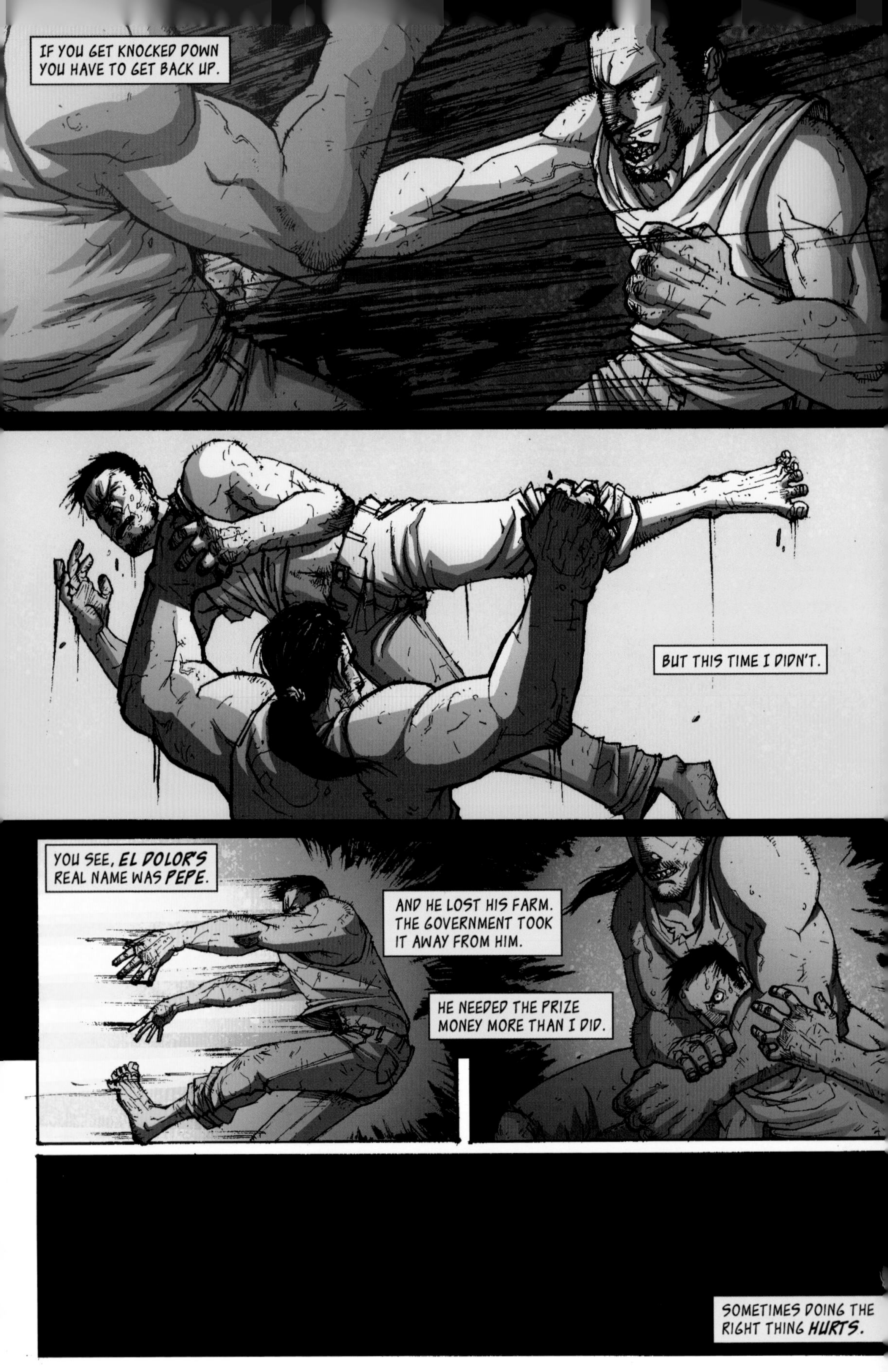
IF YOU GET KNOCKED DOWN YOU HAVE TO GET BACK UP.
BUT THIS TIME I DIDN'T.
YOU SEE, EL DOLOR'S REAL NAME WAS PEPE.
AND HE LOST HIS FARM. THE GOVERNMENT TOOK IT AWAY FROM HIM.
HE NEEDED THE PRIZE MONEY MORE THAN I DID.
SOMETIMES DOING THE RIGHT THING HURTS.

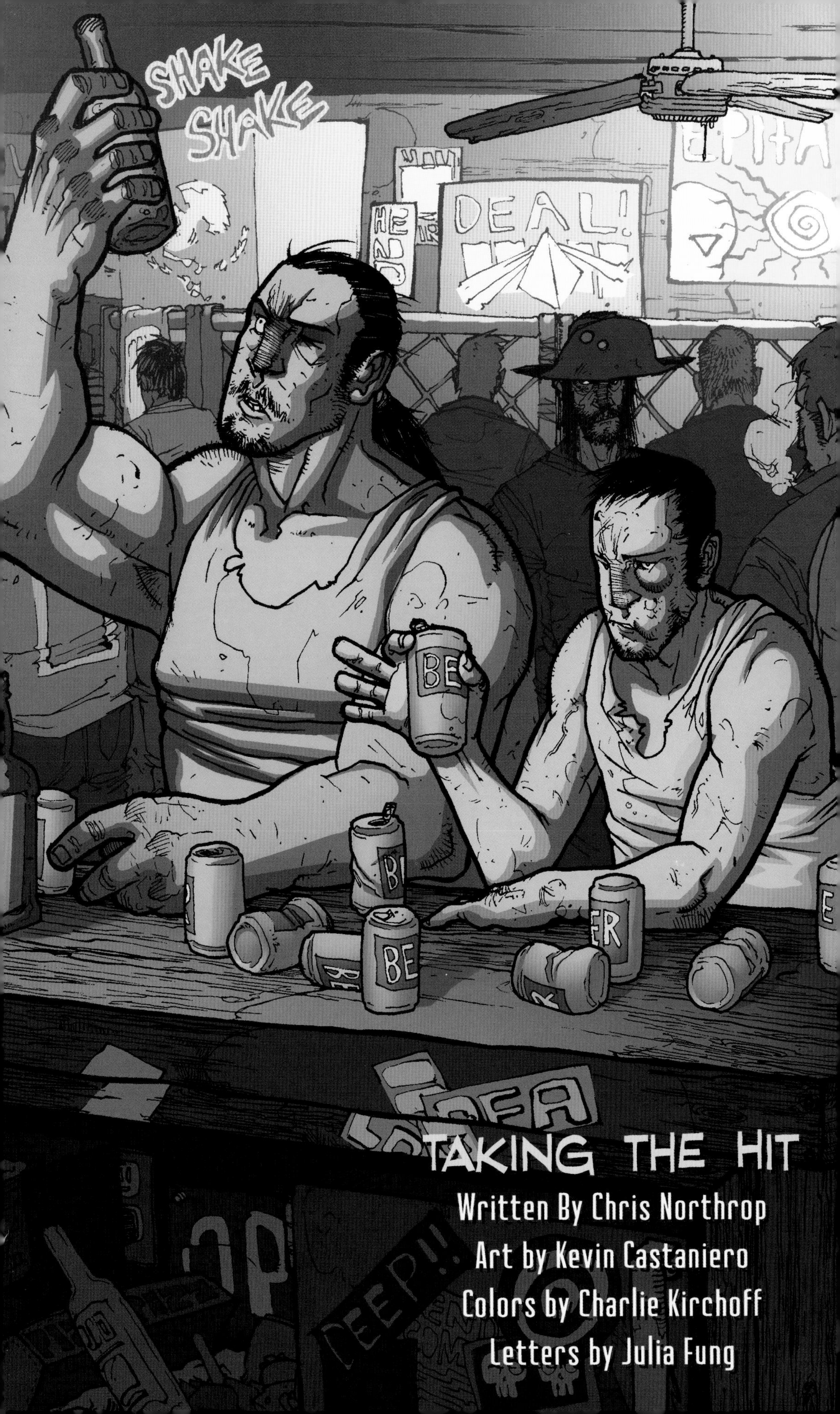

SHAKE SHAKE
DEAL!

TAKING THE HIT

Written By Chris Northrop
Art by Kevin Castaniero
Colors by Charlie Kirchoff
Letters by Julia Fung

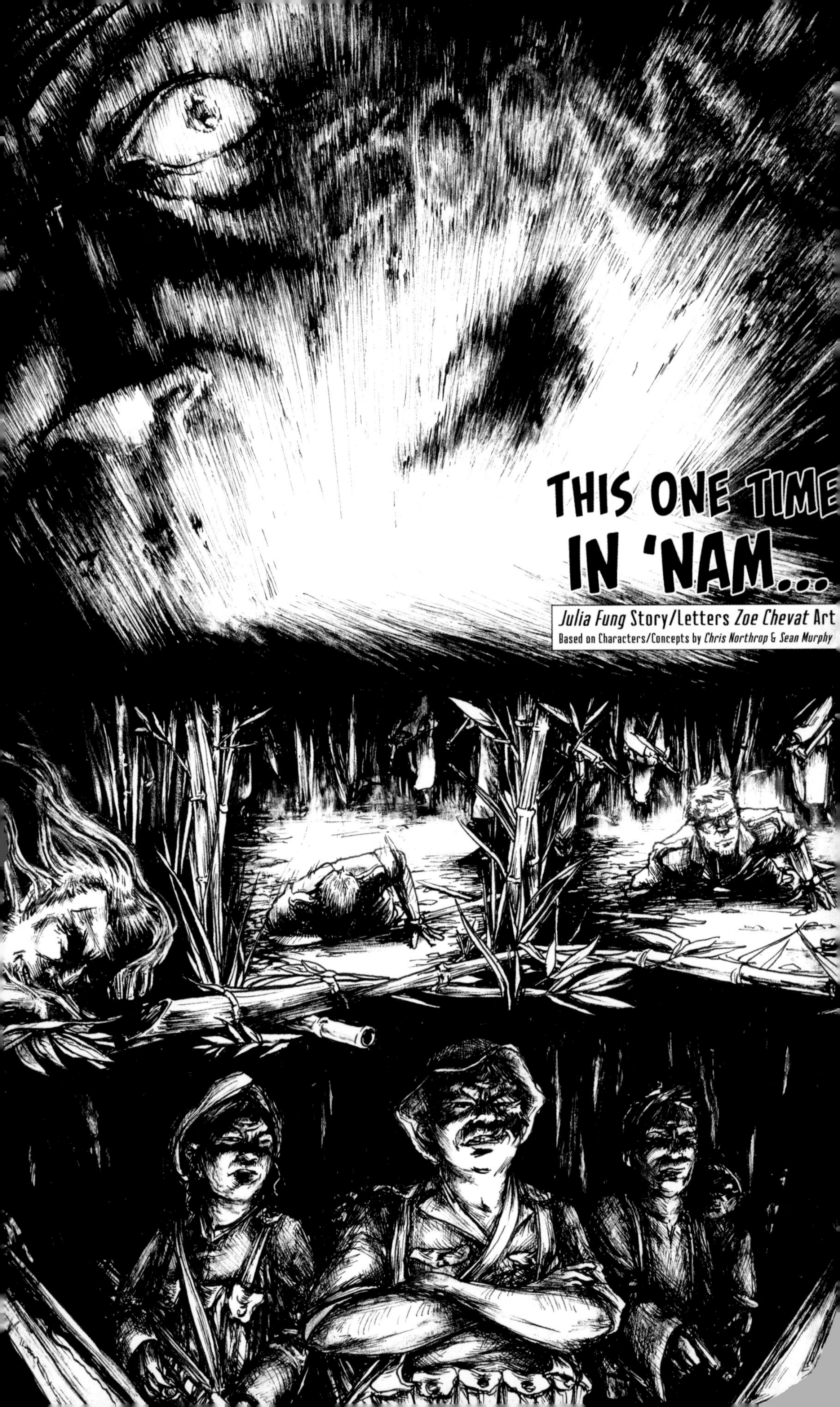
THIS ONE TIME
IN 'NAM...
Julia Fung Story/Letters Zoe Chevat Art
Based on Characters/Concepts by Chris Northrop & Sean Murphy

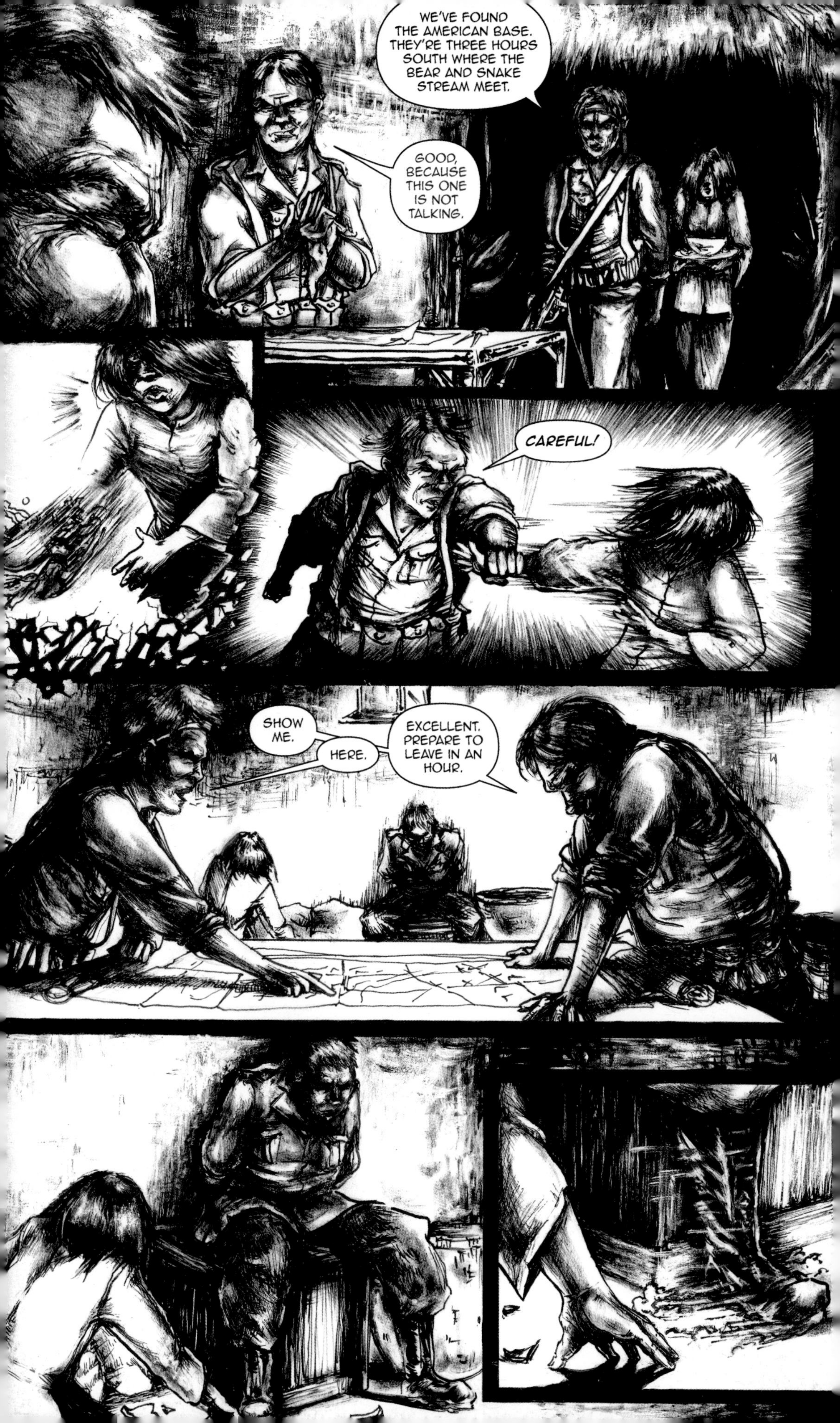
WE'VE FOUND THE AMERICAN BASE. THEY'RE THREE HOURS SOUTH WHERE THE BEAR AND SNAKE STREAM MEET.
GOOD, BECAUSE THIS ONE IS NOT TALKING.
CAREFUL!
SHOW ME.
HERE.
EXCELLENT. PREPARE TO LEAVE IN AN HOUR.

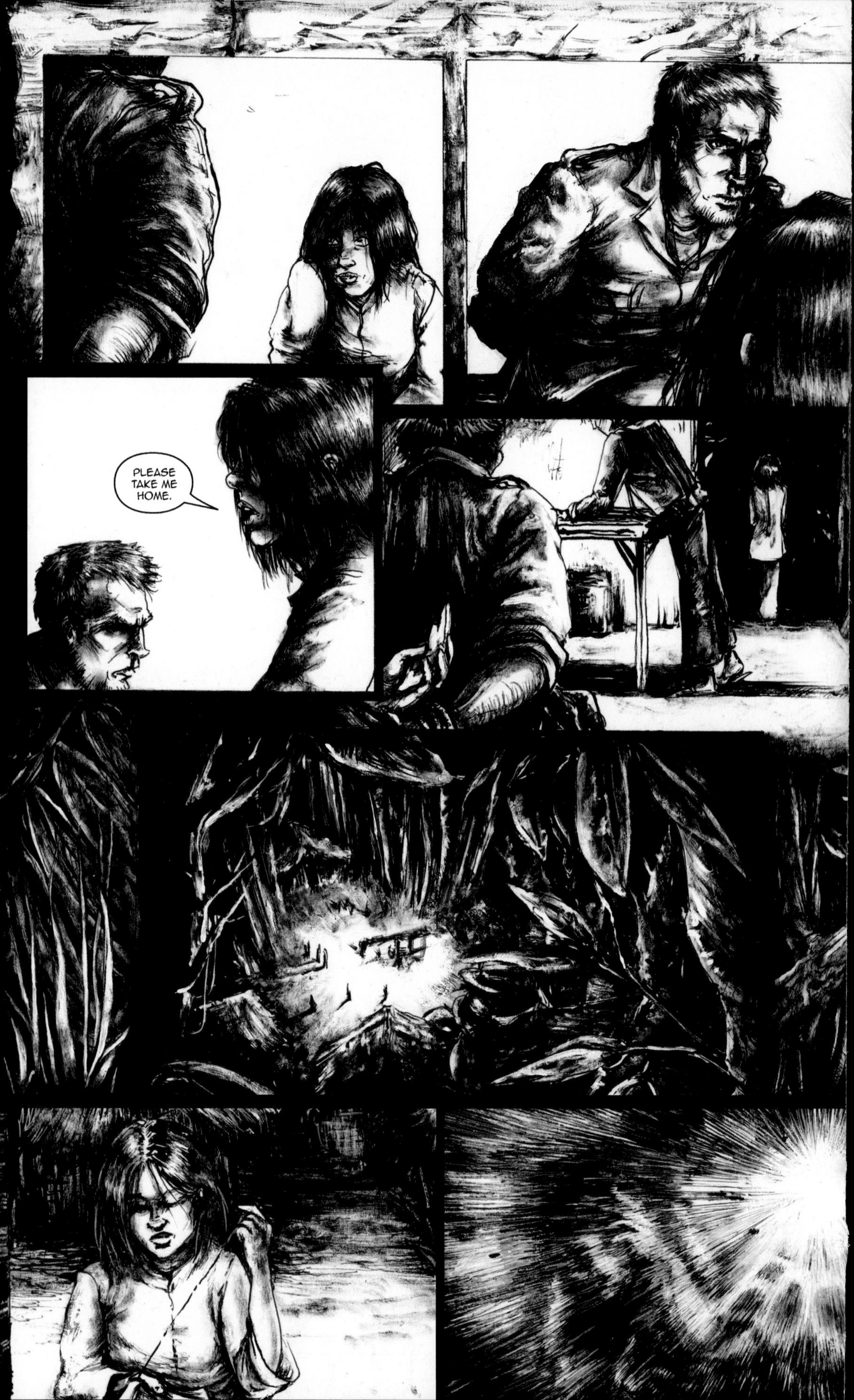
PLEASE TAKE ME HOME.

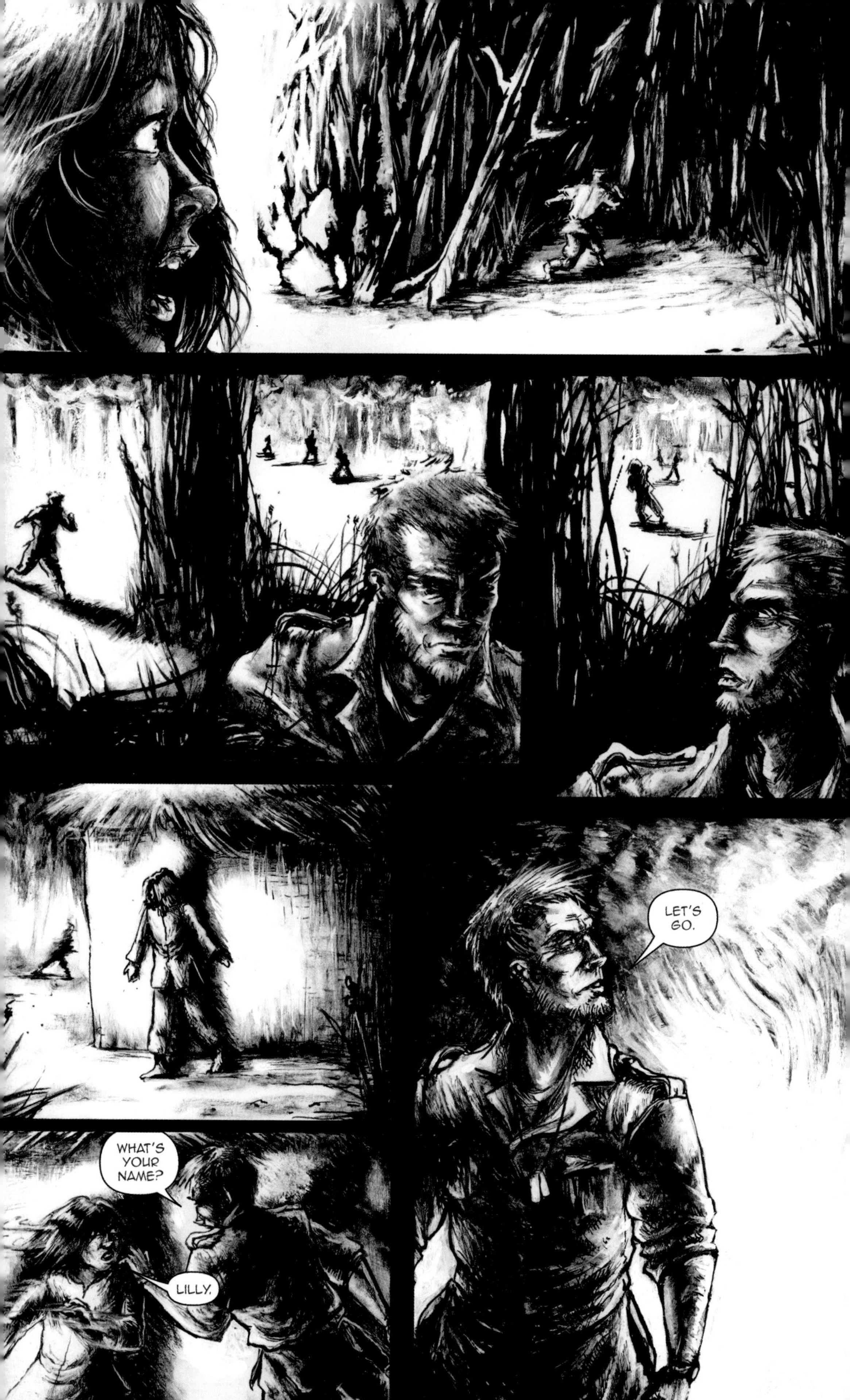
WHAT'S YOUR NAME?
LILLY.
LET'S GO.

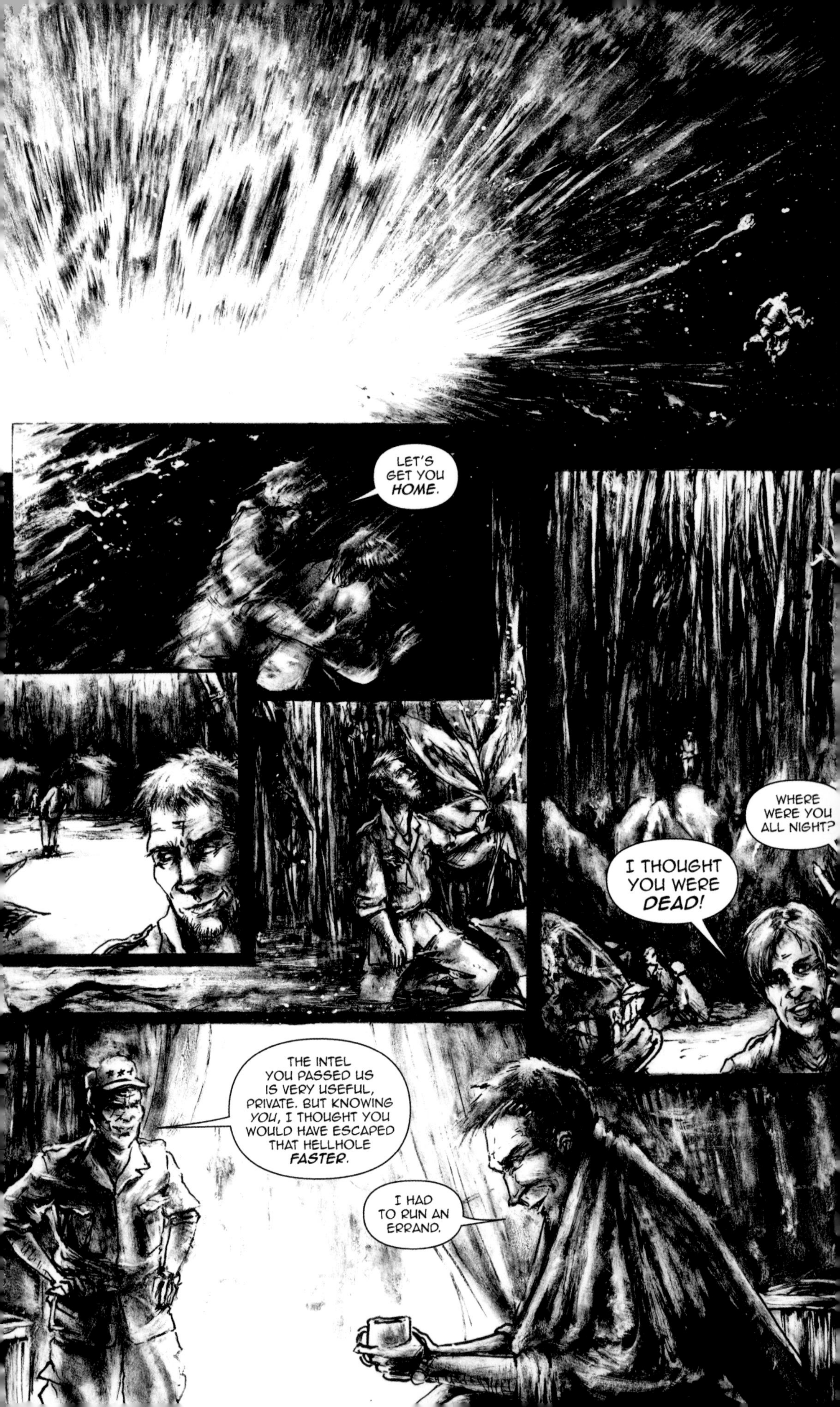
LET'S GET YOU *HOME*.
WHERE WERE YOU ALL NIGHT?
I THOUGHT YOU WERE *DEAD!*
THE INTEL YOU PASSED US IS VERY USEFUL, PRIVATE. BUT KNOWING *YOU*, I THOUGHT YOU WOULD HAVE ESCAPED THAT HELLHOLE *FASTER*.
I HAD TO RUN AN ERRAND.

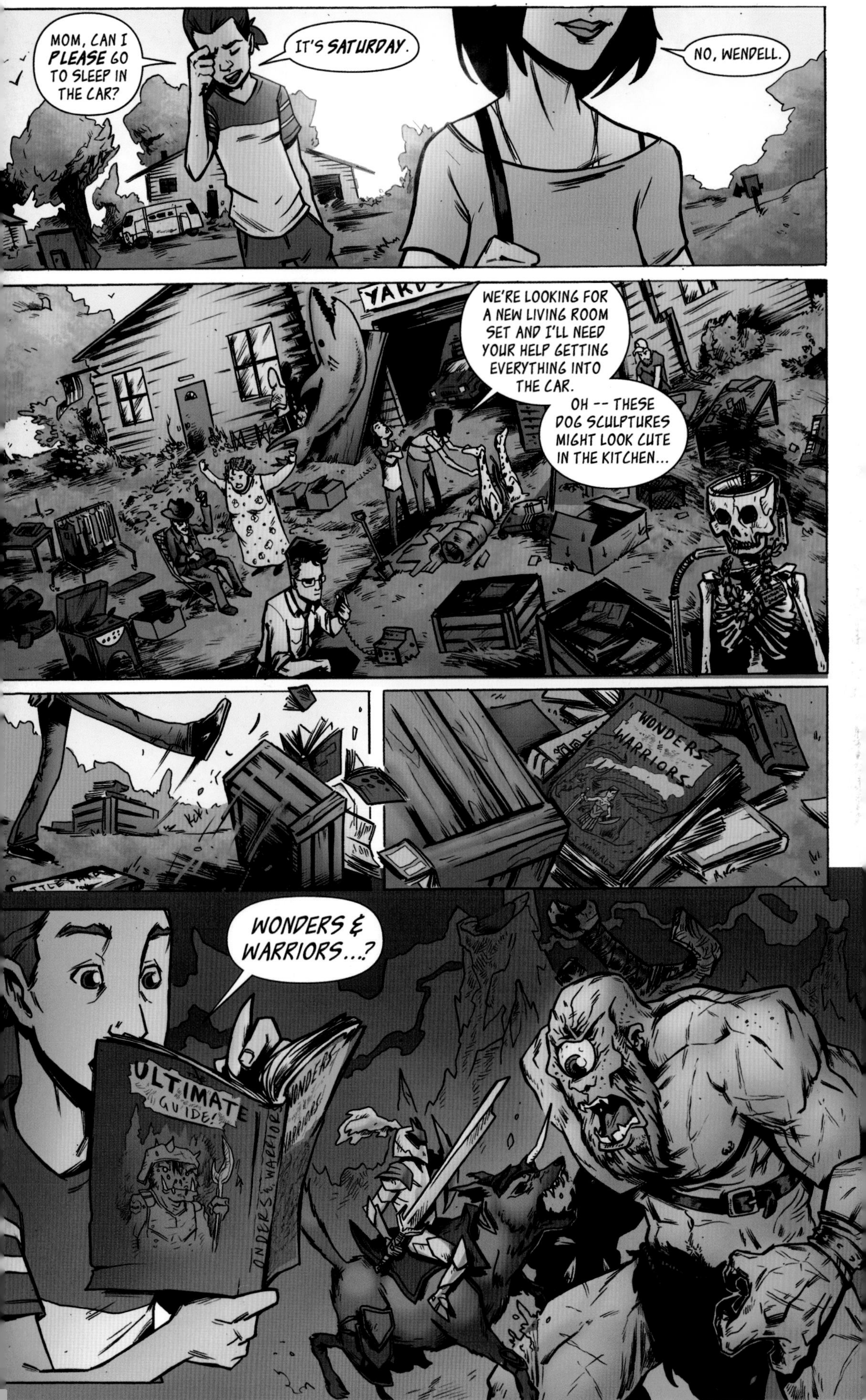

MOM, CAN I PLEASE GO TO SLEEP IN THE CAR?
IT'S SATURDAY.
NO, WENDELL.
WE'RE LOOKING FOR A NEW LIVING ROOM SET AND I'LL NEED YOUR HELP GETTING EVERYTHING INTO THE CAR.
OH -- THESE DOG SCULPTURES MIGHT LOOK CUTE IN THE KITCHEN...
WONDERS & WARRIORS
WONDERS & WARRIORS...?
ULTIMATE GUIDE!
WONDERS & WARRIORS

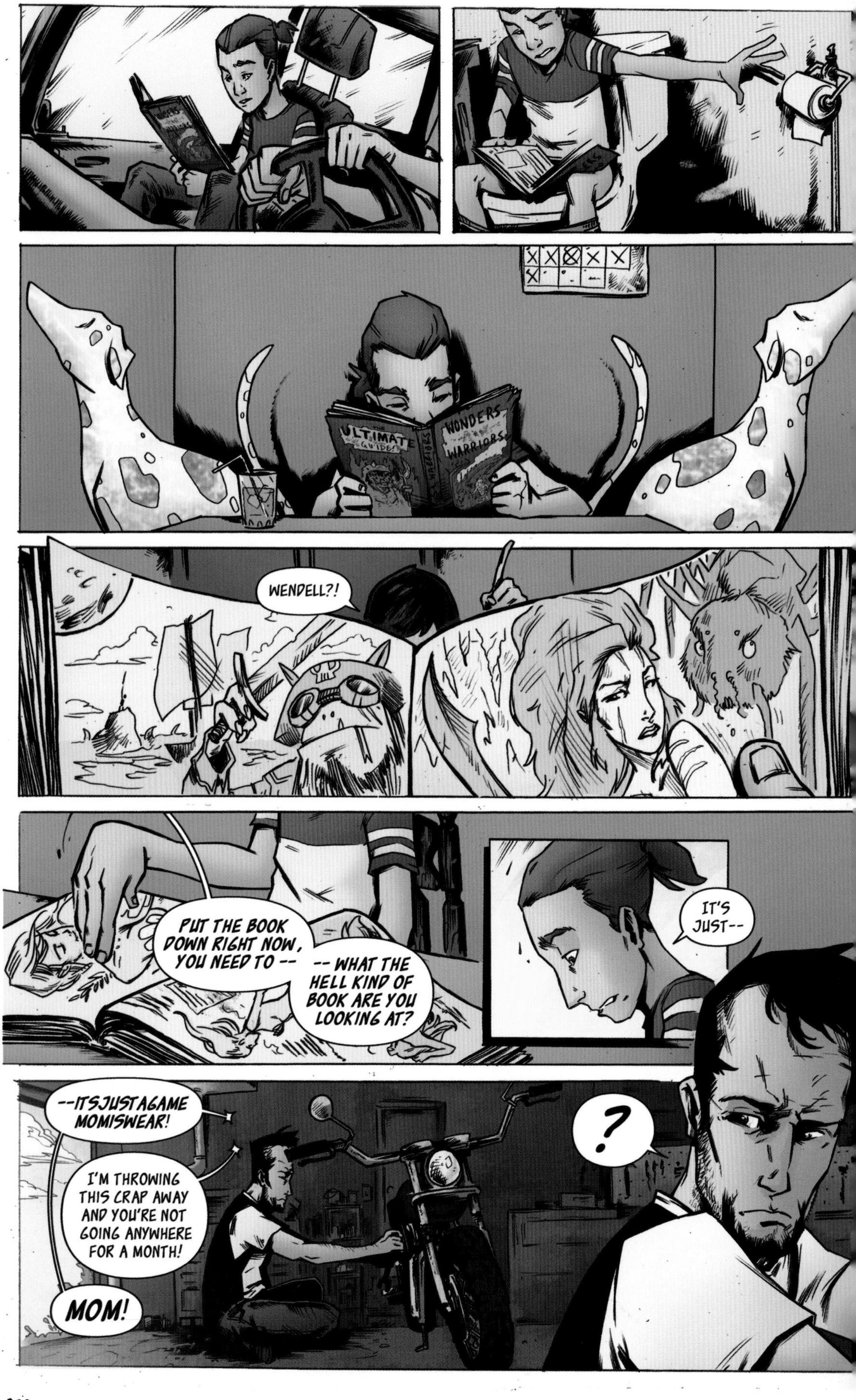
WONDERS WARRIORS
THE ULTIMATE GUIDE
WONDERS WARRIORS
WENDELL?!
PUT THE BOOK DOWN RIGHT NOW, YOU NEED TO --
-- WHAT THE HELL KIND OF BOOK ARE YOU LOOKING AT?
IT'S JUST--
--ITSJUSTAGAME MOMISWEAR!
I'M THROWING THIS CRAP AWAY AND YOU'RE NOT GOING ANYWHERE FOR A MONTH!
MOM!
?

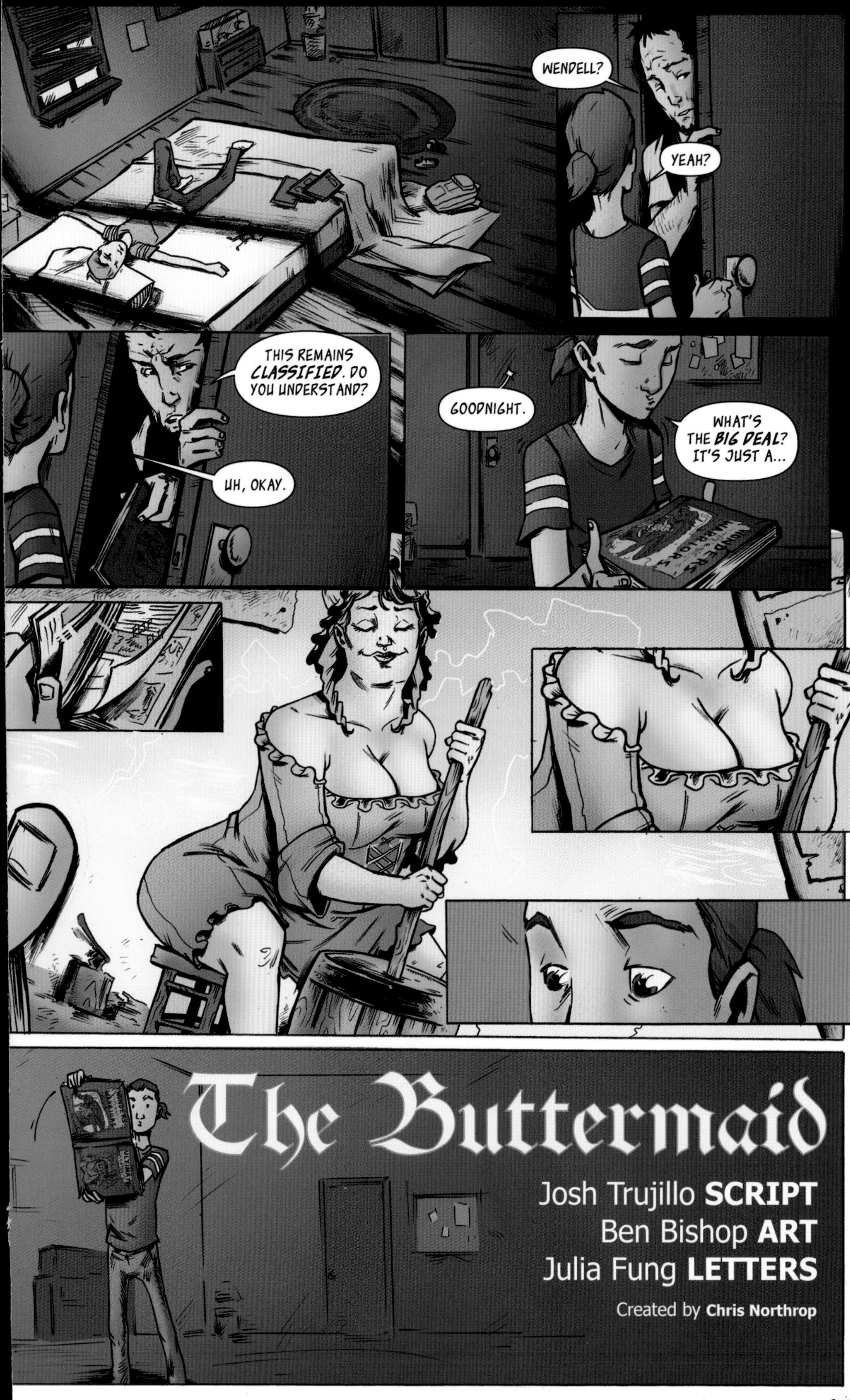

WENDELL?
YEAH?
THIS REMAINS CLASSIFIED. DO YOU UNDERSTAND?
UH, OKAY.
GOODNIGHT.
WHAT'S THE BIG DEAL? IT'S JUST A...
The Buttermaid
Josh Trujillo SCRIPT
Ben Bishop ART
Julia Fung LETTERS
Created by Chris Northrop

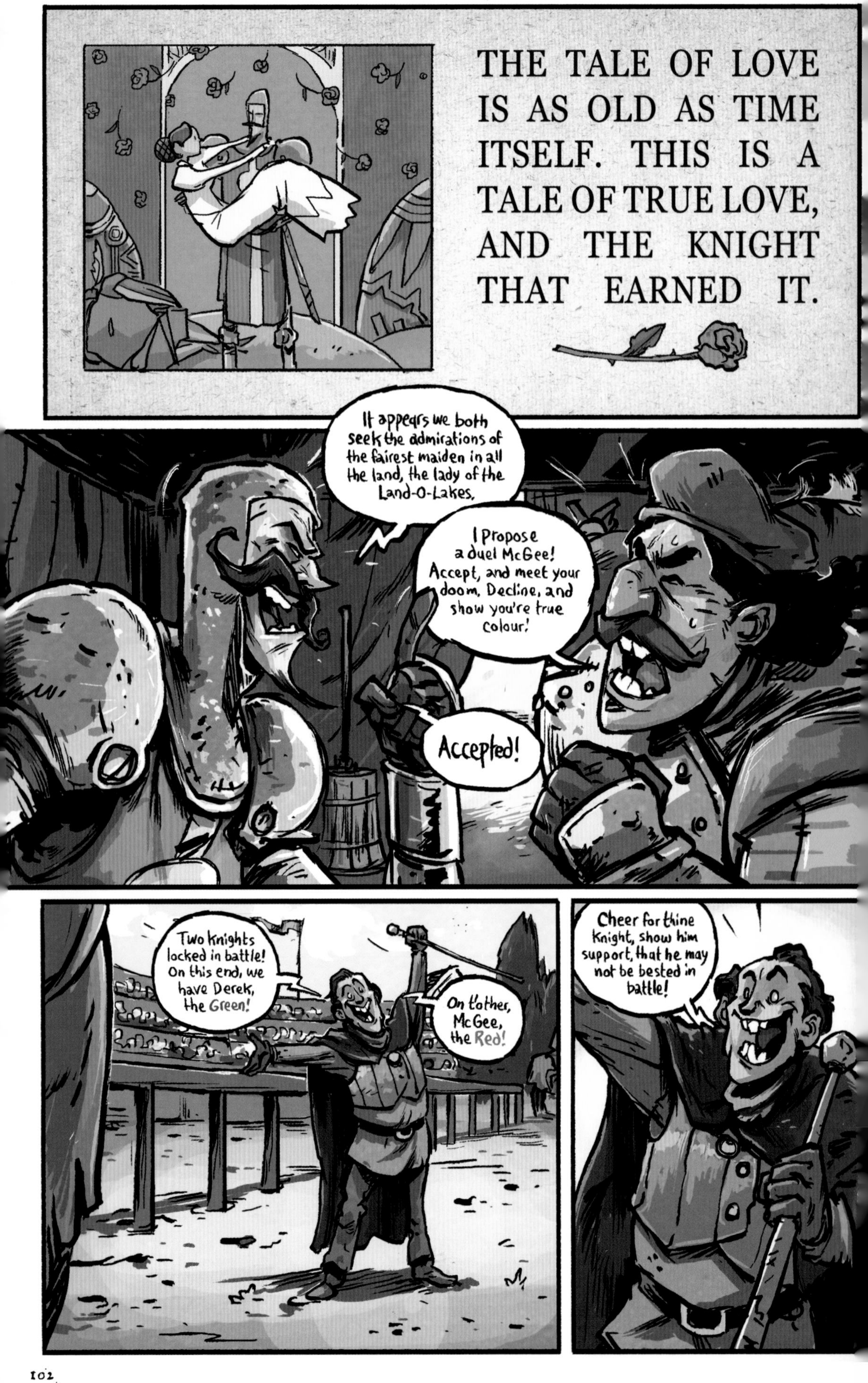
THE TALE OF LOVE IS AS OLD AS TIME ITSELF. THIS IS A TALE OF TRUE LOVE, AND THE KNIGHT THAT EARNED IT.
It appears we both seek the admirations of the fairest maiden in all the land, the lady of the Land-O-Lakes.
I Propose a duel McGee! Accept, and meet your doom. Decline, and show you're true colour!
Accepted!
Two knights locked in battle! On this end, we have Derek, the Green!
On t'other, McGee, the Red!
Cheer for thine Knight, show him support, that he may not be bested in battle!

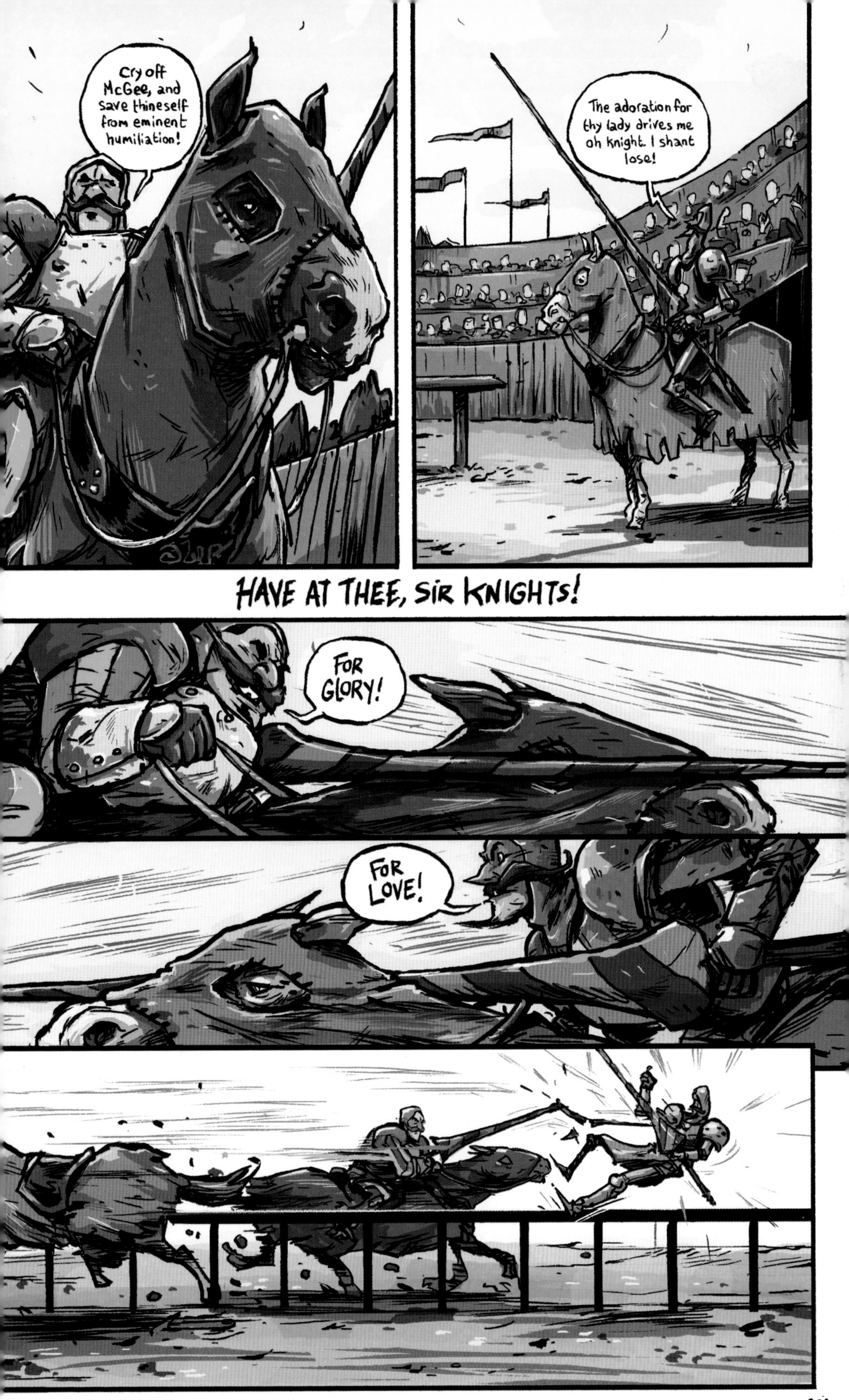
Cry off McGee, and save thineself from eminent humiliation!
The adoration for thy lady drives me oh knight. I shant lose!
HAVE AT THEE, SIR KNIGHTS!
FOR GLORY!
FOR LOVE!

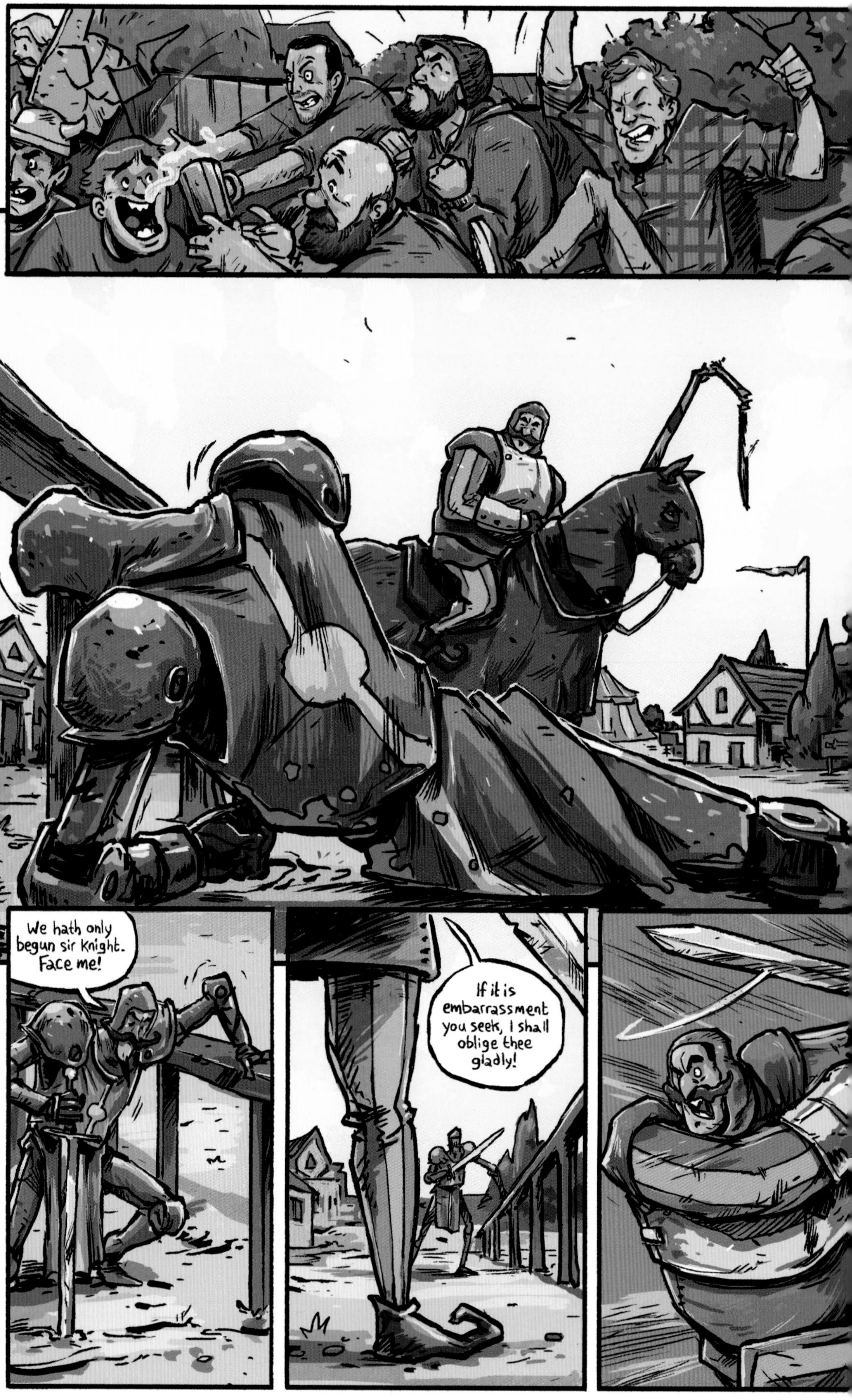
We hath only begun sir Knight. Face me!
If it is embarrassment you seek, I shall oblige thee gladly!

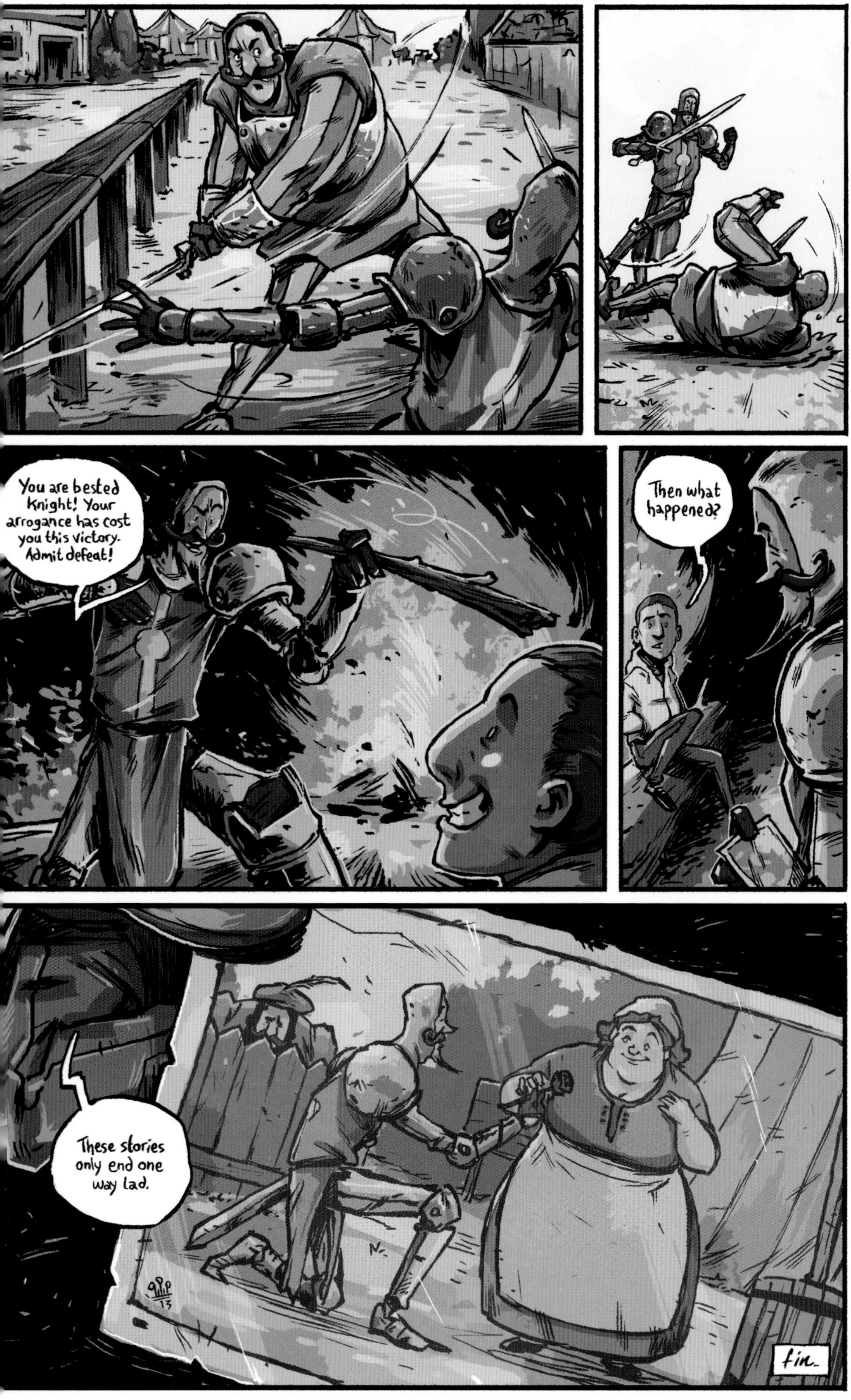

You are bested Knight! Your arrogance has cost you this victory. Admit defeat!
Then what happened?
These stories only end one way lad.
fin.

HEAR YE, **HEAR** YE!

MEASURE A KING'S WEALTH, NOT BY THE COUNT OF **COIN** IN HIS TREASURY, BUT BY THE NUMBER OF GUESTS IN HIS BANQUET HALL...!

THE FOOL SPEAKS **SAGELY**, FATHER...

AYE, JOSEFINA! **VERILY**! AND SO, I ASK THESE LORDS AND **LADIES**...

THANK **ME** NOT FOR THIS FEAST AND PAGEANTRY. LET GRATITUDE SWELL IN **MINE** BOSOM, ALONE -- THANKFUL FOR YE WHOSE PRESENCE **ELEVATES** MY COURT!

THOU **PRATTLE** AS IF TO CONVINCE **THYSELF**...

OCTAVIO! WHAT TREACHERY IS THIS...?!

IF THIS **SEEM** TREACHERY TO THINE **MEAD-ADDLED** MIND, KING FELIPE, THEN A BIGGER **FOOL** THAN THAT JESTER SEE I!

NAY! THE EXILED SERVANT RETURNS, **STRUTTING** INTO THINE COURT WITH INTENTIONS **BARE** AS THE WET NEWBORN.

AND **WHAT**, PRAY TELL, ARE THESE PLAIN INTENTS, OH YE **DISGRACED** VIZIER?

WHY, TO CLAIM THE FETCHING AND EVER-SO-**CHASTE** PRINCESS JOSEFINA'S HAND!

OH, HOW I HATH WISHED TO SUCKLE FROM HER CORSETED DUG...

I INVOKE THE RIGHT OF **PROVOCA-TOR ET PROVOCARE** AND THUSLY PRESENT SIR NESTOR OF AJENJO AS MY PROXY.

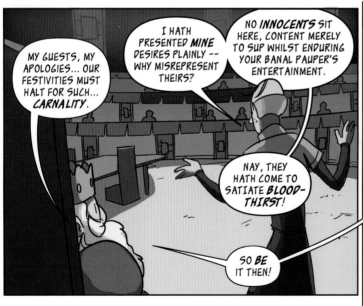

MY GUESTS, MY APOLOGIES... OUR FESTIVITIES MUST HALT FOR SUCH... **CARNALITY**.

I HATH PRESENTED **MINE** DESIRES PLAINLY -- WHY MISREPRESENT THEIRS?

NO **INNOCENTS** SIT HERE, CONTENT MERELY TO SUP WHILST ENDURING YOUR BANAL PAUPER'S ENTERTAINMENT.

NAY, THEY HATH COME TO SATIATE **BLOOD-THIRST**!

SO **BE** IT THEN!

SUCH **OUTRAGE**...

THE **INTENDED** EXHIBITION OF KNIGHTLY PROWESS SHALL INSTEAD BE A **TOURNAMENT**.

A **NOBLEMAN** AMONGST US, VALOR-OUS ENOUGH TO DEFEND MY DAUGHTER'S VIRTUE, SHALL **RISE** TO THIS TASK AND --

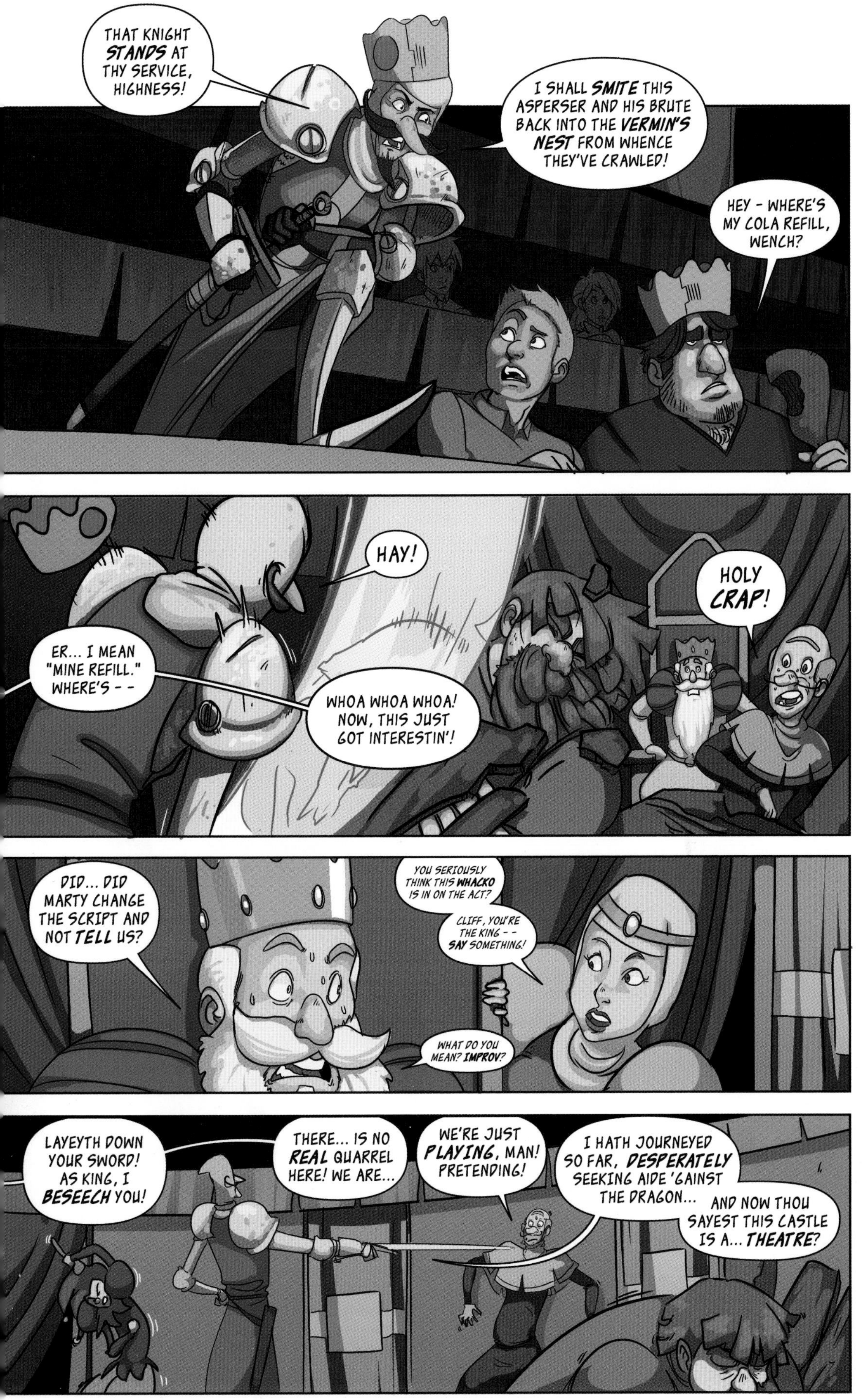
THAT KNIGHT STANDS AT THY SERVICE, HIGHNESS!
I SHALL SMITE THIS ASPERSER AND HIS BRUTE BACK INTO THE VERMIN'S NEST FROM WHENCE THEY'VE CRAWLED!
HEY - WHERE'S MY COLA REFILL, WENCH?
HAY!
HOLY CRAP!
ER... I MEAN "MINE REFILL." WHERE'S - -
WHOA WHOA WHOA! NOW, THIS JUST GOT INTERESTIN'!
DID... DID MARTY CHANGE THE SCRIPT AND NOT TELL US?
YOU SERIOUSLY THINK THIS WHACKO IS IN ON THE ACT?
CLIFF, YOU'RE THE KING - - SAY SOMETHING!
WHAT DO YOU MEAN? IMPROV?
LAYEYTH DOWN YOUR SWORD! AS KING, I BESEECH YOU!
THERE... IS NO REAL QUARREL HERE! WE ARE...
WE'RE JUST PLAYING, MAN! PRETENDING!
I HATH JOURNEYED SO FAR, DESPERATELY SEEKING AIDE 'GAINST THE DRAGON...
AND NOW THOU SAYEST THIS CASTLE IS A... THEATRE?

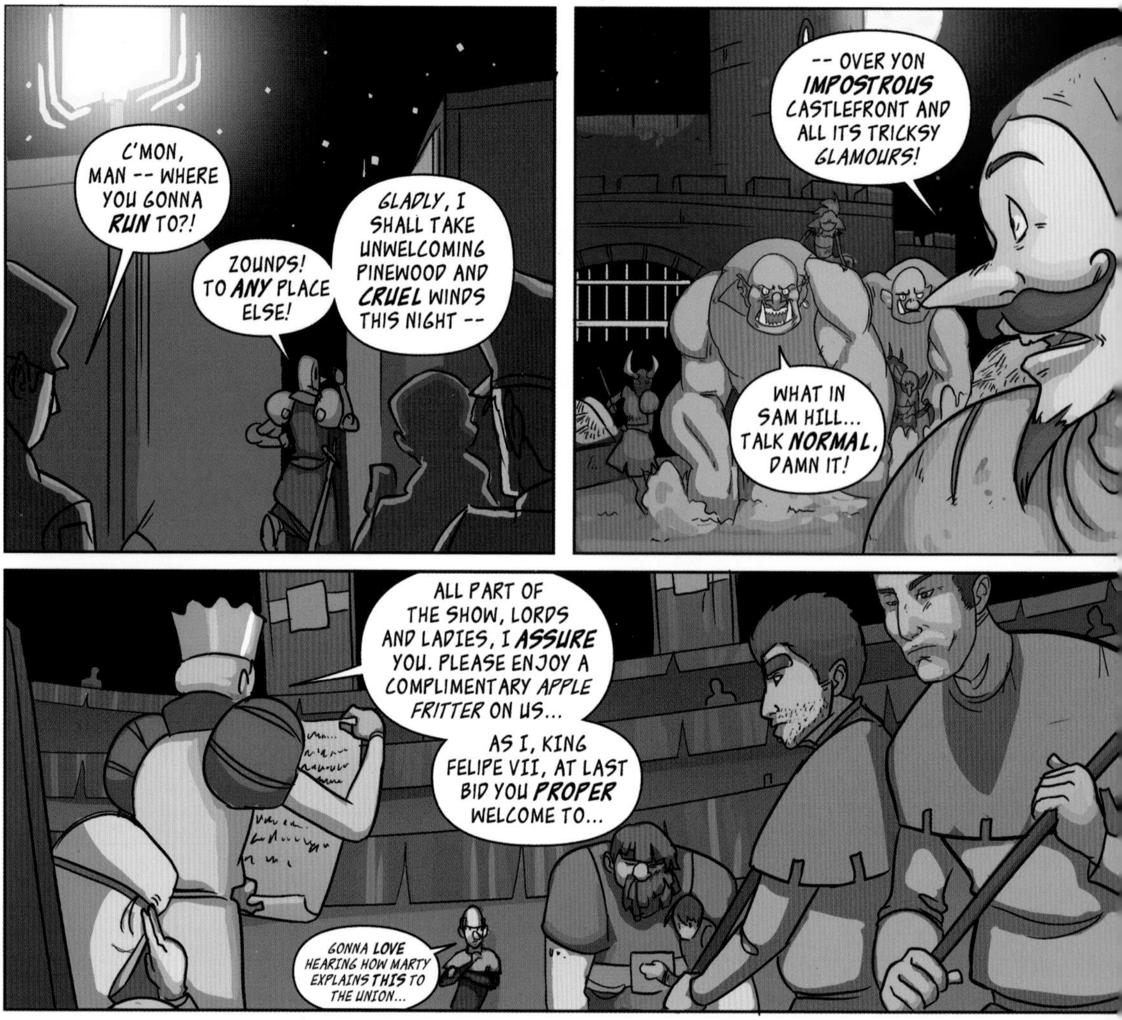
C'MON, MAN -- WHERE YOU GONNA RUN TO?!
ZOUNDS! TO ANY PLACE ELSE!
GLADLY, I SHALL TAKE UNWELCOMING PINEWOOD AND CRUEL WINDS THIS NIGHT --
-- OVER YON IMPOSTROUS CASTLEFRONT AND ALL ITS TRICKSY GLAMOURS!
WHAT IN SAM HILL... TALK NORMAL, DAMN IT!
ALL PART OF THE SHOW, LORDS AND LADIES, I ASSURE YOU. PLEASE ENJOY A COMPLIMENTARY APPLE FRITTER ON US...
AS I, KING FELIPE VII, AT LAST BID YOU PROPER WELCOME TO...
GONNA LOVE HEARING HOW MARTY EXPLAINS THIS TO THE UNION...

"...DINING WITH DRAGONS"

Written by **Tom Pinchuk** Art by **Zack Turner** Letters by **Julia Fung**
Characters and Concepts **Chris Northrop** & **Sean Murphy**

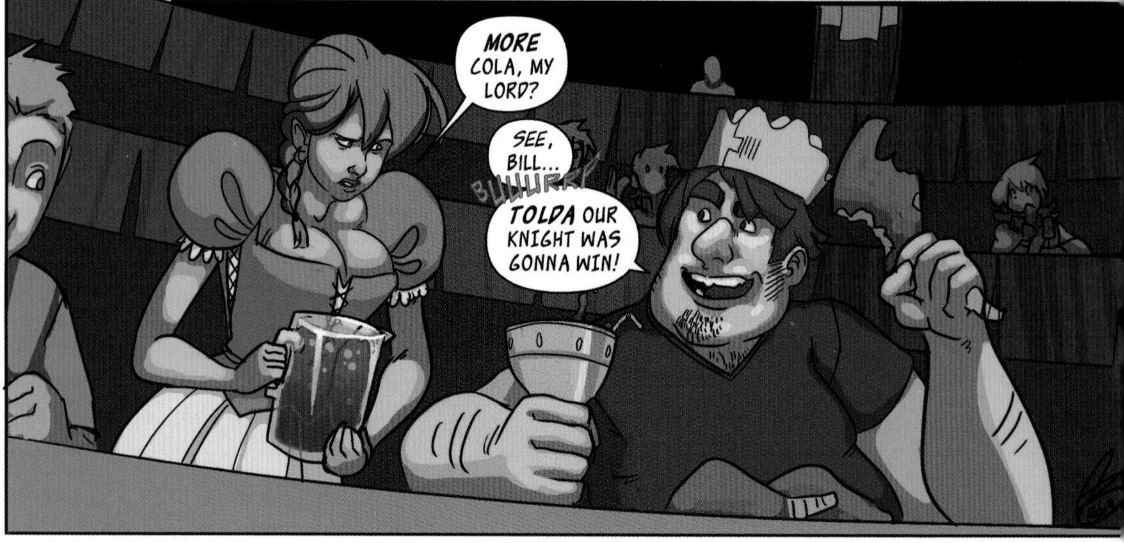
MORE COLA, MY LORD?
SEE, BILL...
TOLDA OUR KNIGHT WAS GONNA WIN!

PIN-UP GALLERY

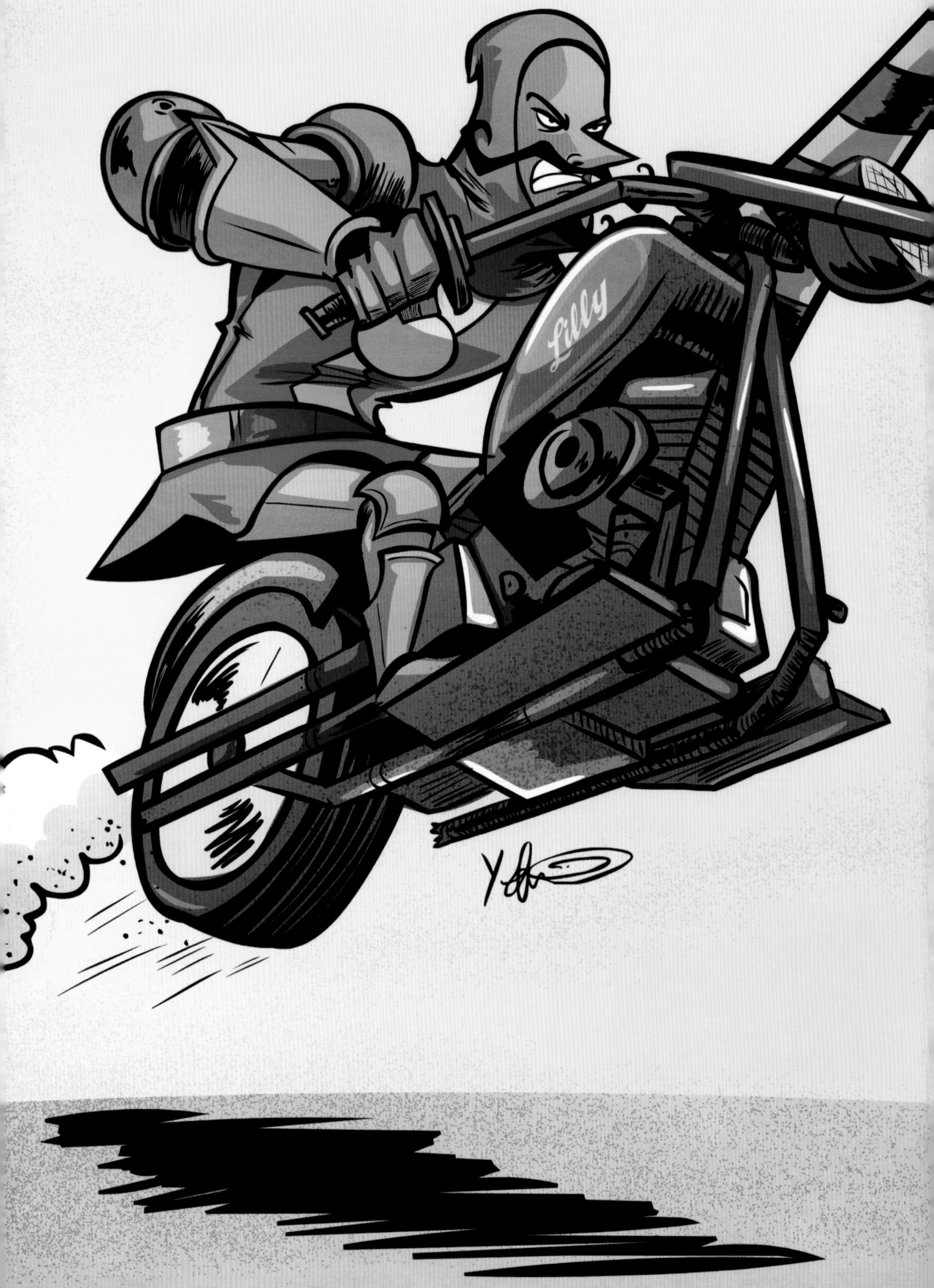
Lilly

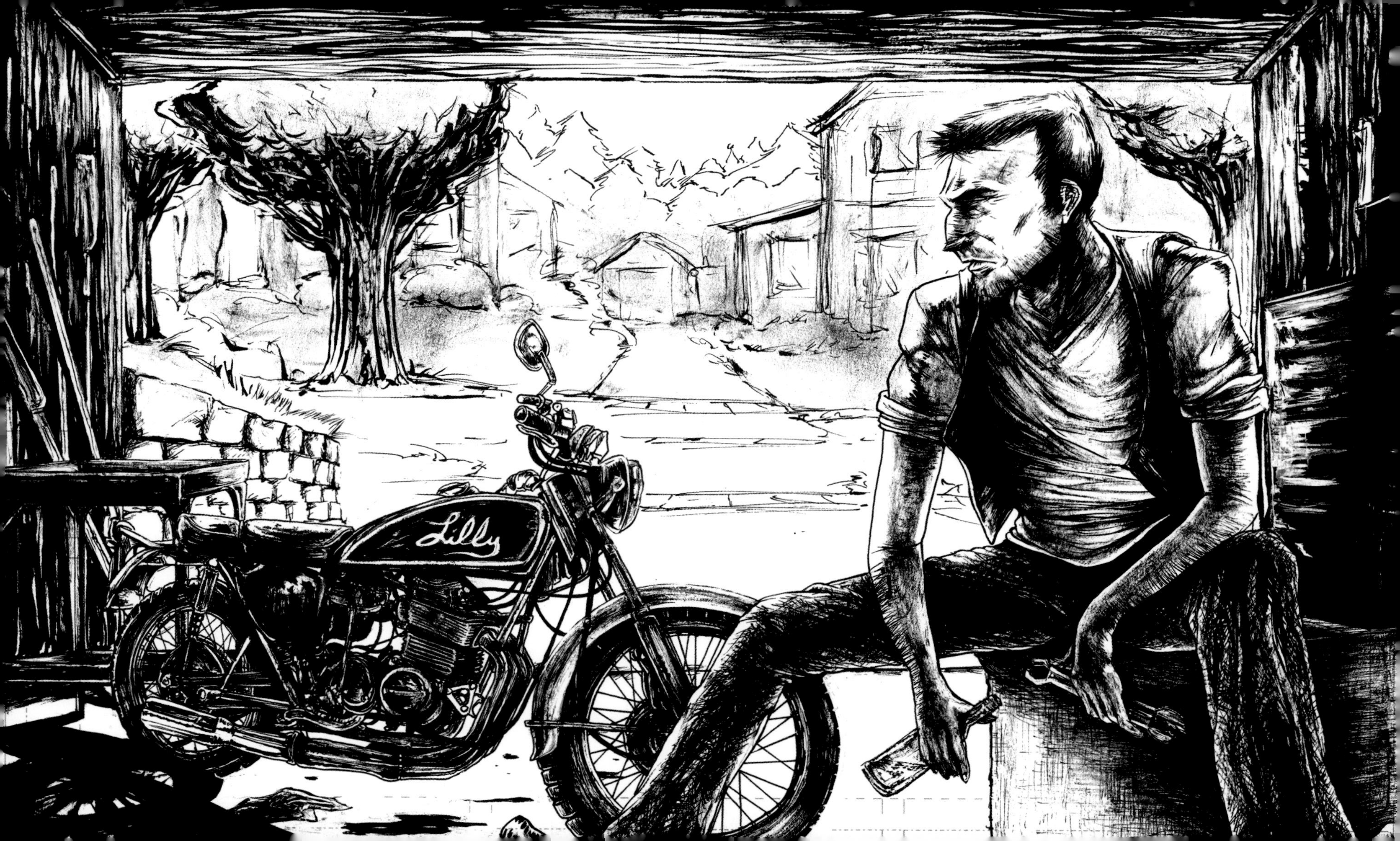
Lilly

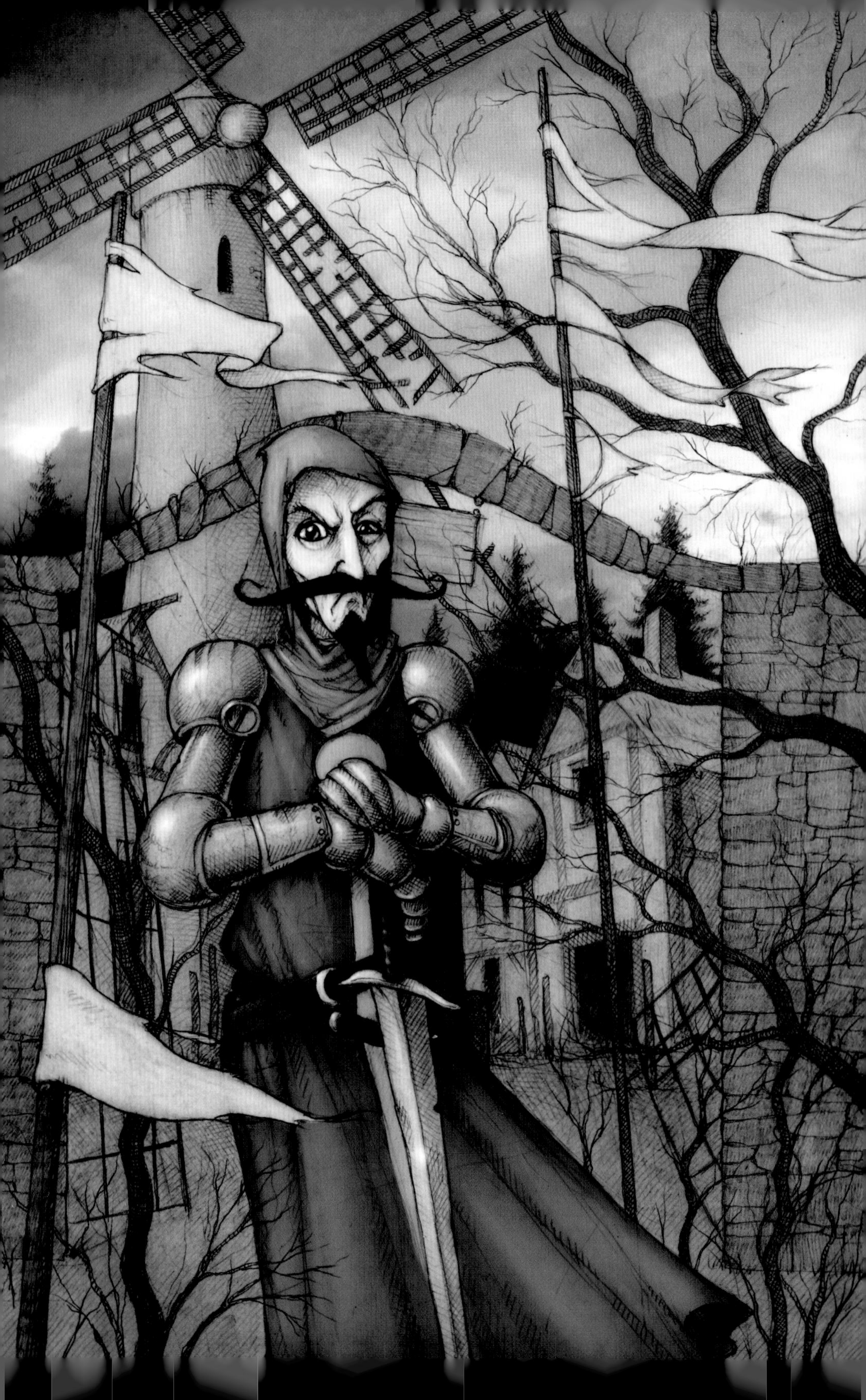

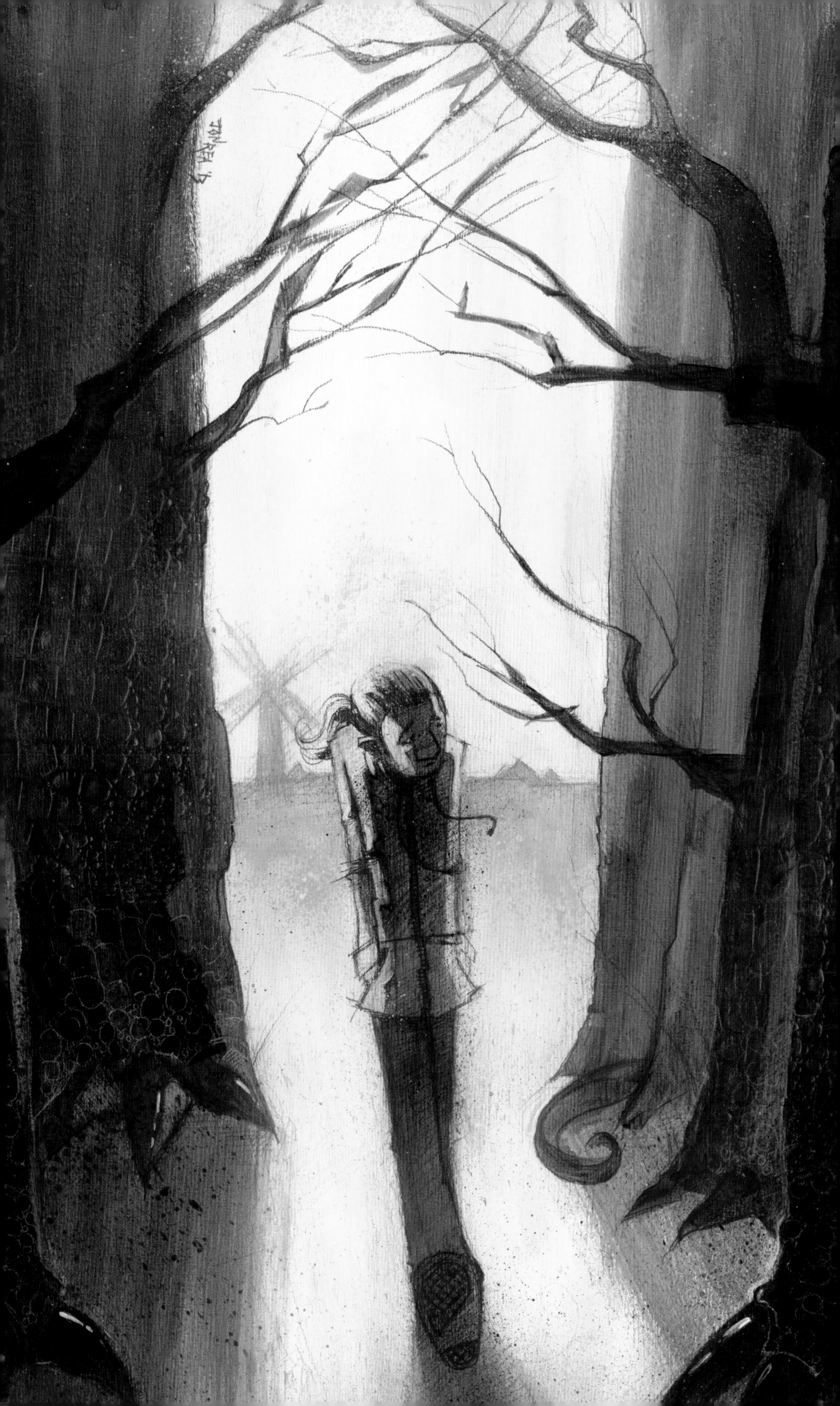

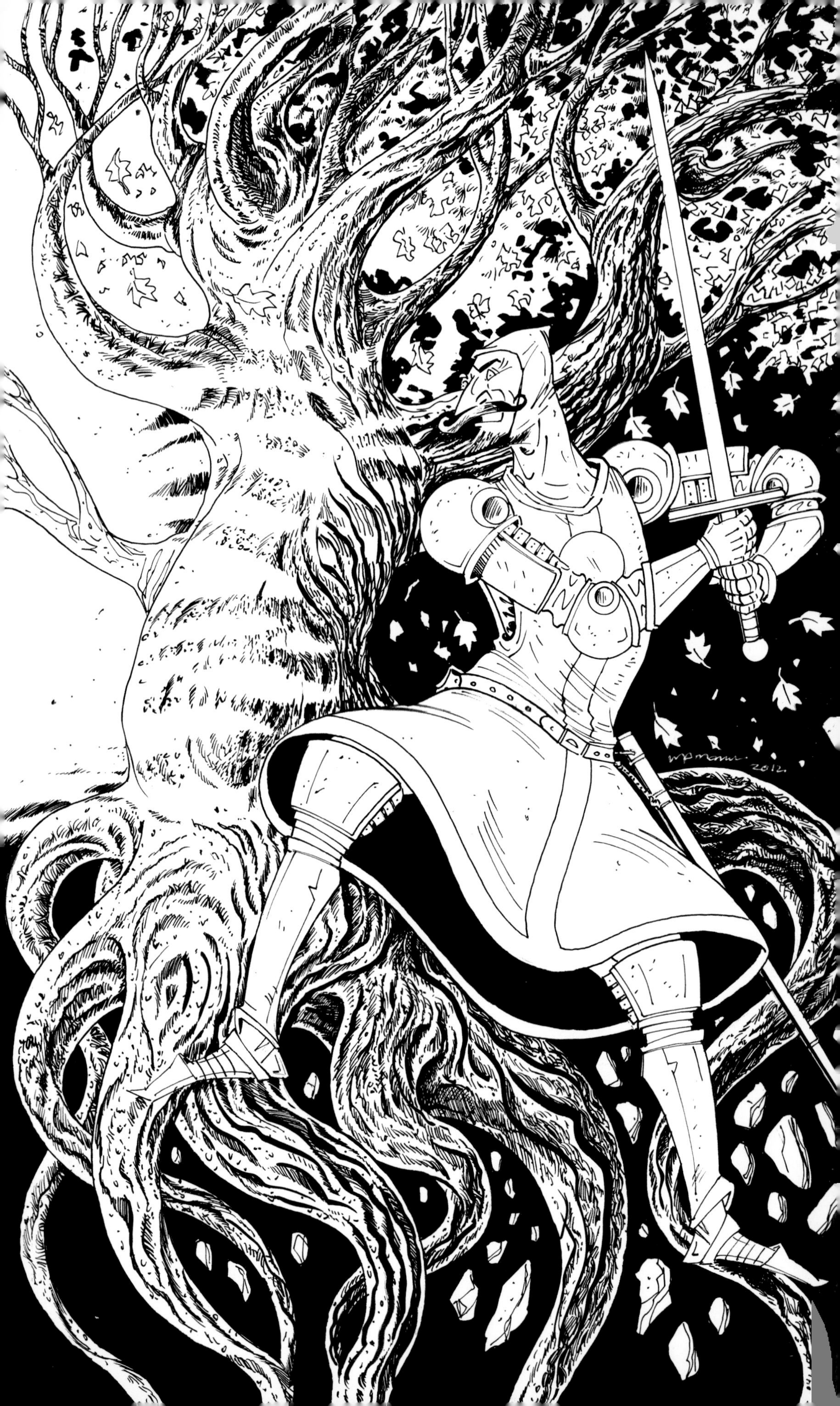

wpmann
2012.

Concept Design by Jeff & Sean

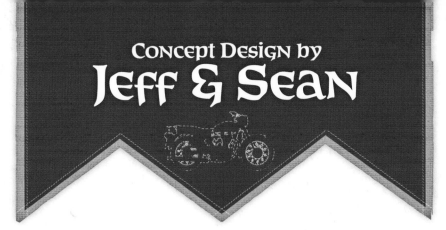

JEFF STOKELY was tasked with creating the world of *Dragons*. Leaves and trees, motorcycles and ringer T-shirts. It had to capture New Hampshire suburbia in the 1980's. As a reference, Jeff built on designs by SEAN MURPHY from 2007. The following is a look at their work.

Character concepts.
(Art by Jeff Stokely)

WENDAL
TED
LORD HABERSHAM McGEE

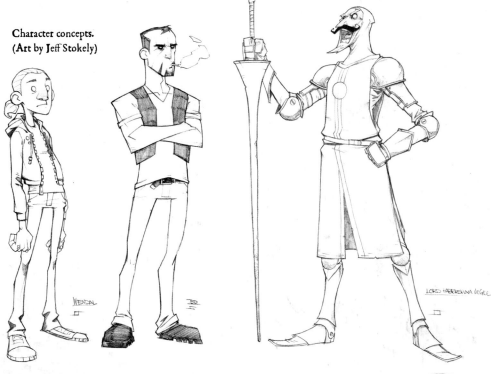

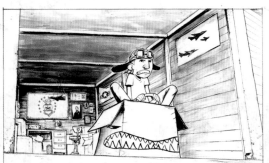

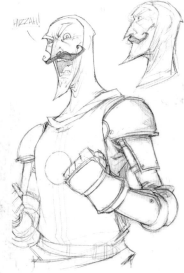

Wendell playing in a storage unit filled with a box of his father's things. It's never said what happened to Wendell's real father, but it's insinuated that he died and was a fighter pilot. In the original script for *Dragons*, Wendell is 13, but he was more interesting as a character at 16. Three years can make a huge difference. (Art by Jeff Stokely.)

HUZZAH!

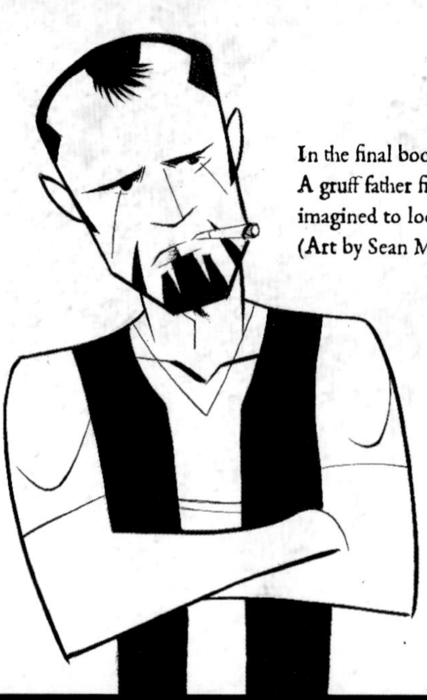

In the final book, Ted retains much of his original look. A gruff father figure with a grumpy gaze. He was always imagined to look like a younger Clint Eastwood. (Art by Sean Murphy, 2007.)

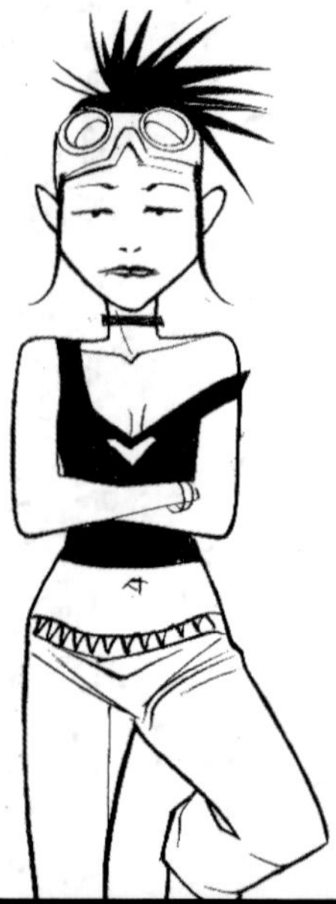

Ted originally had a teenage assistant who helped him with fixing motorcycles. Her purpose was to overshadow Wendell and serve as his potential love interest. In the end, Ted cast a long enough shadow himself. The assistant's name was Lilly and the character was cut in the final version of the story. But her name lives on. Ted's motorcycle is called *Lilly*. (Art by Sean Murphy, 2007.)

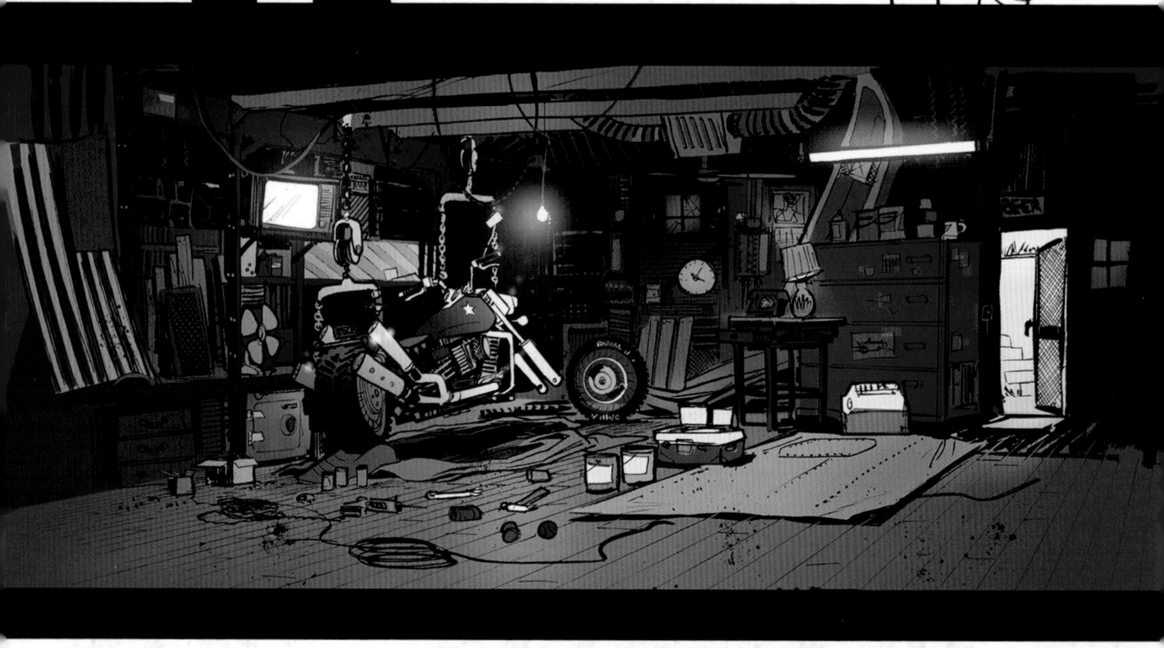

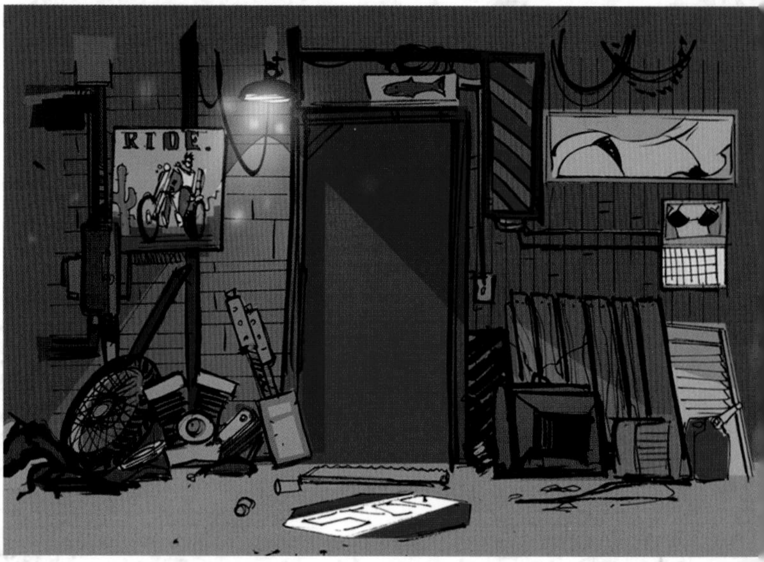
RIDE.

Ted's garage tells you everything you need to know about him. Calendars with photos of women, motorcycle magazines, beer cooler adorned with a few cans of brew, and tool benches. (Art by Sean Murphy, 2007)

The Dragon wasn't designed until we were well into to Chapter 3. We wanted to save it and be just as surprised as the readers when it showed up. There are doubts in the story as to what the dragon actually is, and if it even exists. So when readers get to it finally, it's a big pay off in the last 10 pages or so.

On top of the actual reveal, we wanted it to be a radical design. It was always going to be lumbering and more of a beast than a classic dragon. This allowed a more interesting functionality to it. When it runs, you can feel its weight. You can see how heavy it is. Its wings are small, so it can't fly. The wings are there to fan to flames of its dragon fire. And the quills on its back are there so you cannot jump on. You'd have to attack it from underneath, pretty much the only part where it is exposed and vulnerable. It's painted red, like Habersham, so it clashes with the cold environment.

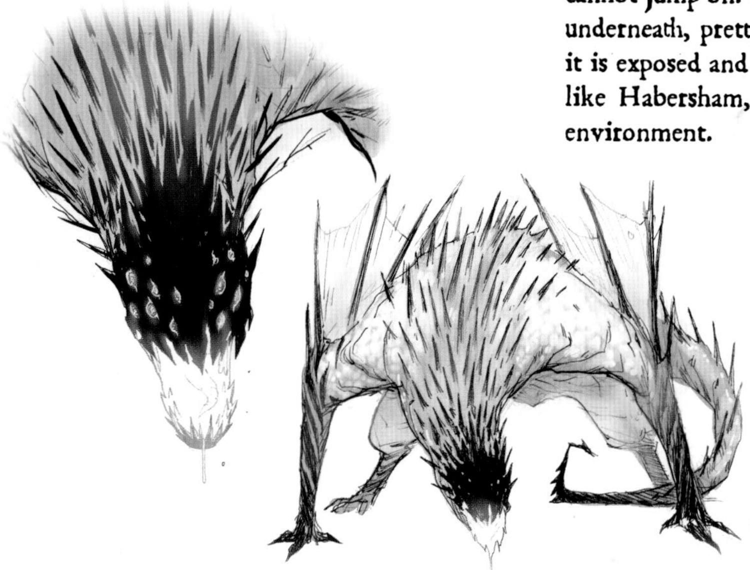

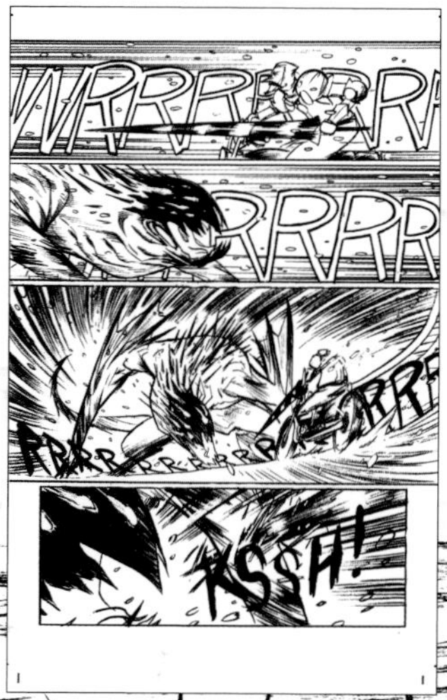
KSSH!

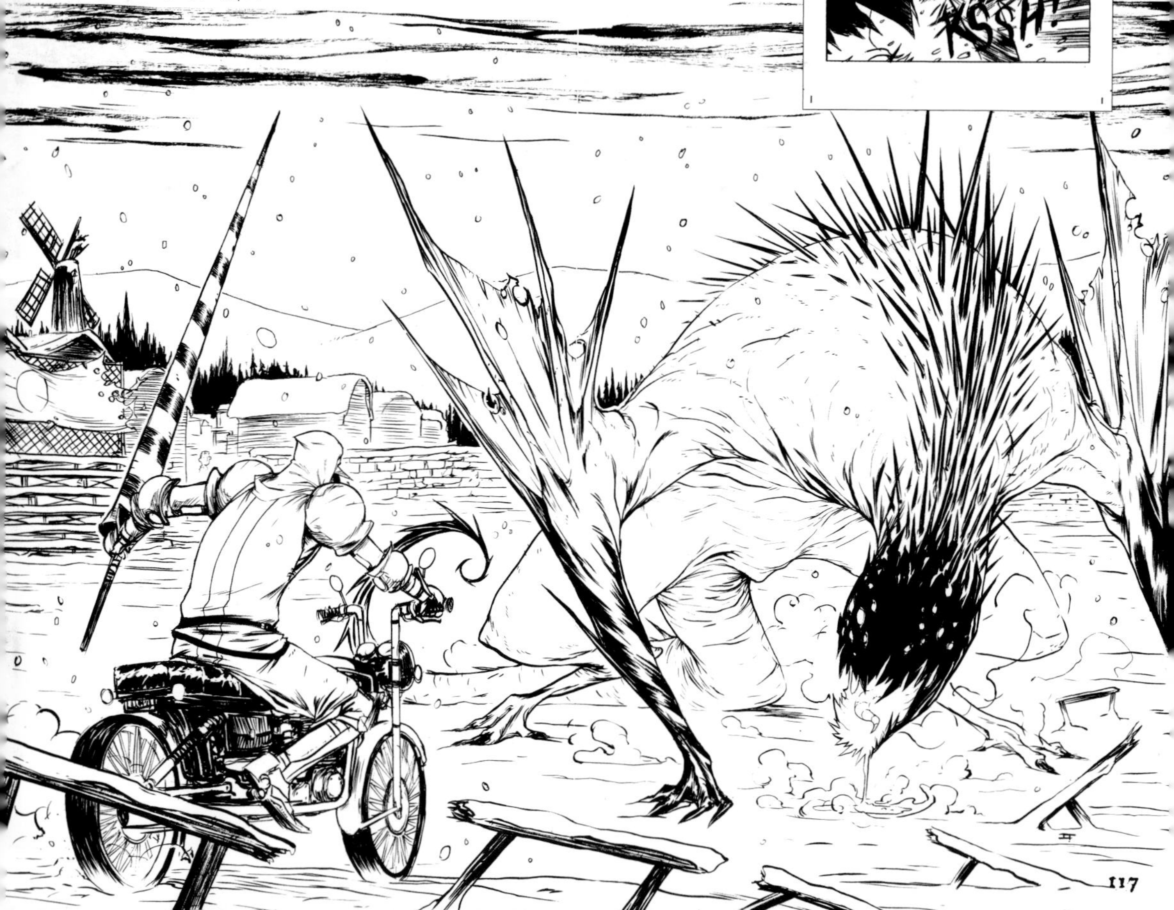
THE REASON FOR DRAGONS - CH4. PG. 6/7 - JEFF STOKELY 2013

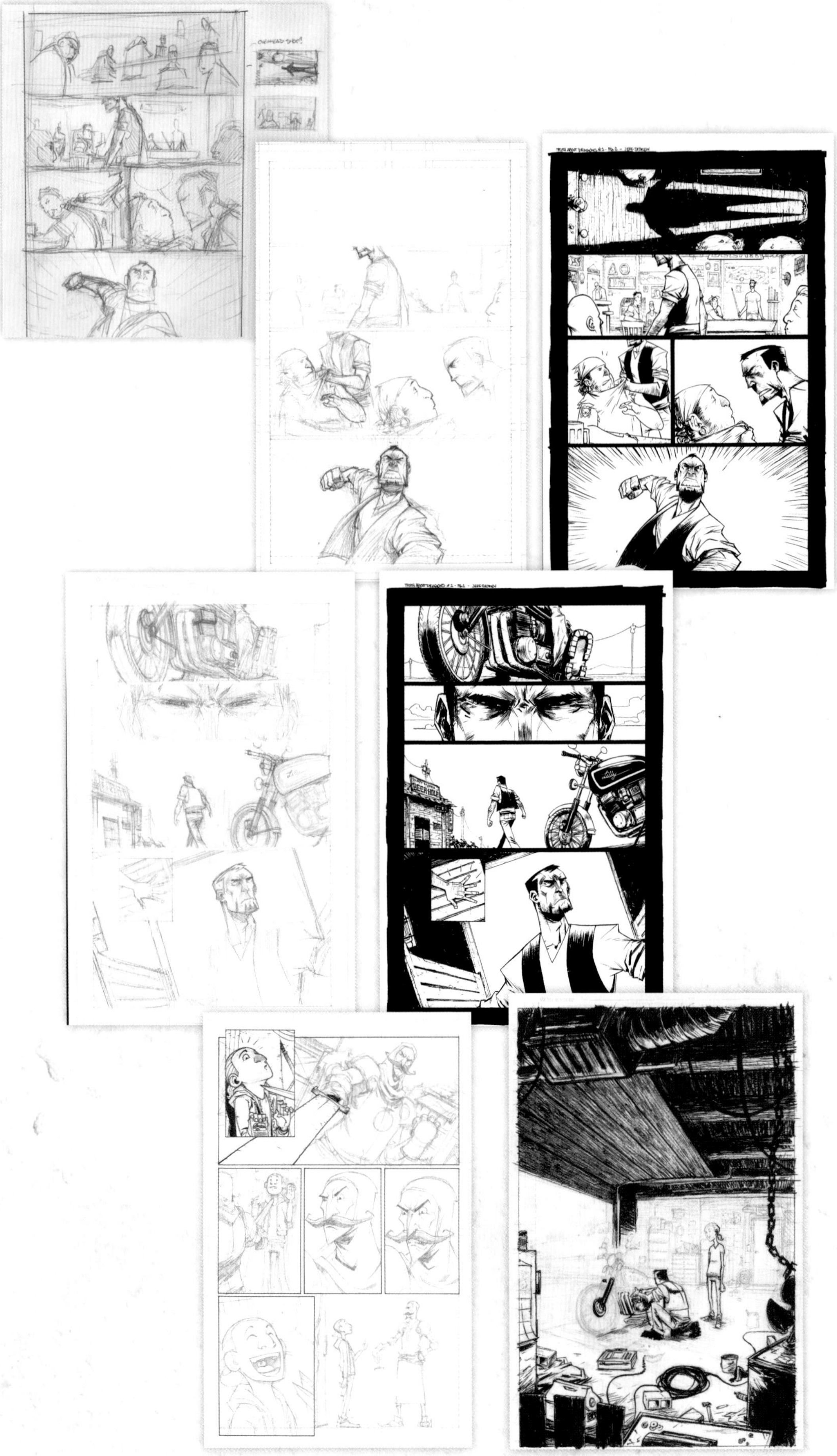
OVERHEAD SHOT!
BEER HOLE

Afterword

I'd like to take a page to thank everyone who worked on this book and those who supported it.

Of course Sean Murphy, who is not only a mentor as far as comic books and writing goes, but also one of those rare friends who you can finish each other's sentences with about the most obscure things flying around in your brains. Thanks for taking me under your wing when I had skill but no direction. Those first two years I moved to Los Angeles were hard but we made it work and had a good time doing so.

Big thanks to Jeff Stokely for taking our designs and breathing humor and pathos into them. You really made the book shine and watching you master that brush pen was a real treat.

Andrew Elder, who set a tone with those first pages of color. I know it was a schedule squeeze but it helped shape everything after it.

My editor Rebecca Taylor, publisher Mike Kennedy, and man about town Joe LeFavi! You three really pushed for this book to come to fruition. Thanks a million for the vote of confidence and all the pep talks along the way when I hit stumbling blocks. I'd also like to thank the EiC Stephen Christy and marketing man Mel Caylo.

To the other artists and writers who worked on all of the shorts and helped expand the little world I built, you did a fantastic job and all brought your own flavor. I'd especially like to thank Zoe Chevat for keeping me company many nights when I was coloring, you helped me keep my head straight.

Speaking of keeping me centered, I'd like to single out and thank Julia Fung, who served as my backbone and my rock while I was working on this, and also developed as quite the letterer. Without your help, this book would have been a lot harder.

David Edward Perry, whose comedy and upbeat attitude has helped me get through some tough times in LA during that formative summer of 2007 when I first moved to Los Angeles.

I'd also like to thank my family. Because of work, I have been stuck in Los Angeles, missing holidays, so I thank you for understanding even if it's caused more distance than just from California to New Jersey.

My Uncle Mike, who passed this last year. He taught me to think with an open mind, reason, laugh at how silly the world can be, and how to paint. If you had the pleasure to know him, his voice rings through this book if you listen closely.

There are a lot of other people, too long to list. But each of you cheered me on in your own way to the completion of *The Reason for Dragons*.

-Chris Northrop
Los Angeles, 2013

Artist Thank You:

I would like to thank Chris Northrop for trusting me with these characters and for taking me on this journey with him. To him and my friends, namely Mark Ashmore, I thank for enduring me and my freelancer deadlines and being there when I was in need. I would like to dedicate my work in this book escapists everywhere and also to my father, who passed while I drew this book. He had a wonderful mustache and was a wonderful storyteller. It saddens me that this is a story he will never be able to read, for I know he would love every page.

-Jeff Stokely
2013

Chris Northrop

was born in Brooklyn, NY. He has had a fascination with story and art from a young age, drawing dinosaurs and writing cartoons in the margins of his school notebooks. After scoring his first job doing animation at The Animation Collective in New York for Nicktoons shows in 2006, he moved from New York to Los Angeles to continue as an animator. After seeing the landscape, he made a left turn into comic books as a colorist and background painter.

Since then Chris has worked for several coloring studios. He makes his home in Hollywood, California where he is fueled by coffee and a love of his profession.

Jeff Stokely

is a California native making his home in Long Beach, toiling away making comics and concept art. He has previously worked on Archaia books including *Fraggle Rock* and *Thrilling Adventure Hour*, and has also worked for companies such as Mattel and BOOM! Entertainment.

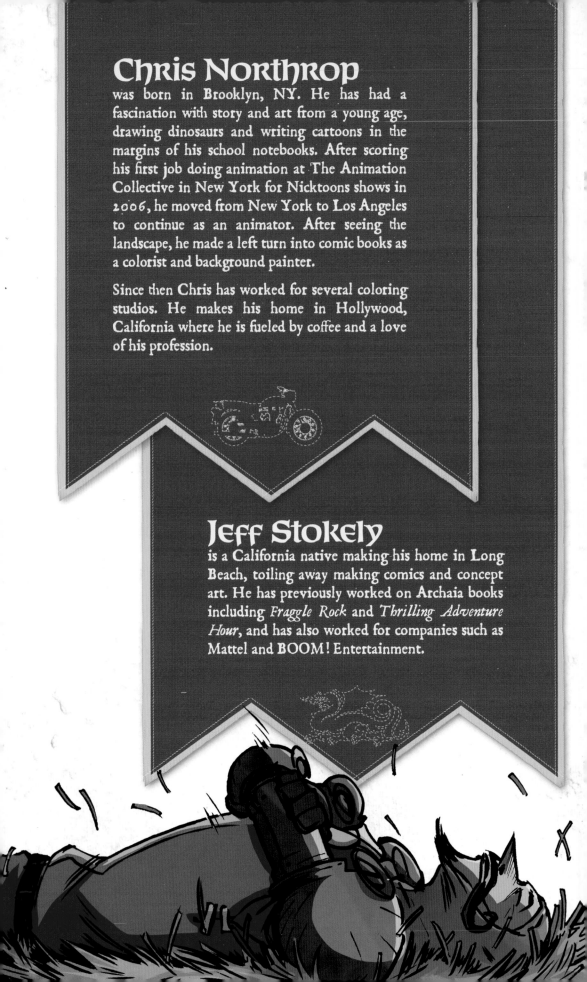